New York City

REAL CITY

REAL CITY

New York City

www.realcity.dk.com

LONDON, NEW YORK,
MELBOURNE, MUNICH AND DELHI
www.dk.com

Produced by
Blue Island Publishing

Contributors
Dahlia Devkota, Rachel F. Freeman, Jonathan Schultz

Photographers
Susannah Sayler, Andrew Holigan

Reproduced in Singapore by Colourscan
Printed and bound in China by Hung Hing Offset Printing Company Limited

Real City first published in Great Britain in 2007
by Dorling Kindersley Limited
80 Strand, London WC2R 0RL

Previously published as New York eGuide, 2005

A CIP catalogue record is available from the British Library.

ISBN: 978-1-40531-798-6

The information in this Real City guide is checked annually.

This guide is supported by a dedicated website which provides the very latest information for visitors
to New York City; please see page 7 for the web address and password. Some information, however,
is liable to change, and the publishers cannot accept responsibility for any consequences arising
from the use of this book, nor for any material on third party websites, and cannot guarantee that
any website address in this book will be a suitable source of travel information.
We value the views and suggestions of our readers very highly. Please write to:
Publisher, DK Eyewitness Travel Guides,
Dorling Kindersley, 80 Strand, London WC2R 0RL, Great Britain.

Contents

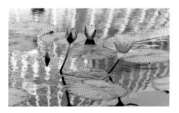

The Guide

Real City New York

Stay ahead of the crowd with **Real City New York**, and find the best places to eat, shop, drink, and chill out at a glance.

The guide is divided into four main sections:

Introducing New York – essential background information on the city, including an overview by one of the authors, the top tourist attractions, festivals and seasonal events, and useful travel and practical information.

Listings – eight themed chapters packed with incisive reviews of the best the city has to offer, in every price band and chosen by local experts.

Street Finder – map references in the listings lead you to this section, where you can plan your route and find your way around.

Indexes – the By Area and By Type indexes offer shortcuts to what you are looking for, whether it is a bar in the East Village or a French restaurant.

The Website

www.realcity.dk.com

By purchasing this book you have been granted free access to up-to-the-minute online content about New York City for at least 12 months. Click onto **www.realcity.dk.com** for updates, and sign up for a free weekly email with the latest information on what to see and do in New York City.

On the website you can:

- **Find the latest news** about New York, including exhibitions, restaurant openings, and music events

- Check what other readers have to say and **add your own comments** and reviews

- **Plan your visit** with a customizable calendar

- See at a glance **what's in and what's not**

- Look up listings by name, by type, and by area, and check the **latest reviews**

- **Link directly** to all the websites in the book, and many more

How to register

❯ Click on the New York City icon on the home page of the website to register or log in.

❯ Enter the city code given on this page, and follow the instructions given.

❯ The city code will be valid for a minimum of 12 months from the date you purchased this guide.

city code: **newyork56482**

introducing
new york

New York buzzes with energy — its adrenaline-fueled, 24-hour lifestyle is always charged with excitement. It also offers some of the best-known shops, bars, restaurants, and clubs in the world. This guide leads you to the latest and the best, opening with the city's top sights and the most fun-packed annual events and celebrations.

INTRODUCING NEW YORK

New York City has never been defined by its icons alone.
Rather, its eight million residents, spread across five
boroughs, lend the metropolis its distinctive character:
a heady mix of stubbornness, creativity, and boundless
ambition. Defiance in the wake of the 9/11 terrorist attacks –
as evidenced by the will to put an even bigger tower on the
site of the World Trade Center – is said to have brought the
city together, but most New Yorkers can tell you that NYC
has been riding a swell of civic pride for the last two decades.

Jonathan Schultz

Renewal, Rebirth, Revitalization

For someone taking the subway to Times Square for the
first time in 15 years, say, or for a lifelong Manhattanite
picking up roots and moving to (gasp) Brooklyn, it's
obvious that New York – the same city that flirted with
bankruptcy in the 1970s and 80s – has experienced an
unprecedented turnaround. Neighborhoods with names
heavy with foreboding such as the "Meatpacking
District" and "Hell's Kitchen" are no longer areas that
locals tell you to avoid; they're where you peruse Stella
McCartney's fall collection or grab a fantastic meal. Yes,
the city has changed, and most would say for the better.
But while dilapidated Lower East Side tenements are
being renovated, and raucous bars and bistros are
supplanting generations-old street-level shops, New
Yorkers are confronting a new set of dilemmas: how much
is too much, and at what point does a neighborhood
sacrifice its core identity in the name of upward mobility?
These questions are being fiercely debated in every
borough, and make for great conversation-starters.
However momentous the city's recent changes might

seem, there are larger forces at work. New York is, and
always will be, a city of immigrants. Ellis Island processed
its last new arrival over half a century ago, but, in just the
past 20 years, Flushing in Queens has blossomed into
one of the most vibrant Chinese immigrant communities
in the country. Spanish Harlem, long the cultural heart of
the city's Puerto Rican (aka "Nuyorican") community,
now counts thousands of Haitian, Dominican, and
Mexican residents. Just steps from Macy's, West 32nd
Street is a disorienting delight, charged with the neon
signage and aromas of South Korea. New York is in a
continual state of cultural evolution, and each new wave
of immigration brings further dimensions and ever more
vitality to the city.

The Endless Smorgasbord

New York serves more foods from more countries than
any city on earth, but diversity is just one part of the
city's remarkable culinary landscape. Above all,
New Yorkers keep chefs honest, and innovation for
innovation's sake is rarely rewarded here. Many of the

a city primer

city's top chefs themselves eat from the local Chinese takeout when they've finished their shift, or buy their meats at a typical neighborhood delicatessen, or grab a bite at the street-corner hot dog and pretzel carts on their way to work. Maybe it's because of this that New York chefs tend to be very down to earth and that classic New York fare often finds its way onto even the haughtiest menus – even if only as a Dr. Brown's Cream Soda served at a top sushi restaurant.

Vibrant Culture

Culture is the lifeblood of any city, but few are as blessed as New York with the range and quality of its performing arts programs, exhibitions, and museum collections. Yet in order for culture to remain vital it must be adaptable – in its forms, ideas, and environment. With rising rents in Manhattan, artists led the charge into Brooklyn's Williamsburg neighborhood and Queens' Long Island City back when these were considered undesirable areas. Residents never lose sight of their city's timeless cultural gems – the Met,

MoMA, Whitney, and The Cloisters – but added to those venerable Manhattan institutions are places such as the Brooklyn Museum, with its new glass entrance pavilion, and hot contemporary galleries such as P.S.1. With culture competing for attention all over this city, the museums are kept on their toes, and it's often when an institution surprises you that the biggest impressions are made. For the Guggenheim Museum's First Fridays event series in 2006, club DJs and a fashionable crowd packed Frank Lloyd Wright's celebrated building. When the last song played, attendees exited onto the genteel Museum Mile, sweaty and ecstatic. Would Solomon Guggenheim, champion of abstract art in all its forms, have approved? We're inclined to say yes.

✓ The Good Value Mark

Cities can be expensive, but if you know where to go you can always discover excellent-value places. We've picked out the best of these in the Restaurants, Shopping, and Hotels chapters and indicated them with the pink Good Value mark.

INTRODUCING NEW YORK

This guide brings you New York as its residents live it, picking out a gem of a shoe store here, a little-known bistro there, and bringing you the bustling charms of neighborhood streetlife. But whether you're here for a week or for a lifetime, few can resist the lure of such well-known pleasures as a Circle Line cruise to Liberty Island on a spring day, or the fun of Rockefeller Center's ice-skating rink in winter. These are the enduring attractions that have impressed generations of New York visitors and natives alike.

Museum of Modern Art

8 E5

11 West 53rd St. bet. 5th and 6th Aves • 212 708 9400 • Ⓜ 5 Ave./53 St.
≫ www.moma.org Open 10:30am–5:30pm Wed–Mon (to 8pm Fri)

When it reopened in 2004, MoMA immediately reasserted itself as the world's preeminent modern art museum. Augmenting the block-buster temporary exhibitions and staggering permanent collection is a brilliant film program, included in the price of admission *(see p107)*.

Empire State Building

6 E3

350 5th Avenue at West 33rd Street • Ⓜ 33 St.
≫ www.esbnyc.com Observatory open 8am–midnight daily

Seventy-mile panoramic views are reason enough to scale what is once again New York's tallest building, but also take time to admire the handsome Art Deco design. Look out for details such as the dazzling gold-and-silver-plate reliefs in the lobby. **Adm**

Times Square

5 D2

West 42nd Street & Broadway • Ⓜ Times Square
≫ www.timessquare.com

Bathed in the 24-hour radiant glow of American consumerism, Times Square is a dazzling, dizzying spectacle. Broadway theatergoers spill forth from its famous playhouses from mid-afternoon to midnight, crowding sidewalks illuminated by billions of watts of electronic billboard power.

For the very latest on New York go to ≫ **www.realcity.dk.com**

top attractions

Brooklyn Bridge
2 F3
Ⓜ Brooklyn Bridge–City Hall

Since it opened in 1883 as the largest suspension bridge in the world, John Augustus Roebling's span, connecting the brownstone-lined streets of Brooklyn Heights to the stately buildings of Lower Manhattan, has been far more than just a means of conveyance. It is iconic, and its pedestrian path is a favorite of cyclists, strollers, and movie-makers.

Ellis Island
1 A5
212 344 0996 • Ferry from Battery Park • Ⓜ South Ferry
≫ www.ellisisland.com Open 9:30am–5pm daily (extended hours in summer)

Scrutinizing medical examination displays, the baggage room, and ships' documents, visitors can appreciate how this city of immigrants took shape amid the turmoil of the 20th century. The Circle Line boat passage also affords breathtaking views of Lower Manhattan. **Adm**

Guggenheim Museum
10 E4
1071 5th Avenue at East 89th Street • 212 423 3500 • Ⓜ 86 St.
≫ www.guggenheim.org Open 10am–5:45pm Sat–Wed, 10am–7:45pm Fri

Frank Lloyd Wright's Guggenheim building has been accused of upstaging the work it houses. Yet when you walk down the spiraling rotunda, viewing works by the Cubists and Abstract Expressionists, or when you peruse the Impressionists' paintings in the annex, it is evident that here art and space interact harmoniously *(see p110)*.

≫ *The themed guided tours at MoMA are a smart way to approach this colossal museum*

INTRODUCING NEW YORK

Statue of Liberty 1 A5

212 269 5755 • Ferry from Battery Park • Ⓜ South Ferry
>> www.nps.gov/stli Open 9:30am–5pm daily (extended hours in summer)

A gift from France to the United States, Lady Liberty was completed in 1886 and became a potent symbol for arriving immigrants. Though the observation deck in the crown has been closed since 2001, you can scale the stairs of the base for rewarding harbor views. **Adm**

Central Park 7 D1

>> www.centralparknyc.org • Ⓜ 72 Ave.

More than just the city's rolling green acres, Central Park is a stage for Shakespeare, a concert venue for Bach, and a theater for all of humanity. In warm months, it teems with cyclists and strollers, Frisbee-flingers, and sunworshippers, while in the snowfalls of winter, the park's bridges and boughs are draped magically in white.

American Museum of Natural History 7 C1

Central Park West & 79th Street • 212 313 7278 • Ⓜ 81 St.
>> www.amnh.org Open 10am–5:45pm daily

The AMNH is a place to marvel at the wonders of planet Earth, with reconstructed dinosaur skeletons, life-size recreations of ocean creatures, and tools from ancient civilizations among its 30 million specimens and artifacts. The adjacent Hayden Planetarium captures the cosmos with state-of-the-art projection technology. **Adm**

top attractions

Ground Zero
`1 C3`

Viewing from Church Street • Ⓜ Fulton St.

The 1,776-ft (540-m) Freedom Tower and 9/11 Memorial and Museum are slated for completion by 2012. Still being debated is the content of the museum, which currently calls for an open-air memorial below ground. Currently, visitors can appreciate the enormity of the Twin Towers' footprints from a viewing bridge on Church Street *(see p101)*.

Rockefeller Center
`6 E1`

West 48th & 51st Sts bet. 5th & 6th Aves • 212 332 6868 • Ⓜ 47–50 Sts
≫ www.rockefellercenter.com Concourse open 7am–midnight daily

A network of 14 commercial, cultural, and residential buildings in the heart of Midtown, Rockefeller Center epitomizes the city-within-a-city ideal championed in the 1930s. At its heart is the famous outdoor ice-skating rink, presided over by a golden Prometheus in repose.

Metropolitan Museum of Art
`8 E1`

1000 5th Avenue • 212 535 7710 • Ⓜ 86 St.
≫ www.metmuseum.org Open 9:30am–5:30pm Tue–Sun (to 9pm Fri, 8pm Sat)

For its sheer breadth of scope, the Met has no equal, and visitors should consider which collections are of most interest before tackling this art behemoth. Currently, the Met is nearing completion of a 10-year renovation program that will allot more space to its Greek and Roman holdings *(see p109)*.

≫ *Upmarket shops and fashion houses line the 5th Avenue side of the Rockefeller Center*

INTRODUCING NEW YORK

Spring's arrival recharges New Yorkers, sending everyone outdoors to explore their city afresh. St. Patrick's Day brings millions onto the streets of Manhattan, but for a quieter celebration of the season many venture to Brooklyn's Botanic Garden to witness the brief, energizing display of cherry blossoms. Summer, hot and sultry, offers the greatest number of cultural events, with outdoor concerts, parades, and neighborhood festivals.

St. Patrick's Day Parade
www.saintpatricksdayparade.com

New York is tinged with emerald green for St. Patrick's Day, a time to celebrate and eulogize about Ireland and all things thereof – most potently Guinness and whiskey, which are consumed in alarming quantities way into the night. The parade itself is a jaunt down Fifth Avenue, with marching bands and dancing, and millions of Irish Americans and far more besides enjoying the spectacle and joining in with the festivities. **17 Mar**

Tribeca Film Festival
www.tribecafilmfestival.org; late Apr–early May

Since it began in 2002, the Tribeca Film Festival has attracted hundreds of thousands of cineastes eager to view, debut, and discuss films of all scales and styles. Everything from Hollywood blockbusters to 10-minute, student-produced animated shorts are featured. Every year the festival attracts more attention, so check the website's booking page as early as possible for the hot tickets. Robert De Niro was one of the instigators of the festival, and the director Martin Scorsese has programed themed series in past years. The festival box office is at 20 Harrison Street between Greenwich and Hudson Streets (Map 1 C1), and events take place in a variety of venues in the downtown area. **Apr–May**

Cherry Blossoms at Brooklyn Botanic Garden
www.bbg.org; first weekend in May

Blooming on 220 trees adjacent to the world-renowned Japanese Hill and Pond Garden (Map 13 D4), the cherry blossoms are celebrated for one weekend. Traditional Japanese dances are performed, music is played, and there are origami workshops, Japanese animated films ("anime"), and samurai sword demonstrations. **May**

Ninth Avenue Food Festival
www.hellskitchen.bz/info/ninthavenuefoodfestival.shtml

Held to raise money for community groups in Hell's Kitchen, the Ninth Avenue Food Festival is a celebration of the neighborhood's many ethnicities, primarily

spring and summer

through their various cuisines. Stages are set up for music and dance performances, and there are stalls selling clothes and jewelry too, but essentially the festival is about filling the belly with food from at least four continents: Argentinian to Vietnamese, Polish to Ethiopian. This festival is extremely popular with native New Yorkers, their taste buds happy aroused at the prospect of clams and oysters, Spanish chorizo, Greek baklava dripping with honey, spicy gumbos, jambalaya, and roasted pork in mole sauce. **Mid-May**

Outdoor Concerts
www.summerstage.org
www.celebratebrooklyn.org/celebrate

Central Park's eclectic SummerStage outdoor concert series (Map 8 E2) might host superstar Sri Lankan hip-hop artist MIA one night and the New York Philharmonic the next. Meanwhile, across the East River in Prospect Park (Map 13 D5), Celebrate Brooklyn! has more of a neighborhood flavor, with jazz, indie pop, and plenty of Latin salsa. **Jun–Aug**

Museum Mile Festival
www.museummilefestival.org; 6–9pm second Tue in Jun

For one June evening, the stretch of Fifth Avenue known as the Museum Mile (82nd to 105th Streets) closes to traffic, and its venerable art museums waive admission charges. However, three hours to do the Met or the Guggenheim is a little tight, and it's better to simply soak up the street scene. Local artists lead art workshops, and musicians, dancers, and jugglers perform. **Jun**

Parades
www.nationalpuertoricandayparade.org; 2nd Sun in Jun
www.hopinc.org (Gay Pride); last Sun in Jun

The Puerto Rican Day Parade takes over Fifth Avenue from 42nd to 86th Streets, and ranks among the city's largest and most festive celebrations, with over 100,000 marchers and 3 million spectators. The Gay Pride March (check website for current route) commemorates the 1969 Stonewall riots in West Village, a galvanizing moment in the Gay Pride movement. The parties and club nights built around Gay Pride are legendary. **Jun**

INTRODUCING NEW YORK

The metamorphosis of Central Park into a sea of bright yellow, rusty red, and mellow orange foliage heralds the fall. This is the time for the marathon to snake through the city's five boroughs, and for New Yorkers to head for the warmth of comedy theaters and concert halls. Winter might bring record snows one month and mild days the next. Yet not even the weather's mercurial nature can detract from the fairytale spirit of the holidays.

West Indian Day Carnival

www.wiadca.com; first Mon in Sep

This carnival has been taking place in Brooklyn since 1967 when the event was moved from Harlem, where it began in the 1930s. Today it brings around 4 million revellers onto the streets on and around Eastern Parkway (Map 13 D4), where there are countless food stalls selling jerk chicken, salt fish, and coconut bread. The parade of wonderfully dressed masqueraders, carnival floats, steel bands, and sound systems sets off at 11am and continues until 6pm. **Sep**

Feast of San Gennaro

www.sangennaro.org

Get a taste of old Little Italy during the grandest festival on the calendar for Italian New Yorkers. For 11 days, the spiritual heart of the neighborhood – Mulberry Street between Canal and East Houston Streets – teems with vendors selling sausage-and-pepper, fruit ice, and Italian pastries. Processions featuring effigies of San Gennaro take place throughout the festivities. **Mid-Sep**

Comedy Festivals

www.nycomedyfestival.com
www.nycundergroundcomedy.com

New York is well known for its pedigree of stand-up comedians, and in fall there are two major festivals: the NYC Underground Comedy Festival in mid-September, and the New York Comedy Festival in mid-November. Using a mix of venues across the entire city, the NYC Underground Festival primarily showcases rising talent, mixed with some well-known names, and hosts the Bill Hicks Spirit Award for thought-provoking comedy. The more high-profile NY Comedy Festival two months later is geared more toward established comedians, such as New York comedians Susie Essman, Joy Behar, and Lisa Lampanelli. **Sep/Nov**

New York Marathon

www.ingnycmarathon.org; first Sun in Nov

Attracting 35,000 athletes and over two million spectators, the marathon weaves from Staten Island to Central Park before a victor crosses the finish line.

fall and winter

Check the website for the route map. Most spectators congregate along Central Park; head to an outer borough to get a closer look at the action. **Nov**

Carnegie Hall & Lincoln Center Holiday Performances
www.carnegiehall.org; www.lincolncenter.org
www.nycballet.com

Come December, Carnegie Hall turns its attention to seasonal favorites, with performances by the Vienna Boys Choir and Musica Sacra. The New York City Ballet's staging of George Balanchine's *The Nutcracker* at Lincoln Center is a hallowed holiday tradition. Evening and weekend performances sell out quickly, but off-peak tickets are far more readily available. **Dec–Jan**

Emerald Nuts Midnight Run
www.nyrr.org; 31 Dec

Start off the new year with a 4-mile fun run in Central Park. DJs play to warm up the runners from 10pm, then the race kicks off at midnight, with fireworks blazing overhead. Register via the New York Road Runners website by 26 December. **Dec**

Restaurant Week
www.restaurantweek.com

What began as an effort to attract local diners to their neighborhood restaurants has evolved into one of the city's most hotly anticipated events. Manhattan's most acclaimed restaurants offer three-course, prix-fixe lunch and dinner menus that rarely venture above $20 and $35 respectively. Check the website for participating restaurants and dates. As well as the winter celebration, there is a summer Restaurant Week in June. **Jan or Feb**

Hot Chocolate Festival at City Bakery
www.hot-chocolate-festival.com

More than 20 novel varieties of hot chocolate join the menu during February at City Bakery *(see p43)* to melt away the city's winter doldrums. Each day serves up a different special, and some unlikely successes of the past include chili pepper, beer, and banana. **Feb**

INTRODUCING NEW YORK

From pedicab to stretch limo, and with bikes, blades, bus, taxi, and train in between, many modes of transportation are available in New York. The city is easy to orient yourself in – a grid of roads covers much of Manhattan, with streets (west–east) and avenues (south–north) numbered in order. Don't bother hiring a car, or you will spend half your time stuck in traffic or looking for a parking space. Use the subway and walk whenever possible.

Arrival

Whether it's your first or hundredth time coming into New York, the approach by air, sea, or road should inspire you with glimpses of the Statue of Liberty, Brooklyn Bridge, and a familiar spread of skyscrapers. Once you've arrived at one of the airports or major train or boat terminals, there are various options for getting into the heart of the city.

Note that because of security precautions, left luggage facilities have been suspended in all stations.

John F. Kennedy Airport

Also known simply as JFK (for the former U.S. president), this is the biggest of the three main airports and is used primarily for international and Los Angeles flights. Once through customs, choose either a yellow cab ($45 flat rate to Manhattan plus tolls), express bus, the Air Train, or subway. Don't accept unsolicited taxi rides.

Private car services such as **Carmel** offer competitive pricing that's a little cheaper than yellow cabs, but you need to call them for a pick-up. **Super Shuttle** offers shared van rides. Allow 45–60 minutes for car and express bus services to and from Manhattan.

The AirTrain (**www.panynj.gov/airtrain**) connects the terminals and takes you to Jamaica Station, from where you can take a LIRR (Long Island Rail Road) train to Penn Station. It's also possible to take the Air Train to the Howard Beach subway stop, from where you can take the A train on the subway to midtown (about an hour).

Newark International

Taxis from Newark can be pricey. To save money, take the **Newark Airport Express Bus** or shared **Super Shuttle** van, or the monorail to Newark Penn Station, which connects with New York's Penn Station and the PATH trains. Allow 45–60 minutes.

LaGuardia Airport

If you're heading to Columbia or the Upper West Side, you can take the M60 bus for a mere metrocard swipe *(see below)*. Otherwise, share a **Super Shuttle** van or take a private car or **New York Airport Bus**. Yellow cabs offer a shared taxi ride option to keep fares lower. Allow 20–40 minutes.

Penn Station

Located close to Madison Garden, between 32nd and 33rd streets and 7th and 8th avenues, this train hub serves New Jersey Transit and Amtrak trains. It also connects with many subway lines.

Grand Central Station

This station serves Metro-North trains and many subway lines. The main entrance is on 42nd Street, between Vanderbilt and Lexington avenues. Even if you don't need to take a train, you should come to view the beautifully refurbished main terminal. Free tours are offered on Wednesdays at 12:30 by the Municipal Arts Society (212 935 3960).

Port Authority

The Port lies between 8th and 9th avenues, from 40th to 42nd streets. It serves numerous bus lines and offers a gateway to all points in the Continental U.S., Canada, and Mexico.

Getting Around

The subway may be crowded in rush hours, but it's usually the fastest mode of transportation. New York is a pedestrian-friendly area too.

Subway Trains & Buses

The **MTA** (Metropolitan Transit Authority) is responsible for the 24-hour system of city buses and subways. The **metrocard** works for both. You can purchase a set amount of rides or unlimited day, week, and month metrocards, which are cost-efficient for frequent trips (prices are listed on the website). Machines take credit cards and cash; note that booth attendants don't accept large bills.

One swipe ($2) allows you to enter the subway system for an unlimited time and distance, often with a free bus transfer. Buses take metrocards or exact change of $2 in coins.

For the very latest on New York go to ⟫ www.realcity.dk.com

After midnight, trains are less frequent and some express lines run local, making many stops. Keep in mind that nights and weekends are the prime time for track work, so pay attention to announcements on service suspension or re-routing. After midnight, buses stop anywhere on the route upon request, even if it's not an official stop.

Taxis

Yellow cabs are the official New York taxis. The meter starts at $2.50 with $0.40 increments for every 1/5 of a mile, or after 2 minutes if you're stuck in traffic. There's a $1 weekday peak hour surcharge from 4–8pm; the night surcharge (after 8pm) is $0.50.

Taxi drivers have a reputation for being reckless or rude, but most are friendly. The white light in the middle of the sign on top of the car signals that it's ready for hire; if the whole sign is lit, then it's off duty. Most yellow cabs are limited to four passengers.

Other Options

It's pricier than a cab, but the human-powered pedicab is fun and can often dodge through traffic jams. Some drivers are also licensed tour guides.

PATH trains connect the 33rd Street and 6th Avenue, and World Trade Center stops with Hoboken, Jersey City, and Newark for $1.50 – useful for getting to the NJPAC (see p137).

Ferry services operate around the Manhattan coast and offer crossings to New Jersey. Special summer services on **New York Waterway** also connect downtown piers with a super beach at Sandy Hook, New Jersey.

New York has a network of scenic cycle paths, the best of which stick to the periphery of Manhattan or parkland in the outer boroughs. Cycles can be rented from Metro Bicycles (**www.metrobicycles.com**) and A Bicycle Shop (212 691 6149) (**www.a-bicycleshop.com**).

Tours

Big Apple Greeters are trained volunteers giving free, personalized walking tours of neighborhoods. Guides are also trained to give tours to the disabled (212 669 8159; **www.bigapplegreeter.org**). By water, Circle Line (212 563 3200; **www.circleline42.com**) offers tours circumnavigating Manhattan, or shorter ones sailing in the Harbor or just up the Hudson or East rivers.

Helicopters

Besides getting you to the airport or the Hamptons, helicopters are a fun way to get a bird's eye view of the city. Various tour themes and lengths are available from **Liberty Helicopter**.

Walking & Eco Tours

Notable walking tours include Big Onion (**www.bigonion.com**) and I'll Take Manhattan Tours (732 270 5559; www.newyorkcitywalks.com). New York City Audubon (**www.nycas.org**) has a naturalist slant, offering tours of the parks or out on the water. You can also paddle a kayak in the Hudson for free at the Downtown Boathouse (**www.downtownboathouse.org**). In Harlem, there are three excellent cultural tours (see p169).

Directory

Amtrak Rail
800 USA RAIL • www.amtrak.com

Carmel Car Service
212 666 6666
www.carmelcarservice.com

Grand Central Station
718 330 1234
www.grandcentralterminal.com

Greyhound Bus
800 231 2222
www.greyhound.com

JFK Airport
718 244 4444
www.kennedyairport.com

LaGuardia
718 533 3400
www.laguardiaairport.com

Liberty Helicopter
212 967 6464
www.libertyhelicopters.com

MTA
Subway/Bus/LIRR/Metro-North info
www.mta.nyc.ny.us

Newark Airport Express Bus
www.olympiabus.com

Newark International
973 961 6000
www.newarkairport.com

New Jersey Transit
800 772 2222 • www.njtransit.com

New York Airport Bus Service
www.nyairportservice.com

New York Waterway
800 53 FERRY

NY/NJ Port Authority
For airports, bridges, tunnels, bus and train stations
212 435 7000
www.panynj.gov

PATH
800 234 7284

Super Shuttle
212 BLUE VAN
www.supershuttle.com

INTRODUCING NEW YORK

Whether you need to find a decent public restroom, an accessible subway stop, or a WiFi hotspot for your laptop, knowing the basics in any new place is useful. While this section offers practical help with some basic questions, remember that in spite of an alleged gruff exterior, New Yorkers are generally happy to offer guidance to the uninitiated. The key to getting information from a native is not to be shy and to ask for what you need directly.

Disabled Organizations

Since 2002, the City of New York has been committed to ensuring that all 158,738 street corners are ramped for wheelchair accessibility. Work isn't fully completed yet, but the majority have now been tackled.

Most MTA buses are equipped with lifts for wheelchairs, but only a select few subway stations are accessible. Reduced fare options are available for public transportation.

For subway maps in Braille call 718 330 3322. Hands On! is an organization providing sign language interpretation for films, theater productions, and museum exhibits. Hospital Audiences, Inc. offers an audio service for blind theatergoers and museum visitors.
• **Hands On!**
212 740 3087; TTY use relay 711
• **Hospital Audiences, Inc.**
888 424 4685; TTY 212 575 7673

Emergencies and Health

There are several good **emergency rooms** *(see Directory)*. You can also find details of all types of New York hospitals at **www.citidex.com**. The site lists walk-in centers, which are good for less urgent ailments. All of the 24/7 pharmacies belong to one of the three big chains: **CVS**, Rite-Aid,

and **Duane Reade**. Remember that health insurance is essential.

Gay and Lesbian Travelers

A great place for up-to-date information is **The Lesbian, Gay, Bisexual & Transgender Community Center**. This is open daily from 9am–11pm and welcomes drop-in visitors. *The New York Times* has been recognizing same-sex unions in its Sunday "Society" pages since 2002.

Listings/What's On

Time Out New York is an informative weekly, with a bias towards Manhattan. The bi-weekly, free *L* magazine (**www.thelmagazine.com**) focuses on events in Brooklyn and below 23rd Street in Manhattan; it can be found in the orange boxes on the streets, usually near another good freebie, the *Village Voice* (**www.villagevoice.com**). The *New York Magazine* features more mainstream events. The Friday *Weekend Guide* section to *The New York Times* (**www.nytimes.com**) highlights cultural events.

Money

A credit card (or two or three) is essential in New York, especially for booking a hotel room or if you want to

hire a car. Visa, MasterCard, Amex, and Diners Club are accepted by the majority of businesses. Traveler's checks are also widely used. Indeed, many businesses accept payment in traveler's checks instead of cash, but the checks must be in denominations of U.S. dollars. Traveler's checks in U.S. dollars can be exchanged for cash at most banks in New York, but other currencies are difficult to exchange. Before traveling, check with your bank to see if you can use your debit card in the U.S. In many New York stores, you will be asked to key in your debit card PIN rather than sign your name. This isn't the case in restaurants, however.

Opening Hours

Most **shops** are open by 9am, and regular closing time is 5–6pm, and later on Thursday. Many shops are open daily, including Sundays and holidays. However, some establishments choose to close on Mondays for a break. The same goes for most sightseeing attractions – including **galleries** and **museums**.

Hip clothing stores and record shops downtown tend to stay open until at least 8pm on a regular basis. Record shops may be open until midnight or even 1am. Some shops with late closing hours may open at 11am. **Restaurants** billed as "late-night" usually serve until 1 or 2am; standard serving hours are until 10:30–11pm. **Bars** tend to close between midnight and 1am during the week, staying open until around 3 or 4am on Friday and Saturday nights.

Phones and Communications

Check coverage with your cellphone provider before traveling, or hire a phone. Note that U.S. companies charge you to make and receive calls.

Verizon payphones on the streets charge 50 cents for an unlimited time on any local call. Some public phones charge only a quarter for a local call, but time is limited. Note that you must dial the full code 1 212 for any number within the 212 area code.

There are many Internet cafés. If you have a wireless laptop, then look for the free WiFi hotspots. Starbucks coffee shops have WiFi, but you pay for the T-Mobile connection. Free wireless connectivity can be found in Bryant Park and many of the small parks found downtown, including City Hall and Bowling Green Park. Check **www.wifihotspotlist.com/ny/html** for updates of new areas. Many libraries have free Internet connectivity too.

Sales Tax

A sales tax of 8.625% is added to most things that you purchase, including to restaurant and bar bills.

Security & ID

Since 9/11/01, more attention is paid to security in public areas. Unattended bags and packages are treated with suspicion and removed.

Stay aware of who is around you when you're gazing up at skyscrapers (a dead giveaway that you're a tourist). Take some form of photo ID if you plan to go bar- or club-hopping (the minimum age allowed is 21). Even if you're sporting a walker and grey hair, many nightclub bouncers won't let you in without ID.

Tipping

The general rule of thumb is that you tip **restaurant serving staff** 15%–20% of the bill. (Salaries in the industry are very low, so most staff really do rely on tips). If you're mathematically challenged, then double the listed tax which will give a 17.25% tip. **Beauticians** and **taxi drivers** should receive a 15–20% tip, although many people offer drivers just over 10%. **Bartenders** usually receive $1–3 per round. For hotel **room service**, offer a 15% tip, unless a service fee is included in the bill; hotel **porters** get $1–2 per bag.

Tourist Information

The New York Convention & Visitors Bureau operates a visitor information center on Seventh Avenue and updates the official NYC tourist web site. Also try **www.ny.com** and **www.visitnewyork.com**. Many locals use **www.newyorkmetro.com** to find things to do, eat, and buy. For up-to-date local news, weather, and information, try **www.ny1.com**.

Washroom Facilities

There's a noted lack of public facilities in New York, which results in many a crossed leg. Natives are known to dash into hotel lobbies or a local Starbucks to find the nearest "rest" facilities. To work out where the good public washrooms are before you venture out, check **www.thebathroomdiaries.com**.

Directory

24/7 Pharmacies
CVS 1396 2nd Ave. at 71st St.
(& other locations) 212 249 5699
www.cvs.com

Duane Reade
224 West 57th St. (& other locations)
212 541 9708
www.duanereade.com

Cellphone Rental
212 832 7143
www.roberts-rent-a-phone.com

Crime Victims Hotline
212 577 7777

Directory Enquiries
Dial 1 (area code) 411
or 1 (area code) 555 1212

Doctors on Call
212 737 2333 (24/7 service)

Emergencies
911

Emergency Rooms
St. Vincent's Hospital
West 11th Street at 7th Avenue
212 604 7998

Bellevue Hospital Center
462 First Avenue at 27th Street
263 7300

Urgent Care Center NY Hospital
525 East 68th Street
212 746 0795

Government Info & Services
311 (non-emergencies)

The Lesbian, Gay, Bisexual & Transgender Community Center
208 West 13th Street,
212 620 7310
www.gaycenter.org

National Organization on Disability
www.nod.org

Tourist Info
810 7th Ave. between 52nd & 53rd Sts
212 484 1200
www.nycvisit.com

restaurants

New York is one of the world's finest cities for dining out, whether you aspire to a table at one of the most fashionable restaurants, or simply want to pick up something cheap and tasty from a café or from a street vendor. Myriad restaurants cover every cuisine imaginable, the food served up on anything from banana leaves to porcelain plates. The following pages provide a snapshot of NY's dining scene.

RESTAURANTS

Regardless of expense or distance traveled, dining out in
New York feels special. Residents of course have their
fail-proof standbys: the bubbling hot pots at Grand
Sichuan, the juicy Porterhouse at Peter Luger. But we also
revel in receiving a hot tip from a friend, or stumbling upon
a hidden gem during an aimless Sunday stroll. New York
reveals an intimate side of itself through its restaurants,
and locals are always eager to discuss their favorite spots
with visitors ... here are a few of mine.

Jonathan Schultz

Local Flavor

An insistence on local ingredients whenever possible set these
eateries apart. Specials at the **Mermaid Inn** *(see p35)* are usually
caught around Long Island Sound; Chinatown's **Golden Unicorn**
(see p29) draws fans of local soft-shell crabs in summer, and **Blue
Smoke** *(see p45)* barbecues succulent meat from upstate New York.

Best Pizzerias

The city's most beloved import is baked the old-fashioned Neapolitan
way (in a coal-burning oven) at **John's of Bleecker Street** *(see p39)*,
while spicy variations at **DiFara** *(see p58)* inspire pilgrimages from all
five boroughs. At the nouvelle end of the spectrum, Mario Batali grills
his pizzas and tops them with surprising ingredients at **Otto** *(see p38)*.

Breakfast and Brunch

Only the heartiest appetites need apply at **Annie's** *(see p51)*, where
generous servings of pancakes rule. West Village is the city's brunch
destination, but at the weekend go a little further west to **Florent** *(see
p42)* in the Meatpacking District. And don't miss out on the savory-sweet
pleasures of dim sum in Chinatown – join the flock at around 11am daily.

choice eats

Hot Tables

Sake after sake, maki after maki, **Blue Ribbon Sushi** *(see p37)* keeps diners wanting – and ordering – well past midnight. For dinner with a bit of culinary theater, **Ouest** *(see p53)* is a handsome restaurant with a bustling on-view kitchen, while history is your dining companion at **Peter Luger** *(see p59)*, perhaps the most fabled steakhouse in the land.

Late-Night Bites

East Village and Lower East Side bar-crawlers have their choice of post-midnight munchies, from fortifying borscht at **Café Veselka** (144 2nd Ave., Map 4 E2) to piping-hot fries at **Pommes Frites** *(see p40)*. Quirky diner **Florent** *(see p42)* acquired a new clientele purely by accident after the Meatpacking District's transformation into a clubbers' paradise.

Global Cuisine

NY is famous for street food, and you really should try a delicately spiced vegetable crepe from Washington Square pushcart **NY Dosas** *(see p41)*. Austrian standards are done emphatic justice at **Wallsé** *(see p41)*, and the intensely garlicky roast chicken at **El Malecón II** *(see p54)* puts the Dominican Republic on your plate ... and on your breath.

Restaurants

66 *Chinese with a twist* `1 D1`
241 Church Street (at Leonard St.) • 212 925 0202
» www.jean-georges.com
Open lunch & dinner daily (to midnight Mon–Thu,
to 1am Fri & Sat, to 10:30pm Sun)

A restaurant in the empire of prestigiously gifted chef
Jean-Georges Vongerichten, 66 has a chic, minimalist
interior, immersed in shades of white, silver grays,
and black. The lofty space, with a view to the kitchen
above a row of fish tanks, attracts style slaves and
foodies alike. Dishes draw on Chinese influences, and
are produced with the customary Jean-Georges flair –
specialties include Peking duck, the 66 sesame
noodles, sweet and sour two-flavored shrimp, steamed
cod, Vietnamese coffee-flavored sorbet, and five-spice
vanilla ice cream. The evening is when 66 is at its
liveliest best – if you haven't reserved, imaginative
cocktails ease the wait for a table. Lunch is cheaper,
with a reasonable prix-fixe menu. The check is accompanied by light, green-tea fortune cookies. **Expensive**

Montrachet *quality food and wine* `1 D1`
239 West Broadway (between Walker & White Sts)
212 219 2777
» www.myriadrestaurantgroup.com/montrachet
Open dinner only Mon–Thu & Sat, lunch & dinner Fri

This has one of the best cellars in the country, a wine
selection to match its *haute cuisine*, and a sommelier
to advise without a trace of condescension. The
dining space is relaxed and comfortable. **Expensive**

Acappella *gourmets and grappa* `1 C2`
1 Hudson Street (at Chambers St.) • 212 240 0163
» www.acappella-restaurant.com
Open lunch & dinner Mon–Fri, dinner only Sat

This ever-popular NY haunt produces delicious
northern Italian food. Along with seasonal variations,
the menu boasts well-prepared lamb and fish as well
as superb pasta and pesto dishes. The waitstaff are
indulgent and serve free grappa. **Expensive**

28 ✓ *Good value*   For the very latest on New York go to » www.realcity.dk.com

Peking Duck House *perfect poultry* `2 E1`

28 Mott Street (between Pell St. & Chatham Sq.) • 212 227 1810
Open all day from 11:30am daily

Chinatown's bustle carries into this restaurant on busy nights, and the Peking duck leaves little wonder why: crisp skin and succulent meat are served with sliced cucumber, scallions, and tangy-sweet sauce. Service can be brusque, and other dishes are fairly standard, but the bird is transcendent. **Moderate**

Golden Unicorn *a beacon in Chinatown* `2 F1`

18 East Broadway (at Catherine St.) • 212 941 0911
Open all day daily; dim sum 9am–3:30pm

Deep in Chinatown lies this shrine to the indulgent Cantonese tradition of dim sum. Late on Sunday mornings, the 1,000 seats of a pleasantly appointed dining room fill with families eager to sample petite plates of shrimp dumplings, roast pork buns, and sweet egg custards. Dinner is a quieter affair. **Cheap**

Balthazar *timeless brasserie* `3 D5`

80 Spring Street (between Broadway & Crosby St.) • 212 965 1785
>> www.balthazarny.com Open from 7:30am daily (to 1am Mon–Thu, to 2am Fri & Sat, to midnight Sun)

Parisian in style, Balthazar has retained its popularity through consistently good bistro fare. The menu changes throughout the day, catering for breakfast, lunch, dinner, and through to after hours. Sublime desserts, and weekend brunch is a winner. **Moderate**

Mercer Kitchen *hip French/American* `3 D5`

99 Prince Street (at Mercer St.) • 212 966 5454
>> www.jean-georges.com
Open breakfast, lunch & dinner daily

The Mercer is all about keeping things simple and chic. The SoHo location attracts the trendsetters; the menu attracts the foodies. Its setting is casual, with tables, banquettes, and bar seating surrounding an open-plan kitchen. **Moderate**

>> *Cheap: under $14 for a main course; moderate: $14–25; expensive: over $25*

L'Ecole *gastronomy defined*

3 D5

462 Broadway (at Grand St.) • 212 219 3300
>> www.frenchculinary.com/lecole
Open lunch & dinner Mon–Fri, dinner only Sat

A restaurant that ticks all the right boxes: set in a prime location, it has a bright, airy interior with huge windows, serves excellent food and offers bargain prices. L'Ecole is indeed a school, and the students of the French Culinary Institute use the patrons as their willing guinea pigs. It's a wonderful arrangement – diners indulge in three-, four- and five-course meals without having to sell off the family silver, while students have a chance to hone their skills. You can order à la carte, but the prix-fixe menu is great value.

These students are potentially star chefs, and the menu reflects that ambition by offering dishes rooted in both traditional and contemporary French cuisine. Creations such as poached sole with shrimp and mussels in a cider cream sauce, eggplant and red pepper terrine, and tea flan served with madeleines demonstrate the challenging nature of the cooking. If you prefer simpler fare, omelet with shoestring potatoes won't disappoint. Even the delectable bread is made on the premises. The menu changes every six weeks.

You'll be hard-pressed elsewhere to find such a winning combination of bright atmosphere and first-rate cooking at these prices. **Moderate**

Jane *creative American fare*

3 D4

100 West Houston Street (between Thompson Street & La Guardia Place) • 212 254 7000
>> www.janerestaurant.com Open all day from 11:30 (11 Sun)

Jane takes the food you may already know and adds special touches, subtly reinventing but not disguising the main ingredients. Meat and salmon burgers reign supreme, though the juicy fruit-purée cocktails give them a run for their money. **Moderate**

Cafe Gitane North African spices

4 E4

242 Mott Street (at Prince St.) • 212 334 9552
Open all day from 9am daily

French/North African offerings such as fragrant cous cous and spicy mergüez sausages draw the area's fashionable youth. In summer, the sidewalk tables are hotter commodities than the designer sandals in the neighboring boutiques, but the cozy dining room holds plenty of charm too. **Cheap**

Cafe Habana Cuban/Mexican café

4 E4

17 Prince Street (at Elizabeth St.) • 212 625 2001
Open all day from 9am daily

Flavorful specialties from this bustling corner café inspire devotion among Nolita's beautiful people, who eye one another over delicious Cuban pork sandwiches, huevos rancheros, and corn on the cob. Quench your thirst with a chelada: Mexican lager with lime juice and salt. **Cheap**

Bereket late-night Turkish belly-filler

4 F4

187 East Houston St. (at Orchard St.) • 212 475 7700
Open 24 hours daily

Rare is the downtown resident who, after a night of barhopping, hasn't relished the succulent lamb shawarma sandwich, fresh hummus or tangy, stuffed vine leaves at this East Houston institution. For what is essentially a Turkish fast-food restaurant, Bereket offers surprisingly subtle, authentic eats. **Cheap**

The Elephant French/Thai fusion

4 F4

58 East 1st Street (between 1st & 2nd Sts) • 212 505 7739
>> www.elephantrestaurant.com
Open lunch & dinner daily

Reds and golds dominate the whimsical, evocatively lit dining room, where couples sip luscious Elephant Martinis – vodka, cassis, and pineapple. Don't miss Sticky Rice – chicken and pork steamed with rice and vegetables in lotus leaf wrapping. **Moderate**

'inoteca *great small plates* `4 F4`
98 Rivington Street (at Ludlow St.) • 212 614 0473
Open breakfast, lunch & dinner daily

A happening corner wine bar/restaurant, 'inoteca is perfect for a few glasses while you munch on a selection of snacks, known as "small plates." These include cheeses, a generous helping of sliced meats, panini, and salads. Weather permitting, you can sit outside for high-caliber people-watching. **Moderate**

WD-50 *adventurous American* `4 G4`
50 Clinton Street (between Rivington & Station Sts)
212 477 2900
>> www.wd-50.com Open dinner daily

Chef Wylie Dufresne built his reputation on taking risks and you can try some of his delicious experiments in this simple, clean restaurant. Rabbit sausage with avocado or lamb with hibiscus-date purée are typical attention-grabbers. **Expensive**

Cube 63 *unique sushi in a stylish setting* `4 G4`
63 Clinton Street (between Rivington & Station Sts)
212 228 6751
>> www.cube63.com Open lunch & dinner Mon-Sat

Having worked in top sushi kitchens, brothers Ken and Ben Lau carry priceless expertise into their sleek restaurant. Mellow light illuminates the sushi counter, while young professionals share *omakase*: a sampler platter of wildly creative rolls. BYOB. **Moderate**

Alias *deceiving appearance; convincing menu* `4 G4`
76 Clinton Street (at Rivington St.) • 212 505 5011
Open dinner daily (to 11pm Mon–Thu, to 11:30pm
Fri & Sat, to 10pm Sun) ✓

Don't be misled by the kitsch signage; there's no spam on the menu. Alias serves imaginative dishes, such as lamb spare ribs, duck confit, and candied avocado. It has become a Lower East Side institution, and the prix-fixe Sunday menu is a bargain. **Moderate**

Le Souk *North African dining* `4 G3`
47 Avenue B (between 3rd & 4th Sts) • 212 777 5454
» www.lesoukny.com Open dinner daily

With the arrival of trendy restaurants, boutiques, and bars in recent years, Alphabet City (easternmost part of the East Village) has seen its profile rise considerably. But the neighborhood conceals some of its best assets behind a gritty urban cloak. Le Souk is a fine example of this – a fantastic North African restaurant that, externally, does little to distinguish itself from the surrounding neighborhood grocers and bars. An unassuming shell, however, belies a sultan's treasure trove of African textures, tones, and delicacies within. Fashionable groups dine shoulder to shoulder on plush banquettes, while the adjacent bar area has low, Moorish tables, floor pillows, and softly lit iron lanterns. Meze plates serve as a prelude to the arrival of ceramic tajines filled with aromatic cous cous, tangy mergüez sausages, and garlicky mussels. After 9pm, belly dancers gyrate between the tables. **Moderate**

Bao 111 *modern design meets Vietnamese food* `4 G3`
111 Avenue C (between 7th & 8th Sts) • 212 254 7773
» www.bao111.com Open dinner daily

Architect/chef Michael Huynh prepares brilliant Vietnamese cuisine in this sleek space of his own design. Diners – many of them artists and fashion models – rest on crimson banquettes sipping fragrant *pho* soup or browsing Bao's eclectic dessert menu. Black sesame ice cream, anyone? **Cheap**

Le Tableau *French/Mediterranean cuisine* `4 F3`
511 East 5th Street (between Aves A & B) • 212 260 1333
» www.letableaunyc.com Open dinner daily

Wonderful French food in a button-sized hot spot. The menu changes often, but the produce is consistently flavorful, with dishes such as pork loin with maple yam purée, gorgonzola, and porto reduction. Try the early evening prix-fixe three-course menu for super savings. **Moderate**

Restaurants

Pylos *taverna in Alphabet City* 4 F3

128 East 7th Street (between 1st & A Aves) • 212 473 0220
➤➤ www.pylosrestaurant.com
Open dinner Mon–Sat, brunch Wed–Sun

Many worlds lie within eight blocks of the 2nd Avenue subway station: the Orthodox Jewish Lower East Side, Ukrainian East Village, and Chinatown, for example. Most surprising of all, however, is the spirit of the Aegean that hides amid Alphabet City's hard-rocking bars. Pylos is a handsome Greek taverna, with stucco walls, blue shutters, and earthenware jugs hanging from the beams. Gastronomes from all over the city worship the *dolmathes* (stuffed vine leaves) here. Another popular dish is *arnaki yiovetsi* – stewed lamb chunks redolent of clove, oregano, and tomato, served on toothsome *orzo* grains. Knowledgable staff help you navigate the encyclopedic Greek wine list. Save room for the *galaktobaureko* – these flaky, custard-filled phyllo triangles covered in warm honey are perhaps Pylos's greatest temptation. **Moderate**

Yaffa Cafe *pitta stop* 4 F3

97 St. Mark's Place (between 1st & A Aves)
212 674 9302 Open 24 hours daily

Day and night, punk rockers and poets flock to this offbeat eatery on St. Mark's. After last call at the neighborhood's bars, Yaffa's leafy, festively-lit back patio fills with hungry revelers eager to curb their impending hangovers with home-made pitta bread, hummus, and other tasty Middle Eastern fare. **Cheap**

Freemans *hipster lodge* 4 E4

Freeman Alley, off Rivington • 212 420 0012
➤➤ www.freemansrestaurant.com
Open dinner daily, brunch Sat & Sun

At the end of Freeman Alley lies a buzzing New England eatery where Lower East Side carnivores tuck into dishes such as roasted trout, braised duck leg, and seared filet mignon – all under the glazed gaze of moose heads mounted on the wall. **Moderate**

Paul's Palace *huge hamburgers*   `4 E3`

131 2nd Avenue (at St. Mark's Pl.) • 212 529 3033
Open all day daily

The quintessential American hamburger experience.
From the linoleum countertop and checkerboard
tablecloths, to the cheeky burger descriptions posted
above the well-seasoned grill, Paul's is a greasy
charmer. Go in for peerless 1/2-pound burgers and
extra thick milkshakes. **Cheap**

Mermaid Inn *seafood, New England style*   `4 E3`

96 2nd Avenue (between 5th & 6th Sts) • 212 674 5870
≫ www.themermaidnyc.com Open dinner daily

With its framed nautical charts, ship diagrams, cabin
lamps, and rustic tables, this classic fish house would
seem more suited to the Maine Coast. But the modern
rock soundtrack and style-conscious local clientele
anchor the proceedings in urban bohemia. When
restaurant mogul Jimmy Bradley unveiled this oddity
on edgy Second Avenue in 2003, it was an instant hit.

The inn is extremely popular, and you'll generally
have to wait for your table at the weekend. This is when
the seafood bar comes into its own, providing Nova
Scotia oysters on the half shell. Once seated, you can
continue with roasted mussels or feather-light clam
fritters before considering the mains. Depending on
the season, these might range from classic grilled
salmon through tender pan-fried skate wing to the
popular lobster salad sandwich. Complimentary
cups of lemon pudding cap the meal. **Moderate**

Morning Coffee and Afternoon Tea

New York's plentiful "coffee shops" are great for
cheap food and people-watching, but, ironically, not
for coffee. For a real, European-style coffee, you
need to seek out the city's best cafés. For excellent
cappuccinos, go to **Via Quadronno** *(see p225)*, and
if you want to pick up a quick espresso, stop at the
orange mobile **Mud Truck** (on Union Square) or the

Mud Spot (permanently parked on 9th St.). **Joe** *(see
p224)*, in the West Village, also does great coffee.
    The **Palm Court at the Plaza Hotel** (reopening fall
2007) serves a formal afternoon tea. **Tea &
Sympathy** is cozy and casual, offering scones and
perfectly brewed tea. **Lady Mendl's Tea Room** is
upmarket and their scones are divine. *(For all, see
p226.)* For something funkier, try **Teany** *(see p74).*

≫ *For a full list of recommended cafés, see pp224–5; for tearooms, see p226*   `35`

Restaurants

Angelica Kitchen *incredible vegetables* `4 E2`

300 East 12th Street (between 1st & 2nd Aves)
212 228 2909
>> www.angelicakitchen.com Open all day daily

A vegan pioneer since 1976, Angelica earns high marks for cooking with extremely fresh ingredients grown using sustainable methods. This would be reason enough to lure environmentally aware citizens to the charming, Tuscan farmhouse-inspired dining room. Yet Angelica's greatest asset is perhaps the chef's ability to coax dazzling flavors out of the most basic ingredients. Omnivores will be hard pressed to note the absence of cream in a rich butternut squash soup, or bemoan the missing corned beef in a warm tempeh (a soybean preparation) Reuben sandwich.

Vegan approximations of American classics are on the menu alongside such exotica as *hiziki* and *kombu* (Japanese seaweeds), and *daikon* (a root), which bolster the Kinpira salad. Service is friendly and the waitstaff are happy to explain the dishes. **Cheap**

Sobaya *noodle seduction* `4 E2`

229 East 9th Street (between 2nd & 3rd Aves)
212 533 6966
Open lunch & dinner daily

The menu explains that soba buckwheat noodles contain vitamins and protein, and are especially good to eat after drinking alcohol. Well, if that doesn't explain the crowds, then it must be the authentic Japanese flavors. Big bowls of stomach-pleasing noodle soup are the main focus, served with fresh scallions and your choice of extras, such as vegetables, duck, tempura, and yam. Appetizers include fried mushroom with shrimp paste, spinach with sesame sauce, and selected sushi-style dishes. A comprehensive sake menu offers a guide to the level of fullness and flavor of each type.

The decor is typically Japanese in its simplicity and sense of order. The friendly waitstaff are generally hip Japanese transplants sporting navy samurai bandanas on their heads. **Cheap**

The Spotted Pig *English-style gastropub* `3 C2`
314 West 11th Street • 212 620 0393
>> **www.thespottedpig.com** Open lunch & dinner daily

Modeled on cozy English gastropubs, The Spotted Pig offers a menu of steamed cockles and roll mops (pickled herring), as well as chargrilled burgers and salads. They don't take reservations, but that leaves time to nurse a pint or two of ale amid a congenial crowd while waiting. **Moderate**

Blue Ribbon Sushi *the freshest fish* `3 C4`
119 Sullivan Street (between Prince & Spring Sts)
212 343 0404
Open noon–2am daily

Like its West Village brother *(see below)*, the SoHo outpost of Blue Ribbon obsesses over the freshness of ingredients. Here, the main ingredient is raw fish. Try sitting at the sushi counter rather than the popular back room for faster service. **Expensive**

Blue Ribbon Bakery *Old World delights* `3 C4`
33 Downing Street (at Bedford St.) • 212 337 0404
Open lunchtime to 2am daily (to midnight Sun)

Inside this cozy space, Village sophisticates crowd windowside tables for European indulgences such as foie gras, antipasti, and crusty home-made breads. Ask to be seated downstairs in the wine cellar-like space where diners can watch freshly baked breads come out of the oven. **Expensive**

Tomoe Sushi *Japanese-style delectables* `3 C4`
172 Thompson Street (between Bleecker & Houston Sts)
212 777 9346
Open all day Wed–Sat, dinner Mon (cash or Amex only)

Tomoe presents New Yorkers with some of the freshest fish in the city. That is why, despite a lack of atmosphere in this small sushi joint, people will line up for as much as an hour, just to get a taste of the "real thing." The wait is worth it. **Moderate**

Restaurants

Otto Enoteca & Pizzeria *huge snacks* `3 D3`

No. 15th Avenue (at 8th St.) • 212 995 9559
>> www.ottopizzeria.com Open all day daily

Throngs gather nightly to taste celebrity chef Mario Batali's hearty Italian snack foods. The thin pizzas are grilled (not baked) and topped with a diverse range of ingredients – everything from meatballs to fried duck eggs. Save room for the unique, savory *gelati* (ice creams) and *sorbetti*. **Cheap**

La Palapa Rockola *authentic Mexican* `3 C3`

359 6th Avenue (at Washington Pl.) • 212 243 6870
>> www.lapalapa.com Open all day daily

This place debunks the myth that New York lacks credible Mexican cuisine. The interior evokes Mexico's colonial heartland and cinematic Golden Age, providing a festive backdrop for the robust dishes. Pair fish tacos with a frosty Negra Modelo beer and say "Hola" to heaven. **Moderate**

Babbo *the sophistication of northern Italy* `3 C3`

110 Waverly Place (between MacDougal St. & 6th Ave.)
212 777 0303
>> www.babbonyc.com Open dinner daily

Babbo's reputation as one of New York's top Italian restaurants is due to the quality of its menu, devised by Mario Batali *(see also Otto, above)*. You will need to reserve early or ask about last-minute cancellations.

If your party agrees on a pricier meal, try the culinary adventure of either the traditional or pasta tasting menus. However, the main menu, offering dishes such as beef cheek ravioli and fennel-dusted sweetbreads, is also daring and justly lauded. Take time to peruse the wine menu or discuss the options with the knowledgable sommelier. The Italian selections are extensive and expertly chosen.

Despite the price tag, there's no need to dress up – the converted carriage house, with elegant floral arrangements, provides the panache. You just have to leave room for a dessert and *digestivo*. **Expensive**

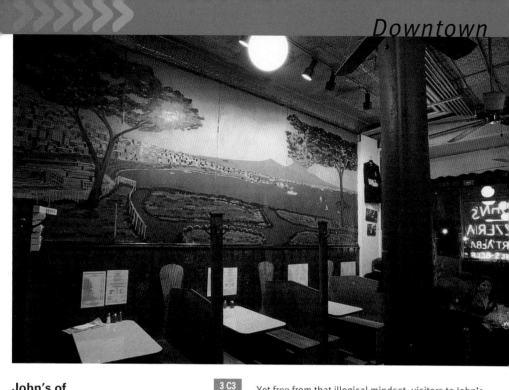

John's of
Bleecker Street *profound pizza*
278 Bleecker Street (between 6th & 7th Aves) • 212 243 1680
>> www.johnsofbleeckerstreet.com
Open lunch & dinner daily (to 1am Fri & Sat); cash only

In this city, pizzeria comparisons are a hot topic and frequently dissolve into shouting matches. Even politicians dare not state their position on pizza, for fear of alienating potential voters. Out of the din, however, one name emerges that inspires more emotion than any other: John's of Bleecker Street.

John's likes to shout about its time-honored credentials: "Est. 1929" is writ large in white letters on its burgundy awning, and rapturous restaurant reviews are plastered to the window. For some New Yorkers, who believe a great pizzeria should be unknown to all but the savviest subway riders, John's very accessibility and fame are sufficient reasons to eliminate it from any discussion of the city's best.

Yet free from that illogical mindset, visitors to John's are in for a supremely satisfying meal.

The restaurant's popularity means that weekend lunch and dinner lines extend to the next storefront, but they move quickly. Once you're inside and seated at a weathered wooden booth, your olfactory nerves will soon react to the unmistakable, heady waft of garlic and romano cheese. To quiet your stomach, start with fresh antipasti and a frosty Peroni lager.

Purists should then opt for the basic cheese and tomato pie, fresh from John's coal-fired oven. What they will be presented with is a thin, smoky, lightly charred crust covered with a bright, slightly acidic sauce, full-cream mozzarella and vibrant spices. Non-purists can choose from garlicky meatballs and other tempting home-made toppings. Once you've chomped your way through a pie, you'll be able to establish your own position in a debate on New York's explosive topic. **Moderate**

Restaurants

Cones *superior ices* 3 C3
272 Bleecker St. (bet. Morton & Jones) • 212 414 1795
Open 1–11 Sun–Thu, 1–1 Fri & Sat (cash only)

What compels a man to drive two hours from Upstate New York to the Village with an empty portable freezer plugged into his car's dash, only to drive straight home again after filling it? Simply this: hand-packed quarts of the best ice cream in the state. True story.

Looking at Cones, there is little to indicate what might stir such passion. It's a tidy parlor, with a few tables and photos of unremarkable sundaes on the walls. But the real show is in the freezer: 32 steel bins brimming with kaleidoscopically colored creams and sorbets, in the tradition of authentic Italian *gelaterias*. *Dulce de leche* and coffee mocha are deliciously rich, whereas tangy fruit sorbets and dairy-free ices present a lighter antidote to the summer swelter. This is why Cones' acclaim stretches from New York to its owners' native Argentina. Still undecided? Brothers Raul and Oscar readily offer tastings. **Cheap**

BB Sandwich Bar *cheesesteak perfected* 3 C3
120 West 3rd St. (between 6th Ave. & Macdougal St.)
212 473 7500 Open 10:30–10 daily

Gary Thompson claims he prepares the best cheesesteak in the city, and the length of the lunch line at his small, upstairs sandwich counter confirms this is no mere boast. Thinly sliced steak is placed on a puffy Kaiser roll, then topped with marinated onions, spicy tomato relish and white American cheese. **Cheap**

Food on the Hoof

Many downtown snack stops cater to people with bite-sized budgets and a desire to keep moving. Irresistible pork and vegetarian wontons can be had in the Lower East Side's **Fried Dumpling**. West Villagers swear by **Mamoun's** fresh, crispy falafel and tangy hummus, and **Pepe Rosso's** bright, delicious Italian specialties. Eat them while watching life's rich pageant in Washington Square Park. For late-night barhoppers, **Crif Dogs** offers sustenance in the form of Chihuahua hot dogs (wrapped in bacon and topped with avocado and sour cream). Or draw a barrage of envious glances on Second Avenue with a paper funnel full of fries from **Pommes Frites,** topped with any of their 25 tasty sauces. For all addresses, *see p216.*

   For the very latest on New York go to ≫ www.realcity.dk.com

NY Dosas *cheap veggie manna* `3 C3`
West 4th Street & Sullivan Street • 917 710 2092
Open 11–5 Mon–Sat

Even on blustery winter days, NYU students line up at this vending cart at the southwest corner of Washington Square for heavenly vegetarian dosas. The south Indian crepes are filled with root vegetables, chickpeas, and spices, resulting in something far too delicate to be classified merely as "street food." **Cheap**

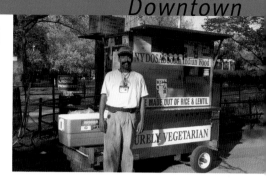

Mary's Fish Camp *chowder heaven* `3 B3`
64 Charles Street (at West 4th St.) • 646 486 2185
➤➤ www.marysfishcamp.com
Open lunch & dinner Mon–Sat

Mary's seafood chowder, and lobster and clam rolls are equal to the best of any New England oceanside restaurant. Add to this the atmosphere of rustic charm, and you see why customers are lured to this tiny space, if necessary waiting outside for tables. **Moderate**

Wallsé *august Austrian fare* `3 A3`
344 West 11th Street (at Washington St.) • 212 352 2300
➤➤ www.wallse.com
Open dinner Mon–Sun, brunch Sat & Sun

Opened by chef Kurt Gutenbrunner in 2000, Wallsé has developed a devoted following. The two-room restaurant has a restful feel, with white linen tablecloths, pale walls, and carefully chosen art work. Many of the clientele are regulars, giving the place an easy-going West Village vibe.

In accordance with Austria's gastronomic traditions, Gutenbrunner produces richly flavored dishes. Besides his famed Wiener schnitzel, other notable dishes include beef goulash with herbed *spaetzle* (a noodle side dish), apple strudel, and *rosti* (a potato and onion side dish) with lobster.

Wallsé also attracts a die-hard band of smokers too, due to its policy of lending all puffing customers beautifully tailored, bright red capes to wear during their stint outside in the cool night air. **Expensive**

Restaurants

Florent *24/7 camp* `3 A2`

69 Gansevoort Street (between Greenwich & Washington Sts)
212 989 5779
>> www.restaurantflorent.com   Open 24 hours daily (cash only)

There's no better place than this for *moules frites* at 3am. Florent offers great home-made soups and a superb weekend brunch. The clientele ranges from daytime workers to outrageously dressed clubbers. Changing messages over the bar will amuse. **Moderate**

Sumile *great fish – raw and cooked* `3 C2`

154 West 13th Street (between 6th & 7th Aves)
212 989 7699
>> www.sumile.com   Open dinner daily

A chic Japanese joint. Chef Josh DeChellis creates innovative dishes, such as tea-smoked eel and black sesame paste with raspberries. The cocktails are fruity and fun, and the menu changes seasonally. There's not a grain of rice in the house! **Expensive**

Tartine *bijou bistro* `3 B2`

253 West 11th Street (at West 4th Street)
212 229 2611 • Open lunch & dinner Tue–Sat,
brunch Sat & Sun; cash only

On a prime corner location that's great for people-watching, Tartine serves consistently delicious light French fare. Croissants are super-buttery, the savory tarts are divine, and the weekend brunch is one of the best deals in town. There's a BYOB policy. **Moderate**

Dining Institutions

Whether for food, tradition, location, or ambience, some classic restaurants in New York just can't be ignored. **Nobu** is renowned for celebrity-spotting and the chef's tasting menu of creative sushi. **The Four Seasons** has been serving Continental cuisine to those with deep pockets since 1959. The space was designed by Mies van der Rohe and Philip Johnson and features Lichtenstein lithographs. **Chanterelle** in Tribeca has been offering classic French and innovative Franco-American cuisine since 1979. For a more casual feel, with first-rate food to boot, **Gramercy Tavern** is another favorite, serving New American cuisine in relaxed surroundings. Finally, **Tavern on the Green** does great brunches. For individual restaurant details, *see pp224–6*.

City Bakery *pastries & chocolate* `3 C1`

3 West 18th St. (bet. 5th & 6th Aves) • 212 366 1414
>> www.thecitybakery.com/index2.htm
Open 7am–7:30pm Mon–Sat, 9am–5:30pm Sun

City Bakery leaves every customer contented. Its salad bar is arguably New York's best, and it also has a huge selection of flaky breakfast pastries, tarts, and decadent tortes. Linger over one of their superb hot chocolates – irresistible with a marshmallow. **Cheap**

Union Square Café *NY favorite* `3 D1`

21 E. 16th St. (bet. 5th Ave. & Union Sq. W.) • 212 243 4020
>> www.unionsquarecafe.com
Open lunch Mon–Sat and dinner daily

Rated as one of New York's favorite restaurants, USC delivers New American cuisine in a relaxed ambience, augmented by fresh flowers and a spacious feel. It's always crowded, so reserve a table early or try for a space at the bar. Go for the daily specials. **Expensive**

Red Cat *creative cuisine in a funky place* `5 B5`

227 10th Avenue (between 23rd & 24th Sts) • 212 242 1122
>> www.theredcat.com
Open dinner daily

Red Cat's funky decor, fabulous food, and seamless service round off perfectly an afternoon spent gallery-hopping. Creative dishes might include chicken with sugarplum and sweet onion sauce, or risotto fritters with blueberry compote. **Moderate**

Grand Sichuan International *bad decor, great food* `5 C5`

229 9th Avenue (at 24th St.) • 212 620 5200
Open all day daily

In style-obsessed Chelsea, this rarity attracts a loyal crowd on the merits of its food alone. For while the decor is stark, the Chinese cuisine is excellent. Try whole fried fish, garlicky sautéed spinach, and addictive pork and vegetable dumplings. **Cheap**

Restaurants

Biltmore Room *plush atmosphere* `5 C5`
290 8th Avenue (between 24th & 25th Sts) • 212 807 0111
>> www.thebiltmoreroom.com Open dinner daily

An entrance through thick velvet curtains adds an air of exclusivity to the Biltmore Room. Beyond the threshold lies a swanky bar and stylish dining room. The bar has its own scene, and people often come just to sip signature cocktails such as the Gin Blossom (infused with basil and combined with elderflower syrup). In the dining area – a mixture of gentlemen's-club tradition and something far more chic – chandeliers hang from the high ceiling, and mirrors amplify the grandeur. Subtle lighting and funky music create a warm mood, and orchids add color.

The attentive staff serve dishes with Asian and Middle Eastern influences, including Algerian spiced lamb, miso-marinated Alaskan cod, and giant prawns wrapped in crispy noodles with avocado and tomato salad and mango salsa. The warm chocolate tart is not to be missed. **Expensive**

Bolo *more than paella* `6 E5`
23 East 22nd Street (between Broadway & Park Ave. S.)
212 228 2200
>> www.bolorestaurant.com Open lunch Mon–Fri, dinner daily

Bolo creates modern interpretations of some of the best traditional Spanish dishes. The menu features inventive tapas, black squid ink risotto, and shellfish and chicken paella. There's a bar, and the atmosphere is upbeat. Good lunch deals. **Expensive**

Tabla *Indian fusion* `6 E5`
11 Madison Avenue (at 25th St.) • 212 889 0667
>> www.tablany.com Open lunch Mon–Fri, dinner daily

Fusing New American and Indian cuisine, Tabla presents dishes such as Goan spiced crab cake and tandoori breads using inventive flavors. A striking staircase divides the colorful formal upstairs dining room from the downstairs Bread Bar, which offers a less formal, slightly cheaper dining option. **Expensive**

For the very latest on New York go to >> www.realcity.dk.com

Tamarind *epicurean spices* `6 F5`

41–3 East 22nd Street (between Broadway & Park Ave. S.)
212 674 7400
>> www.tamarinde22.com Open lunch & dinner daily

Large glass windows, an unfussy modern interior, and cut flowers on each table set the tone. Tamarind has earned several prestigious culinary accolades, and its two proud owners are often seen milling about with diners, basking in positive feedback, no doubt. Such openness also extends to the kitchens, which are surrounded by glass, so you can watch the food being prepared without getting a noseful of every dish.

House specialties include a signature dish of tandoori scallops presented in a fried potato lattice cup, *bhagerey baignan* (eggplant with coconut, sesame, and peanut sauce), Tamarind's chutneys, and a home-made cheese. Lamb and lobster feature prominently on the menu too. The Tearoom offers sandwiches, a vast array of teas, and desserts in a more casual, intimate environment. **Moderate**

Dos Caminos *trendy Mexican* `6 F5`

373 Park Avenue South (between 26th & 27th Sts)
212 294 1000
>> www.brguestrestaurants.com
Open lunch & dinner Mon–Fri, brunch & dinner Sat & Sun

Popular with young professionals, this large restaurant and bar is a vibrant place for margaritas and great Mexican fare. The famed guacamole is prepared at your table, so you can dictate the spice factor. **Moderate**

Blue Smoke *upscale American barbecue* `6 F4`

116 East 27th St. (between Park & Lexington Aves)
212 447 7733
>> www.bluesmoke.com Open lunch & dinner daily

Chef Ken Callaghan smokes spareribs, beef brisket, organic chicken, and sausages over hickory and apple woods, keeping meats flavorful and succulent. The modern dining room fills with boisterous Manhattanites nightly. Excellent beer selection. Live jazz. **Moderate**

Restaurants

i Trulli `6 F4`
wine & pasta in a warm atmosphere

122 East 27th Street (between Lexington & Park Ave. S.)
212 481 7372
>> www.itrulli.com Open lunch & dinner Mon–Fri, dinner Sat

i Trulli's delectable cuisine is true to its roots, which lie in the Italian region of Puglia. Specialties here include the *panelle* (chickpea fritters with goat cheese) and home-made pastas. Try a "flight of wine" (three to taste), and sample cheeses and meats. **Expensive**

Mandoo Bar `6 E4`
Top-notch Korean cooking

2 West 32nd Street (between Broadway & 5th Ave.)
212 279 3075
>> www.mandoobar.com Open all day daily

Cooks bustle about preparing plump little *mandoo* – delicate dumplings stuffed with vegetables, fish, or meat. The salads and seafood dishes are also superb. Avoid weekday lunchtimes when this informal place is packed with local business people. **Cheap**

Artisanal `6 F4`
cheese, please

2 Park Avenue (entrance on 32nd Street) • 212 725 8585
>> www.artisanalcheese.com Open all day daily (brunch served 11am–3pm Sat & Sun)

The revived tradition of fondue-sharing creates a social buzz in the high-ceilinged dining room of this bistro and fromagerie. Various fondues are available, prepared with different cheeses, herbs and oil infusions. Some are traditional recipes, others experimental. Cheese is also the focus of salads, and appetizers such as a three-cheese onion soup. A tarte tatin in a cheddar crust continues the theme into dessert. There are non-cheese selections – *cassoulet* (bean stew), or chicken roasted "under the brick" – but choose at least one course devoted to the star ingredient.

A requisite cheese plate takes on new meaning as the *fromagier* guides you through 200-plus selections. You can also order a "cheese and wine flight" at the bar (three choices of each) and, of course, buy cheese from the shop. **Moderate**

Cho Dang Gol *Korean creations* `6 E3`

55 West 35th Street (between 5th & 6th Aves)
212 695 8222 Open all day daily

Located in the heart of "Koreatown," this establishment is unusual in catering equally to meat-eaters, vegans, and vegetarians. The authentic yet accessible dishes form a perfect introduction to Korean cuisine.

Gop dol bim bap is a good one to try. With this, a heated stone bowl is filled with rice, vegetables (or meat), broth, spicy red paste, and an egg. You mix the ingredients and let some of the rice crisp at the bottom. You can also expect to receive the *ban chan* – little plates of appetizers that come with any meal and include *kim chi* (spicy pickled cabbage).

Cho Dang Gol is also known for its superb leek pancakes and melt-in-your-mouth tofu (bean curd), which is made on the premises, as is an alcoholic drink called Makkuli. The dishes vary in spiciness – ask the waitstaff for guidance if necessary. The lunchtime specials are great deals. **Cheap**

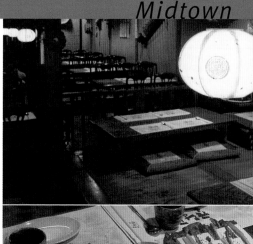

Sandwich Planet *sliced bread sensation* `5 C2`

534 9th Avenue (bet. 39th & 40th Sts) • **212 273 9768**
» www.sandwichplanet.com Open 10:30–8:30 daily

Despite its closet-like dimensions, this pitstop offers a seemingly limitless choice of custom-made sandwiches. Should one of the five tables be available, linger over a signature creation like the Armani: thin prosciutto, fresh mozzarella, artichoke hearts, and rocket pressed between toasted foccacia. **Cheap**

Mi Nidito *surprisingly good Mexican* `5 C1`

852 8th Avenue (between 51st & 52nd Sts) • **212 265 0022**
Open all day daily

With its gaudy signage hawking dozens of Margarita varieties, this unassuming Hell's Kitchen eatery is not the most obvious place to find some of the city's best Mexican food. But the roasted chicken is irresistible – crisp, succulent, and studded with garlic – and the mango margaritas justify all the hoopla. **Moderate**

Restaurants

Churrascaria Plataforma *Brazilian BBQ* `5 C1`
316 West 49th Street (between 8th & 9th Aves)
212 245 0505
» www.churrascariaplataforma.com Open all day daily

Catering mainly to a post-theater crowd, this Brazilian *churrascaria* is a novel and lively fixed-price barbecue. Guests are led to tables in the capacious, elegant dining room and each given a round disk – one face red, the other green. After trips to the salad bar, the crowd settles in for the impending meat extravaganza.

Display the disk's green side and gracious servers approach, wielding skewers of top-quality roasted meats – sirloin steaks, sausages, prime rib, chicken, and baby lamb chops – and fish such as salmon. When your plate is full, flip the disk to red. When you've emptied it, flip again to green, and repeat the performance until your belly attains the desired level of distension. Plataforma's perfect Caipirinha is a refreshing, albeit potent, palette cleanser of cachaça rum, sugar, and mint over cracked ice. **Expensive**

Genki Sushi *sushi on the roll* `6 E1`
9 East 46th St. (bet. 5th & Madison) • 212 983 5018
» www.genkisushi.com
Open lunch and dinner to 8:30 Mon–Fri, to 5 Sat

A conveyor belt stocked with midtown's freshest fish revolves through the colorful dining area. Take your pick from plates (color-coded according to price) of assembled rolls and succulent sashimi. Lunchtimes are busy, so come early evening if you can. **Cheap**

Ess-a-Bagel *classic snacks* `6 F1`
831 3rd Avenue (at 51st St.) • 212 980 1010
» www.ess-a-bagel.com
Open 6:30am–9pm daily (to 5 Sun)

This spacious midtown shop bakes arguably the city's best bagels. Feel free to linger over any of 14 varieties, coupled with award-winning whitefish salad, Nova Scotia smoked salmon, eggplant salad, or a classic spread of cream cheese. **Cheap**

Acqua Pazza *fresh pasta, seafood & fish* `8 E5`

36 West 52nd Street (between 5th & 6th Aves) • 212 582 6900
>> www.acquapazzanyc.com
Open lunch & dinner Mon–Fri, dinner only Sat

Acqua Pazza – "crazy water" – belies its name with serious Italian food. Octopus, crab, and whole baked fish are typical items on the menu. Pasta infused with espresso is an unusual dish, harking back to the days when coffee was used as a preservative. **Expensive**

Aquavit *Swedish sensation* `8 F5`

65 East 55th Street (between Park & Madison Aves)
212 307 7311
>> www.aquavit.org
Open lunch Mon–Fri, dinner daily, brunch Sun

Swedish chef Marcus Samuelsson, who won a prestigious "Best Chef in New York City" award in 2003, has taken the Scandinavian cuisine at this restaurant to new levels of gastronomic genius. It's not cheap, but worth the price, especially if you sit in the main dining room, which is in an atrium that features an indoor waterfall.

The eponymous aquavit is a potent Scandinavian spirit, double distilled, with flavors added in the second distillation. This and glasses of Carlsberg beer are served alongside house specialties such as herrings. Other favorites include seafood stew in a delicious dill sauce, brioche-wrapped salmon, and Kobe beef ravioli. The restaurant also prepares a beguiling gravlax and tandoori smoked salmon.

Three tasting menus, including a vegetarian option, offer seven-course "Aquavit Bite" meals. Another way to sample many of these flavors at a little less expense is to eat upstairs in the Aquavit Café. The café's kitchen is separate from the restaurant's, but both are overseen by the executive chef. However, Swedish meatballs are available only in the café.

Several house-made and unusual aquavits are available; flavors may include black pepper and vanilla, and pear and cloudberry. **Expensive**

Restaurants

Town *sophistication & pizzazz*   `8 E5`
Chambers Hotel 15 West 56th Street
(between 5th & 6th Aves) • 212 582 4445
» www.townnyc.com
Open breakfast, lunch & dinner daily, brunch Sun

A fashionable restaurant with a fanciful interior and creative Euro-American cuisine. The menu changes seasonally, but signature dishes include, in summer, soft-shell crab. **Expensive**

Norma's *a perfect start to the day*   `7 D5`
At Le Parker Meridien Hotel, 118 West 57th Street
(between 6th & 7th Aves) • 212 708 7460
» www.parkermeridien.com/normas
Open breakfast & lunch daily

Norma's is a swish place, offering one of the most luxurious breakfasts in town: freshly squeezed juice, mango and papaya with cinnamon crepes, mammoth omelets, and French brioche toast. **Moderate**

Geisha *stylish Japanese-American joint*   `8 E4`
33 East 61st Street (between Park & Madison Aves)
212 813 1112   Open lunch & dinner Mon–Sat

Don your best black outfit and blend in with the crowd sipping cocktails while waiting for tables. The menu focuses on seafood with Japanese flavors, such as lobster served with asparagus and mushroom *udon* noodles. Downstairs is hip and fun; upstairs is a bit more subdued. There's a sushi bar too. **Expensive**

Diner Etiquette

Diners – known as "coffee shops" within New York City limits – are part of the quintessential NY experience. They are social levelers, where a poor poet and a business mogul can rub elbows at the counter over omelets. Diner food is comfort food – all-day breakfast fare, including eggs any style, as well as burgers, French fries, and grilled cheese sandwiches. Prices don't dictate the quality of a diner; location, longevity, menu, and staff do. Your server should be courteous, but don't get offended if he/she rushes you during a busy period when tables need to be turned over. Coffee is rarely strong but should always be limitless. Kitchen lingo is part of the tradition: eggs are "sunny-side up" or "(easy) over"; rye toast is placed "whiskey down."

Serendipity 3 *American staples*

8 F4

225 East 60th Street (between 2nd & 3rd Aves)
212 838 3531
>> www.serendipity3.com Open lunch & dinner daily

This is a favorite of Upper East Siders thanks to its satisfying American comfort food. The chicken pot pies, burgers, soups, and salads are, however, mere preambles to dessert: the frozen hot chocolate surely ranks among New York's finest creations. **Cheap**

March *quiet elegance, gourmet food*

8 H4

405 East 58th Street (between 1st Ave & Sutton Pl.)
212 754 6272
>> www.marchrestaurant.com Open dinner daily

Superbly presented food in a renovated townhouse. The gourmet food has a wide range of influences, but there's a discernible Asian accent in the use of raw fish, soy, sesame, and dishes such as shrimp tempura. Outdoor tables from May to October. **Expensive**

Mezzaluna *heart-melting tiramisu*

8 F2

1295 3rd Avenue (between 74th & 65th Sts) • 212 535 9600
Open lunch & dinner daily (cash or Amex only)

A lively and intimate spot for northern Italian cuisine, Mezzaluna excels in freshly made pastas, fish dishes, and brick-oven-baked pizzas. The creamy, light tiramisu is one of the best you'll find in New York. Artistic depictions of half-moons *(mezzaluna)* adorn the walls. Staff are very friendly. **Expensive**

Annie's *hearty brunches*

8 F1

1381 3rd Avenue (between 78th & 79th Sts)
212 327 4853 Open lunch and dinner daily
(to midnight Fri & Sat)

An excellent Sunday brunch (served until 4pm) packs families into this classic New York bistro. Wicked Bloody Marys and generous portions are *de rigueur*. Annie's is also a pancake lover's dream: wholewheat, apple, banana, mixed berry ... take your pick. **Cheap**

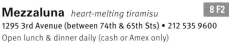

Restaurants

Atlantic Grill *fresh fish, fresh atmosphere* `8 F1`

1341 3rd Avenue (between 76th & 77th Sts) • 212 988 9200
>> www.brguestrestaurants.com
Open lunch & dinner Mon–Sat, brunch & dinner Sun

To please the finicky Upper East Side inhabitants, food, service, and atmosphere have to be of a high order in any establishment here. So the long-standing popularity of the Atlantic Grill attests to its culinary credentials. The restaurant excels at well-prepared, very fresh fish, accompanied by a good wine list, and waitstaff who are both competent and efficient.

A sense of refined informality pervades the spacious dining area, spread throughout two rooms. Additional sidewalk seating is available when weather permits. Specialties include oysters, crabcakes, lightly fried sesame-crusted lobster roll, and barbecued *mahi mahi* (a particularly succulent, slightly sweet fish). There are also daily specials, and you can order small plates from a sushi bar. Book ahead to reserve a table or be prepared to wait – it's worth it. **Moderate**

Candle 79 *fine meat-free dining* `8 F1`

154 East 79th Street (between Lexington & 3rd Aves)
212 537 7179
>> www.candlecafe.com   Open lunch & dinner daily

An upscale restaurant offering wonderful vegetarian and vegan masterpieces, Candle 79 pushes the limit of what you might expect from a meatless menu. Many a dedicated carnivore is won over by the flavors and textures experienced here. Inventive dishes include squash and wild mushroom risotto, and porcini-crusted *seitan* (a meaty wheat protein concoction) with garlicky greens and a wild mushroom red wine sauce.

In addition to organic wine, sake, and beer, the list of non-alcoholic juices and tonics is heavenly. Options such as an elderberry extract with apple and lemon, and an orange juice, coconut, and banana smoothie are divine. The less-formal sister business, Candle Café (1307 3rd Avenue at 75th St; 212 472 0970), also offers creative green food (tasty salads, wraps, and soups) and has a juice bar at the front. **Moderate**

Sushi of Gari *inspiring sushi* `8 G1`

402 East 78th Street (between 1st & York Aves)
212 517 5340
Open dinner Tue–Sun

The tasting menu at this small, simply decorated treasure enables innovative sushi chef Masatoshi Gari Sugio and his staff to demonstrate their mastery over fish and seafood. An à-la-carte menu is available, but allow the chefs to surprise and delight. **Expensive**

Ouest *first-rate New American fare* `9 B5`

2315 Broadway (between 83rd & 84th Sts) • 212 580 8700
>> www.ouestny.com Open dinner daily, brunch Sun

Ouest is about panache in just about every detail. The bar area is the first thing you'll notice, with its wood-paneled walls, shades of deep red, and old-fashioned fans hanging from the ceiling. Beyond this is a corridor that passes a glazed wine cellar and leads to the main dining area. Stylish round, red-leather booths take up most of the room, with square tables along the periphery. There's balcony seating too, though this is a bit cramped and best avoided. The bright kitchen is open for all to see, and the music adds to the atmosphere, tending toward 20s–40s jazz.

Owner/chef Tom Valenti has been much lauded for pleasing the palate and delighting the eye, here and at other top New York restaurants. Highly sophisticated dishes emerge from his kitchen, such as the intriguingly named "truffled omelet soufflé" with mousseline sauce, or lobster ravioli with a herb salad. Well-sourced game and other roast meats are typical offerings. Specials include braised lamb shanks on Mondays and Tuesdays, and the legendary meat loaf on a Sunday. Allow time to peruse the globe-trotting wine list, which has won awards, or ask for advice if the selection proves overwhelming. By contrast, the dessert selection is short and sweet, and includes a panna cotta that can't be beaten.

Ouest's superior brunch menu also wins plaudits by offering refined breakfast food such as scrambled egg with house-smoked sturgeon. **Expensive**

Restaurants

Picholine *traditional excellence*  `7 C3`
35 West 64th Street (between Broadway & Central Park W.)
212 724 8585
Open lunch Sat, dinner daily

The eponymous picholine (green olive) theme adorns the plates and is evident in dishes, such as caramelized ribs with olive sauce. Picholine is also renowned for its cheese cart. Jackets are required in the main dining room; the front bar is less formal. **Expensive**

Pasha *high-class Turkish* `7 C2`
70 West 71st Street (between Columbus Ave. & Central Park W.) • 212 579 8751
Open dinner daily

A sumptuous eatery fit for Ottoman royalty. The rich, deep-red and yellow dining area is hung with vibrant tapestries. Kebabs, stuffed vine leaves, and dozens of other well-seasoned delights are presented by charming waitstaff. Great pre-theater deals. **Moderate**

El Malecón II *Caribbean specialties* `9 B3`
764 Amsterdam Avenue (between 97th & 98th Sts)
212 864 5648
Open breakfast, lunch & dinner daily

Given New York 's sizeable Dominican population, it is not surprising that some of the best Dominican cooking north of Miami is found here. While the staples do not differ greatly from those used in other Caribbean and many Central American kitchens, nuances make all the difference. Few restaurants get the alchemy quite so right as El Malecón II, younger brother of the Washington Heights original. Diners familiar with the restaurant's namesake – the seaside boulevard in Santo Domingo – might raise an eyebrow at the modest dining room. But one look at the spice-encrusted, brown skins of chickens on rotisseries will quell doubts. A mixed crowd of ex-pat families and students enjoys *mofongo* (sweet plantains mashed with stewed pork), and *asopao con longaniza* (rice in broth with spicy Spanish sausage). **Cheap**

Aix *inspiration from France* **9 B5**
2398 Broadway (at 88th St.) • 212 874 7400
≫ www.aixnyc.com Open dinner daily, brunch Sun

The bright oranges and sky blues in this restaurant evoke the colors of Provence. Rather than focusing on traditional Provençal dishes, however, Chef Didier Virot's menu offers a wider range of creative French fare. The star dish is halibut in a garlic cream with oatmeal porcini cake and walnut sauce. **Expensive**

Symposium *genuine Greek* **11 B5**
544 West 113th Street (between Amsterdam Ave. & Broadway)
212 865 1011
Open all day daily

Symposium has been serving stuffed vine leaves and moussaka for over 20 years to its regulars. Sit in the cozy taverna or walk through the kitchen to the enclosed back garden. The Symposium Salad provides a little taste of many dishes on the menu. **Moderate**

New Leaf Café *urban renewal enterprise*
Fort Tryon Park • 212 568 5323 • Ⓜ "A" train to 190th Street
≫ www.nyrp.org/newleaf Open breakfast lunch & dinner
Tue–Sat, brunch & dinner Sun

All net proceeds from this café, which is set in a converted stone house in Fort Tryon Park, go to the restoration and maintenance of the park. Organic salad leaves and wild salmon feature on the menu. Try to catch the Thursday evening Jazz Night. **Moderate**

Noodle Pudding *consistently tasty Italian* **13 A3**
38 Henry Street (between Cranberry & Middagh Sts), Brooklyn
718 625 3737
Open dinner Tue–Sun (cash only)

Don't let the name deceive you: Noodle Pudding refers to a pasta dish, not Asian food here. *Osso buco* (veal knuckle), *penne arrabiata*, real mozzarella, and panna cotta feature among the Italian staples. Locals pack this casually stylish restaurant nightly. **Moderate**

Restaurants

The River Café *enchanting views & food* `13 A3`

1 Water Street (between Furman & Old Fulton Sts)
718 522 5200
≫ www.therivercafe.com Open dinner daily, lunch Mon–Sat,
brunch Sun (formal dress required in evening)

The River Café began serving sublime food in 1977 and hasn't looked back. In a superb setting directly on the waterfront, with a stunning view of the Manhattan skyline and Brooklyn Bridge, this is probably one of the most romantic dining places in the world. Much of the seating allows couples to gaze out at the scene together. The reputable kitchen tends to gravitate toward unusual meats and seafood. Foie gras, rabbit, suckling pig, and caviar might all feature on the menu, with a token dish for vegetarians. The Maine Lobster is a favorite. For novelty value, order the Chocolate Marquise Brooklyn Bridge – a model in fine chocolate. Lunch is slightly cheaper than the prix-fixe dinner. If just savoring the ambience, go for wine and appetizers in the Terrace Room. **Expensive**

The Grocery *a neighborhood star* `13 B4`

288 Smith Street (between Sackett & Union Sts)
718 596 3335
Open dinner Mon–Sat

The petite Grocery offers New American fare and has long been a favorite with locals. It is praised equally for its use of ultra-fresh ingredients and its service. Dishes tend to be simple, and flavors sing out, as in the juicy and healthily trimmed grilled lamb. **Moderate**

Joya *Thai spice* `13 B4`

215 Court Street (at Warren St.) • 718 222 3484
Open dinner daily ✓

With its industrial-chic interior imparting a level of SoHo sophistication to the quaint Boerum Hill/Carroll Gardens neighborhood, Joya lures discerning Manhattanites across the river. Young professionals flock here for the ambience and the deftly executed Thai dishes that rarely venture above $10. **Cheap**

Park Slope Chip Shop *comfort food* 13 C5

383 5th Avenue (at 6th St.) • 718 CHIPSHOP
>> www.chipshopnyc.com Open all day daily

One of Park Slope's most cheerful eateries is inspired by a British phenomenon in dining. Young families and ex-pat students pining for familiar comfort food relish generous platters of chips, fried haddock, crisps, curries, and fishcakes. Dessert? Fried chocolate candy, of course. **Cheap**

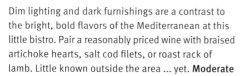

Al Di La *Venetian trattoria* 13 C4

248 5th Avenue (at Carroll St.) • 718 783 4565
>> www.aldilatrattoria.com Open dinner daily except Tue

First-rate food served in a romantic, candlelit setting ensures Al Di La's devoted following. Specials include polenta, gnocchi with fried sage, and grilled sardines. The restaurant doesn't take reservations, so be prepared to have a drink at a neighboring bar while you wait for a table, or go off-peak. **Moderate**

Convivium Osteria *splendid bistro* 13 C4

68 5th Avenue (between Bergen St. & St Mark's Ave.)
718 857 1833
Open dinner daily

Dim lighting and dark furnishings are a contrast to the bright, bold flavors of the Mediterranean at this little bistro. Pair a reasonably priced wine with braised artichoke hearts, salt cod filets, or roast rack of lamb. Little known outside the area ... yet. **Moderate**

LouLou *a taste of Brittany* 13 C3

222 DeKalb Avenue (between Adelphi St. & Clermont Ave.)
718 246 0633
Open dinner daily, brunch Sat & Sun

Cozy LouLou is a great stop before or after a visit to the Brooklyn Academy of Music *(see p135)*. Fish, seafood, and scrumptious crepes are the mainstays of a menu that focuses on the Brittany region of France. Try the lovely back garden. **Moderate**

Restaurants

i-Shebeen Madiba
South African eaterie `13 C3`
195 DeKalb Avenue (between Adelphi St. & Carlton Ave.)
718 855 9190
>> www.i-shebeen.com Open all day daily (to 1am Fri & Sat)

Part Zulu trinket shop, part rustic-style bistro, this place is intriguing. Cosmopolitan locals come for authentic *bobotie* (a curried mince bake) and *potjie bredie* (meat stew in a cast iron pot). There's outdoor seating and live music, weather permitting. **Moderate**

Stan's Place
Southern-style food `13 C3`
411 Atlantic Ave. (between Bond & Nevins Sts) • 718 596 3110
Open all day Tue–Sat, to 5pm Sun

The exterior of this charming Boerum Hill restaurant evokes the spirit of New Orleans with its bright paint-work, shrubbery, and American flag. It's the Creole-inspired food, however, that keeps the locals coming back. Try the pork or catfish po' boy sandwich for lunch; the southern fried chicken for dinner. **Moderate**

DiFara Pizzeria
Neapolitan pizzas
1424 Avenue J (between 14th & 15th Sts) • 718 258 1367
Ⓜ Subway Q to Avenue J
Open all day daily; cash only

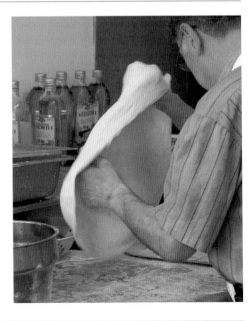

The thin, round pizza of Naples – arguably New Yorkers' most beloved culinary import – is elevated to an art form at this tiny pizzeria in the predominantly Hasidic Jewish neighborhood of Midwood. Producing these transcendent pies behind a cracked linoleum countertop since 1964 is Domenico DeMarco, a master *pizzaiolo* with an obsessive commitment to fresh ingredients and the precise assembly (one blob of creamy mozzarella at a time) of just about perfect pizzas. Translation: you must wait for your food.

Patience is rewarded with the first bite. The robust, basil-laced tomato sauce, crisp crust, light olive oil, and tangy parmigiano reggiano cheese should conspire to put words like "the best" on your lips. They should also distract you from the smoke-stained ceiling, and awkwardly arranged tables – just six altogether. **Cheap**

Relish *classic diner* `13 B2`
225 Wythe Avenue (between Metropolitan Avenue
& North 3rd Street) • 718 963 4546
Open all day daily (to 1am Fri & Sat)

Diners like this usually serve greasy, griddle-fried fare.
But Josh Cohen's seasonal menus feature eclectic
American bistro cuisine at diner-friendly prices: think
chili-rubbed smoked ribs and tomato soup with chèvre
croutons. Locals fill the 1950s-style booths. **Cheap**

Planet Thailand *affordable specialties* `13 B2`
133 North 7th Street (between Bedford Avenue
& Berry Street) • 718 599 5758
Open all day daily to 1am (to 2am Fri & Sat); cash only

The dining room here is cavernous, with towering
windows and gray, industrial walls hung with sweep-
ing paintings by Williamsburg artists. The venturesome
and stylish nibble Thai papaya salads and Japanese
nigiri sushi between sips of warm sake. **Cheap**

Peter Luger Steak House *sizzlers* `13 C2`
178 Broadway (at Driggs Ave.) • 718 387 7400
》 www.peterluger.com
Open all day to 9:45 daily (to 10:45pm Fri & Sat); cash only

Renowned as one of the top meat purveyors in the
country, Peter Luger has been in business since 1887,
and the generations of experience show. The decor is
no-frills, and the menu is simple. Steak – particularly
the Porterhouse – rules. **Expensive**

Bamonte's *old-school Italian* `13 C1`
32 Withers Street (between Lorimer St. & Union Ave.)
718 384 8831
Open all day to 10:30pm Wed–Mon

Home-made pastas and rich sauces reign supreme at
this establishment, which has been in business for
over 100 years. Wonderful photographs on the walls
and a waitstaff who look like they've been here almost
as long are all part of its charm. **Moderate**

shopping

New York is a famously fabulous place to shop. Rich pickings are to be had across the board – in the time-honored department stores of midtown, the designer flagships of Fifth Avenue, and the latest little gem to spring up in buzzing Williamsburg. Follow the lead of New Yorkers and shop where the locals shop – the great delis, bookstores and music outlets downtown, and the funky fashion boutiques in Harlem and Brooklyn.

SHOPPING

Not a city to follow fashion, New York walks the catwalk to its own beat. Getting a handle on Big Apple style requires more than a stroll down Fifth Avenue, and to get an insider's edge you'll need to duck into boutiques in Brooklyn, browse the venerable Manhattan department stores and scan the clothes rails in the retro stores of the Lower East Side. For me though, a day of shopping is never complete without a café pit stop and some downtime for people-watching.

Dahlia Devkota

The Old Guard

Sales staff at **Barney's** *(see p86)* may be a bit standoffish, but can be a wealth of information and make the difference between dressing well and dressing with true style. **Jeffrey** *(see p78)* has amazing customer service, complete with thank-you notes, while **Bergdorf Goodman** *(see p85)* is for those with high-fashion tastes and deep pockets.

Under the Radar

For those who like fashion with street edge, **Alife Rivington Club** *(see p73)* is the place to shop, with its collection of super-cool trainers. At **Nom de Guerre** *(see p93)* fashion imitates art imitating life, and the result is clothes that capture an urban underground spirit. The cool quotient continues at **Mini Minimarket** *(see p92)* in hip Williamsburg.

Snack Attack

Divine cupcakes and a West Village location add up to a line permanently at the door of **Magnolia Bakery** *(see p75)*. **Bonsignour** *(see p76)* is the best place to recharge your batteries with a latte and pastry, and the bench outside is a top spot for people-watching. For a tea selection as long as a Russian novel, check out **Teany** *(see p74)*.

choice shops

Home Front

Pearl River Mart *(see p65)* sells all things Asian, from sake sets to teas and spices at rock bottom prices. Bargains continue at **Housing Works Thrift Store** *(see p89),* where designers and the city's elite donate their pricy goods. **Hable Construction** *(see p72)* offers whimsical yet practical household items, though the price tags are high.

Soothing and Pampering

Among the treatments offered at **Rescue Beauty Lounge** *(see p70)* are manicures and pedicures. At **SCO** *(see p71)* an expert will analyze your skin then mix, shake, and stir pure infusions ranging from willow bark to juniper berries into a bespoke product. To take the pampering home, check out **Fresh** *(see p75)* for beautifully packaged goods.

Fashionista Destinations

Scoop *(see p69)* is all about high living, high dollar, and high fashion – and well-heeled girls can't get enough. At **Kirna Zabate** *(see p67),* designers such as Balenciaga are found next to indie labels. The boutique on the speed dial of every girl and guy in the know is **Marc Jacobs** *(pp68 & 76)* for looks that scream both luxury and cool.

Century 21 *discount designer dressing* `1 D3`
22 Cortlandt Street (between Church St. & Broadway)
212 227 9092
>> www.c21stores.com Open 7:45am–8pm Mon–Fri (to 8:30pm Thu), 10am–8pm Sat, 11am–7pm Sun

This is a goldmine of a department store, so don't let the aggressive crowds scare you away. The discounted designer men's and women's clothes, shoes, makeup, and linens on offer will make the occasional elbow in the ribs well worth the hassle.

The women's shoe department tends to be the busiest and most chaotic, due to weekly shipments from the likes of Costume National, Dolce & Gabbana, and Marc Jacobs. The top floor is the jewel in the crown, though: it stocks the collections of designers such as Armani, Missoni, and Ralph Lauren, but at a fraction of the price you'd pay at the Madison Avenue flagship stores. The only downside to this heavenly situation is the service (often brusque), long lines, and communal dressing rooms.

Kate Spade *stylish accessories* `3 D5`
454 Broome Street (between Mercer & Greene Sts)
212 274 1991
>> www.katespade.com Open 11–7 Tue–Sat, 12–6 Sun

Luxury coupled with whimsy are the key ingredients here. Nylon and leather weekend bags, personalized stationery, and vintage travel books from the 1960s make browsing a delight. (How the beautifully crafted luggage will withstand check-in is another matter.)

Hotel Venus by Patricia Field *Cirque du Soleil meets S&M clothing* `4 E4`
302 Bowery (between Houston and Bleecker Sts)
212 966 4066
>> www.patriciafield.com Open 11–8 daily (to 9 Sat)

Patricia Field – costume designer for the HBO sitcom *Sex and the City* – has designed this store to give free rein to her fantasies. Hip girls, transvestites, and circus performers will find something to make them smile.

Malia Mills *bikinis & maillots* `4 E5`

199 Mulberry St. (between Spring & Kenmare Sts) • 212 625 2311
>> www.maliamills.com
Open noon–7 daily

Take some of the anxiety away from swimsuit shopping with Malia Mills's wide choice of sizes, colors, and styles, which ranges from "pucker shorts" to tankinis and one-piece swimsuits. The assistants will help you find the perfect fit.

Pearl River Mart *Far Eastern treasures* `3 D5`

477 Broadway (between Grand & Broome Sts)
212 431 4770
>> www.pearlriver.com Open 10–7:30 daily

It has never been easier or more fun to get lost in a store. This three-story shrine to everything Asian feels like a cross between a flea market (yes, the prices are that good) and an exotic department store. The elegant Chinese robes, traditional Mandarin dresses, slippers, embroidered bags, and purses would be triple the price in a more conventional store. The simple ceramic bowls and delicate Japanese tea sets are also the same as those found in pricey boutiques.

The kitchen department offers everything you need to prepare an authentic Asian meal: teas, spices, and sauces are available in bewildering quantities. Among the bathroom products are herbal remedies and beauty treats galore. Many of the exquisite Chinese wedding items make stunning accessories or gifts. There's also a selection of cute and colorful kids' clothes, shoes, and toys.

Gifts and novelty items range from funky alarm clocks and butterfly-shaped kites to windchimes, and there's a selection of fascinating traditional musical instruments. This is not to mention the lanterns, the stationery, the bedding, the homewares, and thousands of other items that will make you suddenly feel as if you've developed adult attention deficit disorder. A word to the wise: get here early before the crowds, and keep an eye on the clock – one could easily while away an entire day here.

Shopping

A.P.C. *French utilitarian gear* 3 D4
131 Mercer Street (between Spring & Prince Sts) • 212 966 9685
>> www.apc.fr Open noon–7 Mon–Sat, noon–6 Sun

A true lifestyle store, A.P.C. sells clothing for adults and children, as well as music and objects for the home. The French label carries loose-fitting, neutral-toned work clothes, for looks that can be casual or trendy depending on the accessories. For dyed-in-the-wool Americans, there's a section devoted to denim.

Le Corset by Selima *luxe lingerie* 3 C5
80 Thompson Street (between Broome & Spring Sts)
212 334 4936 Open 11–7 Mon–Sat, noon–7 Sun

The great and the good, from Yoko Ono to Sir Ben Kingsley, have been spotted inside this closet-sized lingerie store. Underwear by Roberto Cavalli and kimonos (new and vintage) will tempt the temptress in you. The hand-dyed corsets are so beautiful that many buyers use them as outerwear.

Barney's CO-OP *hipster clothing* 3 D4
116 Wooster Street (between Prince & Spring Sts)
212 965 9964 Open 11–7 Mon–Sat, noon–6 Sun

If no-brainer shopping is what you're after, then look no further than this wild-child of Barney's New York *(see p86)*, the city's bastion of good style and taste. The CO-OP's eclectic mix of trendy clothes for youngish shoppers takes the Barney's brand in a hipper direction. A vast stockpile of jeans (from Seven to Levi's) for men and women guarantees that you'll find the perfect fit. Other lines – such as Theory, Marc by Marc Jacobs, and Prada Sport – mingle with upscale labels and 1970s-inspired athletic gear from the likes of Puma and Adidas. The handmade hats, funky watches, jewelry, and shoes are quirky enough to warrant more than a second glance – in fact, it's almost impossible to make a bad purchase here. What's more, wearing clothes from Barney's CO-OP is sure to increase your likelihood of getting through the velvet ropes at New York's hot night spots.

Clio *whimsical home accessories* `3 C4`
92 Thompson Street (between Prince & Spring Sts)
212 966 8991
>> www.clio-home.com Open 11–7 Mon–Sat, noon–6 Sun

The focus is on up-and-coming homeware designers from around the world. Unique pieces, such as a walnut cheese board with turquoise inlay, are sold, and look for the Rehabilitated Dinnerware line of revamped vintage serving platters.

Costume National *sleek clothes* `3 D4`
108 Wooster Street (between Prince & Spring Sts) • 212 431 1530
>> www.costumenational.com Open 11–7 Mon–Sat, noon–6 Sun

Ennio Capasa's collection of streamlined clothes for men and women includes pieces you'll want in your closet forever because of their enduring style. The Italian designer's perfectly tailored jackets and skirts appear edgy yet elegant, and each season's shoe collection offers sexy heels and urban-style flats.

Kirna Zabate *wearable avant-garde* `3 D4`
96 Greene Street (between Prince & Spring Sts) • 212 941 9656
>> www.kirnazabete.com Open 11–7 Mon–Sat, noon–6 Sun

Every item here seems to be letting you in on a fashion secret, hinting at what is absolutely "of-the-moment." The two-story boutique is a hot spot for industry insiders, who love the drama of finding Jean Paul Gaultier next to unknown indie labels. Accessories for babies and dogs make the store even more delightful.

Miu Miu *off-beat elegance* `3 D4`
100 Prince Street (between Mercer & Greene Sts) • 212 334 5156
>> www.miumiu.com Open 11–7 Mon–Sat, noon–6 Sun

This flagship store has major browse appeal due to its energetic and flirty designs. While the craftsmanship of parent company Prada can be seen in the details, a let-your-hair-down attitude gives the clothes verve. Miu Miu's fashions may not be cheap, but wearing a shirt that makes you feel happy is priceless.

Shopping

3 D4

Moss *museum-worthy designs*

146 Greene Street (between Prince & W. Houston Sts)
212 204 7100

>> www.mossonline.com Open 11–7 Mon–Sat, noon–6 Sun

This store pleases die-hard design fans as well as
those who just love pretty things. Step into a world of
modern furniture, retro lighting, and Moser crystal.
While many items are ludicrously expensive, others
(like the Lomo cameras) are reasonably priced.

Marc Jacobs *fashion's golden boy* 3 D4

163 Mercer Street (between Prince & W. Houston Sts)
212 343 1490

>> www.marcjacobs.com Open 11–7 Mon–Sat, noon–6 Sun

Given that writer/film director Sophia Coppola is
Jacobs' muse, it's not surprising that every item in
his store has effortless, super-cool style. From his
coveted leather bags to retro-style dresses, jackets,
and shoes, there is little that won't please the eye.

Prada *vast flagship store* 3 D4

575 Broadway (at Prince St.) • 212 334 8888

>> www.prada.com Open 11–7 Mon–Sat, noon–6 Sun

Prada's 24,000-sq-ft flagship in the heart of SoHo
may have become as overexposed as a pop princess's
midriff, but that doesn't mean we won't keep looking.
The elegantly futuristic store, designed by Dutch
architect Rem Koolhaas, retains the flavor of an art
space (the building used to be the downtown arm of
the Guggenheim Museum), and will entice travelers
to visit just to witness architectural history in the
making. Koolhaas included so many technologically
advanced gadgets that even science and technology
magazines covered the store opening.

As for the clothes, they remain beautiful examples
of elegance reinterpreted. For women, the designs do
not slavishly follow fashions, but assuredly set their
own trends. The men's shoes – with the signature red
stripe on the sole of the Prada Sport line – are
staples that never lose their popularity.

Scoop *high fashion*

3 D4

532 Broadway (between Prince & Spring Sts) • 212 925 2886
》 www.scoopnyc.com Open 11–8 Mon–Sat, noon–7 Sun

The price tags may elicit a tiny (involuntary) gasp, but one piece will go a long way in building a great wardrobe. While the store caters mainly to sample-size fashionistas who don't balk at maxing out their credit cards for a poncho, it's a great place to come for the most sought-after pieces from each season.

Dean & DeLuca *a gourmet's mecca*

3 D4

560 Broadway (at Prince St.) • 212 226 6800
》 www.deandeluca.com Open 9–8 Mon–Sat, 10–7 Sun

Should there be a perfect way to stack mangoes, display passion fruit, and organize juice bottles according to the laws of color theory, then Dean & DeLuca will find it. This Aladdin's cave of a gourmet store carries top-quality produce, be it fresh, cured, made locally, or flown in from distant shores. All the produce looks wonderfully wholesome and good. Spices are clearly chosen with care, and the bottles of olive oil from Italy are almost too beautiful to open. And one of the best things about shopping here is that there are always free tasters to sample.

Each department carries delicacies from around the world. The cheese section stocks an ample selection of Goudas and Bries, as well as more exotic delights, such as Brillo de Treviso (a sweet cheese from Italy that is dipped in wine). There are also fine American cheeses, such as the creamy goat's cheese Humbolt Fog. The seafood department carries sushi-grade tuna, and the bakery produces tasty numbers such as Portuguese corn bread – it's good enough to make you throw out the low-carb lifestyle for good.

Head to the back of the store for every type of kitchen appliance you never knew you needed, from sushi trays and crème brûlée dishes to mixers, suede oven mitts, and cedar grilling planks (they keep food moist, apparently). And, lest you become over-whelmed by the choice of food on offer, there is an entire library of cookbooks to help sort things out.

Kate's Paperie *stationery with panache* `3 D4`
561 Broadway (at Prince St.) • 212 941 9816
»» www.katespaperie.com Open 10–8 Mon–Sat, 11–7 Sun

Luddites who prefer the tactile pleasures of pen and paper to the ease of electronic mail should check out Kate's for all their stationery needs. Quirky thank-you cards, giant leather-bound photo albums, fountain pens, stamps, and tactile handmade paper sold by the sheet are here in abundance.

The Apartment *dream apartment loot* `3 D4`
101 Crosby Street (between Prince & Spring Sts)
212 219 3661
»» www.theapt.com Open Mon–Fri by appt only

Once you enter this experimental design studio set up to look like a real apartment, you may have difficulty returning to your own abode. Every aspect of The Apartment has been put together with an eye for what is both minimalist and sensuous. From the multicolored broom in the kitchen to the Philippe Starck fixtures in the bathroom to the Edith Mezard linens on the bed – everything exudes exemplary design. And, of course, everything you see is for sale: the clothes in the closet, the toothpaste in the bathroom, even the food in the fridge. The point of it all? To emphasize that by putting objects in a real setting, design becomes more accessible. The Apartment also hosts "happenings," works with major corporations on brand development, and can be hired to re-style private and commercial spaces.

Rescue Beauty Lounge *nail spa* `4 E5`
8 Centre Market Place (between Broome & Grand Sts)
212 431 0449
»» www.rescuebeauty.com Open 11–8 Tue–Fri, 10–6 Sat & Sun

Ji Baek – the super-stylish owner – has put together NY's most hip beauty salon. As well as pedicures and manicures, Rescue offers many other treatments and all the lotions and potions associated with top-notch aromatherapy, massage, waxing, and brow-shaping.

SCO *customized skincare*

`3 D4`

584 Broadway, 5th Floor (between Prince & Houston Sts)
212 966 3011
>> www.scocare.com Open 11–7 Mon–Fri (Sat by appt only)

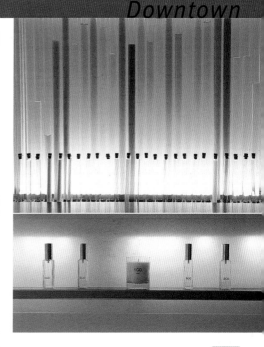

Giant test tubes of pure infusions stand sentinel at the entrance to this tiny, bright, and crisply decorated skincare shop. SCO stands for Skin Care Options, and the products – which include facial cleansers, tonics, and creams, a lip balm, body scrubs, and polishes – are universal to all skin types. The infusions are used to customize them to each person's needs.

The consultant will ask you a series of health-related questions, then mix up a product appropriate to your requirements, choosing from more than 20 natural ingredients: caffeine for toning and tightening skin; vitamins A, C, and E for helping skin renewal; willow bark for its antiseptic properties, and many more. Products are packaged in elegant bottles. Your prescription is filed for repeat orders, and any changes in skin condition can be accommodated.

INA *runway cast-offs*

`4 E4`

21 Prince Street (between Mott & Elizabeth Sts)
212 334 9048
>> www.inanyc.com Open noon–7 daily (to 8 Fri & Sat)

Ever longed for Prada heels but just couldn't afford them? You can find designer goods at a fraction of the original price at this store for girls with high-end tastes but low budgets. Many clothes are brand new, and models sometimes bring in just-off-the-catwalk items.

Calypso *hip hippy beachwear*

`4 E4`

280 Mott Street (between Prince & Houston Sts)
212 965 0990
>> www.calypso-celle.com Open 11–7 Mon–Sat, noon–7 Sun

This famously chic store carries clothes for the girl who spends half the year in Spain's Ibiza and the other half in the Caribbean's St. Bart's. Every item here oozes bohemian beach luxury. Peasant skirts, colorful silk tops, and sandals lend a tropical appeal.

Hable Construction *beautiful interiors* `4 E4`
230 Elizabeth Street (between Prince & Houston Sts)
>> www.hableconstruction.com • 212 343 8555
Open 11–7 Mon–Sat, noon–6 Sun

The Hable sisters named their company after their grandfather's construction business. But instead of building houses, they design pretty, practical things. The canvas pillows, printed boxes, beach towels, and garden accessories will add a dash of fun to any home.

Mayle *dressing up for real life* `4 E4`
242 Elizabeth Street (between Prince & Houston Sts)
212 625 0406
Open noon–7 Mon–Sat, noon–6 Sun

Jane Mayle's vintage-style, super-sexy clothes are on every young Hollywood starlet's must-have list. Actress Kirsten Dunst is among the many fans of Mayle's slip dresses, girly blouses, and slouchy pants. The collection also includes raved-about shoes.

Rafe *eye-catching modern handbags* `4 E4`
1 Bleecker Street (at Bowery) • 877-7 Rafeny
>> www.rafe.com
Open noon–7 Mon–Thu & Sat, noon–8 Fri

Designer Ramon Felix creates glamorous bags and shoes that transport the imagination. His straw-and-leather Corsica bag looks like something Audrey Hepburn could have held, and the St. Germain clutch is pure Parisian chic. There are bags for men too.

Bond 07 by Selima *neo-bohemian looks* `3 D3`
7 Bond Street (between Broadway & Lafayette St.)
212 677 8487
>> www.selimaoptique.com Open 11–7 Mon–Sat, noon–7 Sun

Selima Salaun, known for her optical wear, is behind this NoHo boutique, which caters to women who favor unusual styles. It carries an eclectic selection of bags, hats, dresses, and, of course, glasses, designed by the likes of Cacharel and Tsumori Chisato.

LAFCO *highly coveted beauty products* `4 E4`
285 Lafayette Street (between Prince & Jersey Sts)
212 925 0001
>> www.lafcony.com Open 11–7 Mon–Sat (to 8 Thu), noon–6 Sun (closed Sun in summer)

LAFCO sells exclusive beauty products, including the creams and tonics of Lorenzo Villoresi. This is also the NY base for the entire range of Santa Maria Novella, a coveted Italian skincare line.

TG-170 *clothes that epitomize downtown cool* `4 F4`
170 Ludlow Street (between Houston & Stanton Sts)
212 995 8660
>> www.tg170.com Open noon–8 daily

If you've ever wondered what the cutting-edge kids wear to hip Lower East Side parties, TG-170 will let you in on the secret. The shop stocks small quantities of choice clothes and accessories. Owner Terri Gillis is often here to sort out shoppers' style dilemmas.

ALife Rivington Club *sneaker joint* `4 G4`
158 Rivington Street (at Clinton St.) • **212 375 8128**
>> www.rivingtonclub.com Open 11–7 Mon–Sat, noon–7 Sun

If an exquisite pair of retro trainers is what you're after, you need to be willing to put up with a few headaches. To begin with, ALife pretends not to want to be found – there is no sign out front, and you must ring a doorbell to enter. Such discretion may give you the impression that you've intruded on a members-only club – in fact, their business cards say "members only." But this is all retail theater, and once you're inside the wood-paneled shop any misgivings you have will soon be forgotten.

The knockout shoes are individually displayed, each allotted its own back-lit mahogany shelf space, like a row of rare finds in a local museum. This is fitting, as the items stocked here would be hard to track down elsewhere. Vintage Air Jordans, Nike Air Wovens, and old-school Adidas are just some of the lines available. ALife NYC next door sells clothes.

Shop *fun, feminine finds*   `4 F4`
105 Stanton Street (between Ludlow & Essex Sts)
212 375 0304 Open noon–7 daily

A rack of sexy dresses, lacy cover-ups for the beach, and cashmere sweaters makes Shop feel a little like an intimate dressing room for college sorority girls. The salespeople are extremely friendly too, treating you just like one of the girls. For more standard fare, there's an entire wall devoted to jeans.

Teany *Moby's tea shop*   `4 F4`
90 Rivington St. (between Orchard & Ludlow Sts) • 212 475 9190
>> www.teany.com
Open 10am–10pm Tue–Thu & Sun, 10am–2am Fri & Sat

Electronica music maven Moby has created his own vision of what a teahouse should be (and very teeny it is indeed). The cozy interior is minimalist white, and the sound system reverberates with low-key club music, giving the shop a futuristic Zen-like ambience.

There are over 93 different teas to sample and buy, ranging from the exotic to the highly exotic. Try the Silver Needle (a white tea with a superior level of antioxidants), the Golden Nepal (just because the name is so cool), and the Earl Grey Creme (the real best-seller). Alongside metal canisters of leaf tea, the tiny retail section sells every accessory for the perfect brew, from the teapot – with Teany logo – to cups, glasses, tea caddies, and milk jugs. Don't leave without sampling the vegan/vegetarian menu (organic muffins, delicate sandwiches, and tofu scramble).

Chain Stores

New York has no shortage of chain stores offering reasonably priced fashion. There is a **Gap** on practically every corner – always good for basic T-shirts, jeans, khakis, and bookbags. Equally prevalent is Gap's more upscale sister store, **Banana Republic**. Popular with Wall Street yuppies, Banana offers clean-cut fashion. Prices can be a bit high for fashion with such little soul, but there is always a sale rack with bargains. The all-American, casual-preppy look of **J. Crew** is popular with all age groups, and can even make it into a fashionista's closet. For pseudo-punk flair, try **Urban Outfitters**, where you'll find the latest trends, such as Puma zip-ups, and funky household items like shower curtains and kitchenware. For individual contact details, *see p227–8.*

Subterranean Records *60s–70s vinyl* `3 C3`
5 Cornelia Street (at W. 4th St.) • 212 463 8900
>> www.recordsnyc.com Open noon–8 daily

In the heart of the West Village, Subterranean Records is the kind of music store any die-hard rocker would be hard pressed to fault. Specializing in 70s-era NYC punk and 60s-era rock, the shop is crammed with 7-inch singles and LPs. There's soul, jazz, and blues, too, and plenty of CDs alongside the old-school vinyl.

Fat Beats *hip-hop & def sounds* `3 C2`
406 6th Ave, 2nd Floor (between 8th & 9th Sts) • 212 673 3883
>> www.fatbeats.com Open noon–9 Mon–Sat, noon–6 Sun

Fat Beats caters to DJs and collectors of hip-hop vinyl. If you are a true connoisseur of underground hip-hop, you'll probably have the shop at the top of your NY itinerary. If, on the other hand, you're merely a dabbler in the music, at least go for the experience – especially the too-cool-for-school staff.

Fresh *decadent bath & body tonics* `3 B3`
388 Bleecker Street (at Perry St.) • 917 408 1850
>> www.fresh.com Open noon–8 Mon–Sat, noon–6 Sun

The lotions and potions found here sound more like culinary ingredients than bathroom products. Sugar scrubs, sake bath gel, milk soaps, rice face washes, and soy hand cream are a few of the more exotic creations. All Fresh products are beautifully packaged, making them ideal gifts to take back home.

Magnolia Bakery *classic cupcakes* `3 B3`
401 Bleecker Street (at W. 11th St.) • 212 462 2572
Open noon–11:30pm Mon, 9am–11:30pm Tue–Thu,
9am–12:30am Fri, 10am–12:30am Sat, 10am–11:30pm Sun

Instantly recognizable by the line of happy customers at the door, Magnolia is a Village institution, famed for its beautifully decorated and superb-tasting cupcakes. Don't be shy about guzzling one as soon as you've paid – everyone does.

>> *For a listing of the shops by category, see pp227–9*

Marc by Marc Jacobs *downtown cool* `3 B4`
403–405 Bleecker Street (between Bank & West 11th Sts)
212 924 0026
>> www.marcjacobs.com Open noon–8 Mon–Sat, noon–7 Sun

Ever wondered how models obtain that chic, just rolled-out-of-bed style? Step inside Marc's store, and you too can achieve the look, with a pair of 70s-inspired cords and a bomber jacket – the designer's favorites. The men's and women's stores are next to each other.

Flight 001 *quirky accessories for jet-setters* `3 A2`
96 Greenwich Avenue (at Jane St.) • 212 989 0001
>> www.flight001.com Open 11–8:30 Mon– Fri, 11–8 Sat, noon–6 Sun

Ever thought you could do with a petal pink passport cover? You will be convinced you need more cool accessories and gadgets than 007 after visiting this West Village gem. A mobile spice rack to liven up airplane food, a cigarette lighter that will work in storm-force gales, and adorable laundry bags are among the essentials. For the transcontinental sophisticate, there are *New York Times* trivia games, airplane yoga books, travel candles, and Dr. Hauschka beauty products. This is also your chance to stock up on travel books locating the planet's hippest hotels. Walking-tour CDs of Brooklyn, Manhattan and the Bronx can be burnt on to your iPod, to ensure that you never get lost. Still got money to burn? Then indulge in the silver, hardcase luggage – and look like a traveler who knows how to get there in style.

Bonsignour *coffee & beautiful people* `3 B2`
35 Jane Street (between 8th Ave. & Hudson St.)
212 229 9700
Open 7am–10pm Mon–Sun

Shoppers pack into this Lilliputian space for three reasons: it serves good coffee, even better baked goods, and has the friendliest vibe of any café/bakery in the West Village. The bench outside is a perfect place to sit and watch the world go by.

MXYPLYZYK *eclectic urban homeware* `3 B2`
125 Greenwich Avenue (at Horatio St.) • 212 989 4300
» www.mxyplyzyk.com Open 11–7 Mon–Sat, noon–5 Sun

Keep your hands in your pockets at this unique store, as you're bound to want to touch, stroke, or squeeze *everything*. From puggy banks (pug-dog piggy banks – get it?) to purses resembling Bocce bowling balls, whimsy is the *raison d'être* of almost every item at MXYPLYZYK. (It's pronounced "mixyplitsick," by the way.) Vinyl bowls look like warped LPs, a shiny chrome toaster is suggestive of a prop in a 1950s sci-fi movie, and a nutcracker comes in the guise of a squirrel. Utilitarian products, such as cups and saucers, make the occasional appearance alongside a wealth of semi-useful stuff like salt and pepper dogs, psychedelic plates, wonky glasses, and rubber-bladed desk fans.

There are items for every corner of your home: modern measuring bowls and Japanese dishes for the kitchen, Korres skin care products and giant rubber ducks for the bathroom, a coffee table book of *Turkish Wrestling*, and sleek Martini shakers for your evening cocktails. The most sophisticated pieces (not outrageously priced considering the exclusive West-Village location) include office lamps and metal "industrial-style" jewelry. The point of this store is to bring a little humor and frivolity into the overly studious atmosphere that frequently surrounds contemporary design. Linking all the varied products in this fun store is the perennial question of what is functional design and what is art.

Stella McCartney *high chic/rocker chick* `3 A2`
429 West 14th Street (between Washington St. & 9th Ave.)
» www.stellamccartney.com • 212 255 1556
Open noon–7 Mon–Sat, 12:30–6 Sun

Set in the fashionable Meatpacking District, Stella McCartney's store is a lesson in cool. Green stilettos with plastic cherries dangling off the straps epitomize her vision of elegance with a little *joie de vivre*. The inlaid wood dressing rooms are exquisite.

La Cafetiere *French-style homewares* 3 A1
160 9th Avenue (between W. 19th & W. 20th Sts)
646 486 0667
Open 10–7:30 Tue–Thu, 10–7 Fri, 10–6:30 Sat, noon–6 Sun

Francophiles and those who think a smattering of Provençal style might look good in their homes should head to this shop. While some of the rural-style tableware is pleasant but commonplace, the furniture – such as a weather-beaten armoire – is exceptional.

Jeffrey *boutique department store* 3 A2
449 West 14th Street (between Washington St. & 9th Ave.)
212 206 1272
Open 10–8 Mon–Fri (to 9 Thu), 10–7 Sat, 12:30–6 Sun

A trailblazing store at the edge of the luxuriously gritty Meatpacking District *(see p167)*, Jeffrey is where beautiful people and celebrities shop (you'll often see tinted-glass limousines parked out front). While the store is not large, the stock is a discerning selection, and avant-garde labels such as Dries Van Noten and Balenciaga are much in evidence. This means that you won't have to spend hours digging around for the choicest outfits, but it also means that you won't find bargains either.

The women's shoe department – which takes up the entire center of the store – is quite possibly the best collection of footwear in New York. You'll find sandals made in Capri, Prada flats, Yves Saint Laurent stilettos, Puma trainers, and a selection of other equally stylish brands. Adding to the enjoyment of shopping at Jeffrey are old-school touches, such as formal greeters at the door and an abundance of cheery salespeople.

Oasis Day Spa at Union Square `3 C1`

108 East 16th Street, 2nd Floor (between Union
Square East & Irving Place) • 212 254 7722
>> www.oasisdayspanyc.com
Open 10–10 Mon–Fri, 9–9 Sat & Sun

As its name suggests, Oasis is a peaceful haven in
the middle of one of the most hectic parts of the city.
In addition to spa services and facilities, the shop has
an extensive range of health and beauty products.

ABC Carpet and `3 D1`
Home *beautiful, budget-breaking furniture*

888 Broadway (at E. 19th St.) • 212 473 3000
>> www.abchome.com
Open 10–8 Mon–Fri, 10–7 Sat, 11–6:30 Sun

The six massive floors of ABC will be like the skies of
heaven to many shoppers – there's a vision of
unparalleled beauty wherever you look.

The first floor is an assortment of treasures, such as
hand-blown Venetian glass chandeliers, vintage
nursery furniture from France, and cast-iron Buddha
heads. This level may look like a Parisian flea
market, but don't expect flea market prices.

Walk upstairs to find modern furniture and retro
1960s-style chairs and light fixtures. The third floor
stocks some of the world's finest linens, Frette and
Pratesi among them. Head to floors five and six for
Belle Époque French antiques. Many pieces –
whether rustic cooking pots or formal chairs – would
look at home in a museum.

Many native New Yorkers don't even know about the
top-notch, top-floor restaurants at this extraordinary
store. Le Pain Quotidien is a French-Belgian Bakery
serving breads, pastries, gourmet sandwiches, and
coffee. It's a popular place for brunch. There is also
Pipa, a tapas restaurant, which has a lively atmosphere for larger parties. Lucy is a Mexican barbecue.

Without leaving the store, you can visit the
Mudhoney Salon. This is a full-service luxury hair
salon with a beguiling element of punk set amid the
beauty of East Asian furniture.

Paragon Sporting

3 D1

Goods *clothes and equipment for the sporty*
867 Broadway (at West 18th St.) • 800 961 3030
>> www.paragonsports.com
Open 10–8 Mon–Sat, 11:30–7 Sun

A three-floor megastore for your inner athlete, Paragon offers everything needed for just about any sport you care to mention. The basement is filled to the brim with trainers, including New Balance (the serious jogger's choice), Nike, and Puma. All manner of running paraphernalia is stocked: heart monitors, lap timers, even breathable underwear.

The first floor caters to the more genteel country club set, with tennis rackets, Lacoste shirts, and adorable tennis skirts. There's a wide selection of golf equipment too. Don't miss the large back room for swimwear (from delicate bikini sets made for lounging to serious one-piece Speedos for racing).

The top floor is the preserve of adventure sports: kayaking equipment, diving watches, and a full assortment of camping gear.

Department Stores

Manhattan's department stores are legendary, and visitors rarely feel a visit to New York is complete without venturing to at least one of the city's great shopping behemoths.

Macy's *(see p227)* is usually high on the list; this century-old icon spans a full city block and carries mostly moderately priced goods from homewares to fashion. You'll need to exercise patience, though, as Macy's is always crowded and easy to get lost in. But, if you have time to spare, you will uncover generous sale racks, with all-American brands such as DKNY, Tommy Hilfiger, and Polo.

If you're looking for a more upscale, less crowded variation, **Bloomingdale's** and **Saks Fifth Avenue** *(see p227 for both)* offer not only hundreds of every-day brands but also boutique labels and high-end designer showrooms. Chanel, Stella McCartney,

and Yves Saint-Laurent are among the fashion houses represented at these department stores. During the amazing end-of-season sales, luxury items are reduced by as much as 50 per cent.

Henri Bendel *(see p227)* is much loved by New Yorkers and visitors alike because it feels deceptively more like a boutique than a large department store. This is due, in part, to its clever layout of split levels and winding staircases. Yet the selection here is vast, from hip make-up lines such as MAC and Laura Mercier to private label sweaters. There is a mini boutique of Diane Von Furstenburg wrap dresses and an impressive selection of evening frocks. Unlike the other department stores though, Bendels (as it's affectionately called by New Yorkers) does not sell everything from mixers to mattresses, but limits itself to cutting-edge designers and beauty products. *(See also **Bergdorf Goodman**, p85.)*

Kiehl's *world-famous for beauty products*

4 E2

109 3rd Avenue (between 13th & 14th Sts) • 212 677 3171
» www.kiehls.com Open 10–7 Mon–Sat, noon–6 Sun

Conveniently located just steps away from the Third Avenue stop on the L train, this flagship store for Kiehl's has an awesome product line of plant-based beauty creams, tonics, powders, and soaps. In keeping with the simplicity of the products, the packaging is kept equally minimal.

Grab a basket upon entering and start walking down the rows of cucumber body washes, rose toners, coconut hair conditioners, and more. Friendly and well-informed staff are on hand to answer questions and offer suggestions. A few suggestions for your shopping list: Kiehl's Silk Groom (which does wonders for conditioning and styling hair); the excellent Lip Balm; and Kiehl's Original Musk Oil (which has been known to stop people in their tracks, so intoxicating is its aroma). Kiehl's is also very good at offering free samples of any item you are curious about.

The Strand *the first and last word in books*

3 D2

828 Broadway (at 12th St.) • 212 473 1452
» www.strandbooks.com
Open 9:30am–10:30pm Mon–Sat, 11am–10:30pm Sun

The Strand is a downtown institution, and all visitors to the city should pay a visit here to participate in a New York rite of passage. This is not a bookstore with neatly arranged shelves and space to sit on sofas and sip lattes. And that is precisely why The Strand is so precious to bibliophiles. Books are its sole *raison d'être*, and book-hunters duly crowd the store to scour the shelves for out-of-print books, first editions, and obscure tomes at greatly discounted prices.

A large collection of photography, architecture, and design books sits alongside shelf upon shelf of fiction, from pulp to literary classics. A treasure trove of children's books can be found downstairs. Outside, there are always hundreds of books stacked up, on sale for a dollar each. Whatever you're looking for, there are always astonishing discoveries to be made.

» *A great place to eat on Broadway is L'Ecole,* see p30

St. Mark's Sounds *new & used CDs* `4 F3`

20 St. Mark's Place • 212 677 2727
Open noon–9 Sun–Thu, noon–10 Fri & Sat

This is no place in which to worry about surly service, dust collecting on the CD covers, or the absence of listening booths. However, it is the place to go wild about an amazing selection of used and new CDs of rock, jazz, new wave, soul, and more at prices that rarely go above double digits.

Jazz Record Center *hidden store of jazz jewels* `5 C5`

236 West 26th Street, 8th Floor (between 7th & 8th Aves) • 212 675 4480
>> www.jazzrecordcenter.com
Open 10–6 Mon–Sat

A music store for those who know that jazz isn't just about Miles Davis, John Coltrane, and Dizzy Gillespie. The Jazz Record Center specializes in rare vinyl for true jazz fanatics. Auctions are held via the store's website, through which you can purchase books, magazines, jazz ephemera, and LPs, including coveted first pressings.

Jimmy Choo *shoes that pinch the wallet* `8 E5`

645 5th Avenue (between 51st & 52nd Sts) • 212 593 0800
>> www.jimmychoo.com Open 10–6 Mon–Sat

If the shoe fits (or even if it hurts a bit), don't deny yourself the luxury of owning a pair of status-making Jimmy Choos. There is a style to match any aspect of your life (except maybe hiking): flat sandals for holidays, strappy stilettos for the evening, sporty pumps, and even a bridal collection.

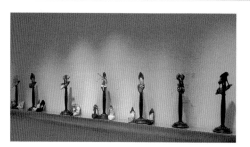

Manolo Blahnik *shoe shrine* `8 E5`

31 West 54th Street (between 5th & 6th Aves) • 212 582 3007
Open 10:30–6 Mon–Fri, 10:30–5:30 Sat

If shoes can be considered works of art, then Manolo Blahniks are masterpieces. Every pair is meticulously hand-crafted, and any woman who wears them gains instant sex appeal (that is, if she can master walking in such dainty heels). Plan on paying a hefty price though: such stylistic wizardry does not come cheap.

Takashimaya *hand-picked exotica* `8 E5`
693 5th Avenue (between 54th & 55th Sts) • 800 753 2038
Open 10–7 Mon–Sat, noon–5 Sun

If you find yourself on the crowded streets of Fifth Avenue, duck into Takashimaya for some peace and tranquillity. A hushed quality fills this six-level store, and the objects therein form a refined selection of goods from around the world (many of them with an Asian influence). Comfort and luxury come in many forms: vintage furniture, state-of-the-art gadgetry, pamperingly soft bathrobes, lacquered bowls, handmade sweaters, and exotic flower arrangements.

The top floor carries deluxe beauty items, such as outrageously decadent silk Japanese slippers that release a perfume as you walk in them. This department also stocks the most coveted and hard-to-find beauty products and fragrances. You'll find ranges by Czech & Speake, Different Company perfumes, and Takashimaya's own T fragrance line.

The slick "lifestyle" floor sells everything from modern dishes to ancient-looking tables and wardrobes. If a one-of-a kind gift is what you're after, there is an endless selection of pretty little things, such as delicate Japanese writing paper and old-fashioned photo albums. Everything is displayed in a sparse Zen-like fashion, and every item is specially selected for its uniqueness and high quality.

The Tea Box Café on the bottom floor is the best place to rest tired feet and reinvigorate the tired shopper. It serves authentic Japanese green teas and bento boxes filled with healthy East-West fusion morsels to munch on.

Shopping

Felissimo *half-gallery, half-boutique* `8 E5`
10 West 56th Street (between 5th & 6th Aves)
212 247 5656
>> www.felissimo.com
Open 11–6 Mon–Thu & Sat, 11–8 Fri

The five-story design house of Felissimo is unlike any other store you'll find in New York – or anywhere else, for that matter. It is a hybrid gallery/design boutique, filled with one-of-a kind products to contemplate and to buy. The owners of Felissimo (which means "beyond happy" in Italian) collaborate with designers from around the world to produce temporary exhibitions. The beautiful and often highly original objects on display may be prototypes for goods not yet mass-produced. Each exhibition has a theme, and aims to make the audience/customers question the effect of design on society. One of the more memorable exhibitions of recent years was "White Out." All five floors were filled with white furniture, clothes, and objects for the duration of the show, which explored the perception of white.

If this all seems a little pretentious, take comfort in the fact that proceeds from the sale of many of the designs go to good causes. A portion of the price of the Tribute Plates – ceramic plates designed by famous actors, designers, and artists – goes to the charity of the designer's choice, as well as UNESCO.

In the gift shop downstairs, you can view and buy more down-to-earth objects, such as modern steel tea pots, metal earrings, funky wrapping paper, T-shirts, and other eclectic but well-designed items.

Niketown *a Nike for everyone* `8 E5`
6 East 57th Street (between 5th & Madison) • 212 891 6453
>> www.niketown.com Open 10–8 Mon–Sat, 11–7 Sun

Much as the name implies, this is, if not quite a town, then certainly a decent-sized village of Nike products. The newest trainers are on display alongside men's and women's workout clothes – cool enough for street wear. If you're less concerned about the latest craze, seek out the Clearance Department for great bargains.

Bergdorf Goodman *old-school charm* `8 E4`

754 5th Avenue (between 57th & 58th Sts) • **800 558 1855**
» www.bergdorfgoodman.com
Open 10–7 Mon–Sat (to 8 Thu), noon–6 Sun

Bergdorf's, as New Yorkers affectionately call this landmark department store, is almost as definitive a symbol of the city as the Statue of Liberty. Located near the Trump Tower and across the street from the Plaza Hotel *(see p189)*, this is where the well-heeled ladies who lunch choose to shop.

The basement level has been converted into the beauty floor. This bright and cheerful space showcases skincare brands, such as La Prairie, and make-up lines including Shu Umera. The Buff Spa is

a manicure/pedicure stand (no appointment necessary). More beauty needs can be fulfilled upstairs at the Susan Ciminelli Day Spa (which is known for its use of soothing, seaweed-based products) and the John Barett Salon.

As for fashion and accessories, everything you could ever need (and didn't even know you needed) is all under the same roof. There's a stunningly fine jewelry selection on the first floor, while a large collection of Marc Jacobs, Gucci, Prada, and Chanel jostles for space on the second floor. The very sophisticated clothes are all displayed as mini-boutiques, showcasing renowned design labels such as Moschino and Dolce & Gabbana.

Dylan's Candy Bar *sugar-lover's dream* `8 F4`
1011 3rd Avenue (at 60th St.) • 646 735 0078
>> www.dylanscandybar.com Open 10am–9pm Mon–Thu,
10am–11pm Fri & Sat, 11am–8pm Sun

Dylan Lauren, daughter of American designer Ralph
Lauren, offers a fantasy for both kids and adults: a
two-story candy store. Not one to do anything run-of-
the-mill, she stocks hard-to-find candy in tins that
you'll cherish long after the contents are eaten.

Barney's New York *hip versus classic* `8 E4`
660 Madison Avenue (at 61st St.) • 212 826 8900
>> www.barneys.com
Open 10–8 Mon–Fri, 10–7 Sat, 11–6 Sun

Too original to be called a department store and too
large to be a boutique, Barney's is unique. Off-beat
clothes by little-known designers are carried right
next to heavy hitters, such as Marc Jacobs and Prada.
The top-floor restaurant lures New York's power elite.

La Perla *luxurious lingerie* `8 E3`
803 Madison Avenue (at 66th St.) • 212 570 0050
>> www.laperla.com
Open 10–6 Mon–Sat

Bikinis and lingerie couldn't be sexier. Glamorous
and risqué tulle-knit bathing suits play peek-a-boo
with the body, while the lingerie selection goes from
nice to naughty in no time at all. The sporty Studio
and saucy La Perla Black collections are included.

Bra Smyth *tailored bras & underwear* `8 E2`
905 Madison Avenue (between 72nd & 73rd Sts) • 212 772 9400
>> www.brasmyth.com Open 10–6 Mon–Sat, noon–5 Sun

Just as no two snowflakes are identical, neither
are two breasts – a fact not lost on Bra Smyth. With
more than 3,000 bras to choose from, and full-
time seamstresses on board to customize each
bra to fit perfectly, falling straps and poking
underwire should never be an issue again.

Anik *city style*

1122 Madison Avenue (between 83rd & 84th Sts)
212 249 2417
Open 10–8 Mon–Sat, 11–7 Sun

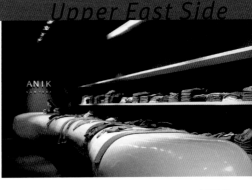

Anik's cashmere sweaters, neutral basics, and figure-hugging jeans are classic New Yorker apparel, and here you'll also find sophisticated women's brands such as Theory and Elie Tahari. There are bargains to be had too, as old stock is rapidly discounted.

Clyde's *boutique pharmacy*

926 Madison Avenue (at 74th St.) • 212 744 5050
➤ www.clydesonmadison.com
Open 9–7:30 Mon–Wed, Fri, 9–8 Thu, 9–7 Sat, 10–6 Sun

Yes, Clyde's is a pharmacy in the sense that you can buy vitamins and cough syrup, but this popular neighborhood institution offers so much more. The store is stocked with high-end beauty and skincare products, candles, and imported bathroom goods.

Christian Louboutin *scarlet soles*

941 Madison Avenue (between 74th & 75th Sts)
212 396 1884 Open 10–6 Mon–Sat

The quirky designs and scarlet soles that mark every Louboutin shoe signify that you've arrived in the style-conscious world of Madison Avenue. Well-heeled fans include New York socialites and Hollywood A-listers. Even if you're not buying, drop by to admire the glorious, Parisian-style interior.

Diane B *clothes & shoes for uptown girls*

1412 3rd Avenue (at 80th St.) • 212 570 5360
Open 11–7:30 Mon–Fri, 10–6:30 Sat; closed Sun in summer

Situated in the lonely shopping territory of the far eastern Upper East Side, Diane B is a good stop for French and Italian women's clothing if you don't feel like venturing downtown. Finding a hot number isn't hard with brands such as Stephan Kelian and Vera Wang, but don't expect to find Prada and Gucci.

Shopping

ABH Designs *creature comforts* `8 H1`
401 East 76th Street (between Lexington & 3rd Aves)
212 249 2276
Open 11–6:30 Mon–Sat

Owner Aude Bronson-Howard's career as a Hollywood costume designer is evident in the items she chooses for her store. Linen napkins with silk trim, Italian plates, down shawls, and faux-mink slippers will bring a touch of luxury to any home.

Searle *coats and cashmere tops* `10 E5`
1124 Madison Avenue (at 84th St.) • 212 988 7318
» www.searlenyc.com
Open 10–8 Mon–Fri, 10–7 Sat, noon–6:30 Sun

What began as a store focusing on stylish top quality sheepskin coats has expanded to include the full gamut of women's clothing. From TSE cashmere sweaters to casual lines such as Blue Dot, Trina Turk, and Lacoste, Searle provides a great mix of styles.

Intermix *must-have clothing* `7 C3`
210 Columbus Avenue (between 69th & 70th Sts)
212 769 9116
» www.intermixonline.com
Open 10–7 Mon–Sat, noon–7 Sun

Intermix is a beacon of style in the relative fashion desert of the Upper West Side. The staff can be less than helpful and prices are high, but the store has an irresistible selection of cool, slinky outfits.

Blades Board & Skate *gear for movers* `7 B2`
120 West 72nd Street (between Columbus & Amsterdam Aves)
212 787 3911
» www.blades.com Open 11–8 daily

The name says it all. Kneepads, goggles, and helmets are among the essential equipment sold here for skateboarders, snowboarders, and inline skaters. Make your choice from an impressive array of skates then head across the street to Central Park.

Housing Works
Thrift Shop *treasures at bargain prices*

306 Columbus Avenue (between 74th & 75th Sts)
212 579 7566
>> www.housingworks.org
Open 11–7 Mon–Fri, 10–6 Sat, noon–5 Sun

This is not just a thrift shop, but a store with heart. It was conceived in 1990 by Keith Cylar and other activists as a not-for-profit shop to help homeless New Yorkers living with AIDS. Housing Works has now become the largest community-based AIDS activist group in the U.S. Cylar passed away in April 2004 after a long AIDS-related illness, but the shop continues his work.

The integrity of the project encourages NY's most stylish residents to donate anything from couches to coveted clothes. It's not uncommon to find sought-after furniture, designer clothes, antiques, and even collectable art. Despite all this, prices remain rock bottom, in contrast to other trendy thrift stores.

Super Runners *jogger's paradise*

360 Amsterdam Avenue (between 77th & 78th Sts)
212 787 7665
>> www.superrunnersshop.com
Open 10–7 Mon–Fri (to 9 Thu), 10–6 Sat, 11–5 Sun

Even if you're not training for the New York marathon, this shop has a running shoe for every terrain, from the gym treadmill to Central Park nature trails. As well as trainers you can buy a watch for checking lap times.

Zabar's *top-notch deli*
2245 Broadway (at 80th St.) • 212 787 2000
>> www.zabars.com
Open 8–7:30 Mon–Fri, 8–8 Sat, 9–6 Sun

Were Zabar's to close, the city could well descend into chaos. Since the 1920s, New Yorkers have relied on this family-run business for all their gourmet kitchen needs, from fine cheeses to the best smoked fish. Don't leave without buying a famous Zabar's coffee.

Xukuma *cool lifestyle store*

11 D4

183 Lenox Avenue (at 119th St.) • 212 222 0490
>> www.xukuma.com
Open noon–7 Wed–Sat, 10–6 Sun

Xukuma, pronounced "zoo-koo-ma," is a lifestyle store for hip city-dwellers. The shop-owners define Xukuma (a word they dreamed up) as "life the way you want it to be." Their vision encompasses homewares – groovy lamps, frames, clocks, etc. – and clothing lines that bank heavily on 1960s/70s-influenced "sista-soul" appeal.

You'll see the lanky, sexy silhouette of a black woman with an Afro (dubbed "X Girl") on everything from T-shirts to posters and cards. Her best cameo is on the tank top and panty sets emblazoned with phrases such as "obey me" and "please me." There's a range of men's underwear with "hustler," "dirty devil," and "bad boy" emblems. Xukuma also stocks gourmet food, teas, and Sia candles, as well as chandeliers and gift baskets.

Demolition Depot *historic artifacts*

12 G3

216 East 125th Street (between 2nd & 3rd Aves) 212 860 1138
>> www.demolitiondepot.com
Open 10–6 Mon–Fri, 10–5 Sat

At this four-story warehouse in Harlem, you'll uncover all sorts of treasures for sprucing up an apartment with touches from a bygone age. There are 19th-century light fixtures, mirrors that once hung in American farmhouses, fireplace mantles, and oil paintings.

Owner and antiques dealer Evan Blum salvages most of his stock from homes and buildings that are about to be destroyed. Because of this, he can buy cheap and sell a beguiling range of architectural pieces – from plumbing fixtures and door furniture to stone sculptures, stained-glass windows, gates and railings – at far more reasonable prices than you'd expect to pay at an auction. Demolition Depot's smaller items include decorative tiles, clocks, old shop signs, and NYC subway signage.

Butter *current trends for women*   `13 B4`

389 Atlantic Avenue (between Hoyt & Bond) • 718 260 9033
Open noon–7 Mon–Sat, noon–6 Sun

Though not completely original by NYC standards, Butter has been a ground-breaking store for Brooklyn, being the first in the neighborhood to offer top-end women's clothing. With lines such as Dries Van Noten, Rick Owens, and Rogan jeans available here, Brooklyn girls no longer have to trek across the bridge.

Bark *one-of-a-kind gifts*   `13 B4`

495 Atlantic Avenue (between Nevins St. & 3rd Ave.)
718 625 8997
Open noon–7 Wed–Sat, noon–6 Sun

"Lifestyle stores" are becoming something of a phenomenon in New York, and Bark (formerly Breukelen) is hailed as the first example of this genre in Brooklyn. In old-fashioned parlance, however, Bark is an interior design store, pre-dominantly stocking pieces for a sophisticated contemporary home – Japanese glass, South African wooden bowls, and jewelry by local artists.

Because the selection offered here is so unusual and distinctive, even Manhattanites are prepared to leave the island once in a while to visit it. Expensive kitchen supplies, such as coffee-makers, handmade ceramic dishes, and stainless steel mixers, offer endless appeal. The wonderfully elegant Diptyque candles are the store's most affordable and best-selling items, but this is not the place for bargains.

Loom *groovy knick-knacks*   `13 C4`

115 7th Avenue, Brooklyn (between Carroll & President Sts)
718 789 0061 Open 11–7 Mon–Sat, 11–6 Sun

Loom is a design store catering to the well-heeled, stroller-pushing crowd of Park Slope. Italian stationery, mod jewelry, and cute little *objets* make wonderful gifts for the friend who has everything. Come and agonize over the discerning selection of glass vases and hand-embroidered bed linen.

Shopping

Nest *clutch of delectable home furnishings* `13 C5`
396a 7th Avenue (between 12th & 13th Sts), Brooklyn
718 965 3491 Open noon–7 Mon, 11–7 Tue–Sat, noon–6 Sun

When graphic designer Jihan Kim and his wife decided to settle down together and have a baby, they also decided to open a store that would combine this cozy time in their lives and their artistic backgrounds. Thus Nest was born (and their baby girl) to fill the niche in Park Slope for off-beat *objets* and furniture for starting a home.

Their range of products for a groovy home include sleek, handmade ceramic vases – made by Kim's aunt – and Japanese mugs with bold graphic prints. Nest also stocks hand-embroidered pillows and stylish window shades, tiny wooden children's chairs in bold colors (really adorable), and space-age Blue Dot desks, made of white Lucite. The perfect buy if space is tight in your suitcase are Nest's giant, adhesive dots, which come in bright colors and are designed to decorate walls, ceilings, and floors.

Mini Minimarket *ironic girly lifestyle store* `13 B2`
218 Bedford Avenue (at N. 5th St.) • 718 302 9337
>> www.miniminimarket.com Open noon–8 daily

A hodgepodge of all things cool, this store has everything for the hipster Williamsburg girl: playful jewelry, fashions from Tokyo, sexy underwear, Gola trainers, and 1980s-inspired tops. The minimarket stocks only small quantities of each item, so it's unlikely you'll find anyone else wearing the same thing.

Spoonbill & Sugartown Booksellers *rare tomes* `13 B2`
218 Bedford Avenue (at N. 5th St.) • 718 387 7322
>> www.spoonbillbooks.com Open 10–10 daily

Books on painting, photography, architecture, and graphic design cater to Brooklyn's bohemians. At the back of the store, you'll find used books on everything from religion to geography. What you won't find is anything off the current *New York Times* bestseller list.

Darr *curiosity shop*

13 B4

369 Atlantic Ave. (bet. Bond & Hoyt) • 718 797 9733
>> www.shopdarr.com
Open 11–7 Tue–Sat, noon–6 Sun

From unusual vintage furniture to prison art, Darr is a world of curiosities. Around every corner lies some peculiar item or other – maybe an anatomical chart or a stuffed chicken. You may just find the perfect gift for the person who thought they had everything.

Nom de Guerre *trend-setting clothes*

13 B2

88 North 6th Street (between Berry & Wythe Aves)
718 387 3363
>> www.nomdeguerre.net Open noon–8 Mon–Sat, noon–7 Sun

Known for its hip urban gear, Nom de Guerre sells sleeveless graphic T-shirts, Sanskrit-adorned hooded sweatshirts, and pinstriped, plaid, and checked blazers, cardigans, and vests. The shop was founded by a creative collective of four friends, their goal being to combine elements and influences from the worlds of art, fashion, and urban subcultures. The result is casual clothing that looks worn in and thrown together, much like Brooklyn itself.

Affiliated stores are located in Tokyo and L.A. All share a common theme of otherworldliness, created by using basement sites that are dressed up to resemble bunkers, tunnels, and even archeological digs. In addition to the clothing line, this store features a curated book selection and Nom de Guerre collaborative products.

Beacon's Closet *vintage clothes trader*

13 B1

88 North 11th Street • 718 486 0816
>> www.beaconscloset.com
Open noon–9 Mon–Fri, 11–8 Sat & Sun

Sick of all your old clothes? Then take them to Beacon's Closet and either sell your garments for cash or trade them for instore credit. In the shop, you'll find lots of secondhand clothing and accessories for men and women. There are also brand-new CDs.

Earwax *sounds to clean out your ears*   `13 B2`

218 Bedford Avenue (at N. 5th St.) • 718 486 3771
Open noon–9 Mon, 11–9 Tue, Thu & Sat, noon–8 Wed, Fri & Sun

Earwax is the antithesis of record store chains: there is no adjoining coffee shop/bookstore and you can't pre-listen to CDs. But what you do get is a hand-picked selection of music that won't let you down. New CDs are biased towards indie rock, while the formidable second-hand section runs the full gamut of tastes.

Calliope *modern consignment store*   `13 B2`

135 Grand Street • 718 486 0697
Open noon–7 Tue–Sat, noon–6 Sun

Part vintage jumble, part contemporary boutique, Calliope is a neighborhood favorite for its unusual selection of clothing and accessories. The newer designs work well with the second-hand pieces – just look at Sarah Luna's frocks, with their nod to 1970s-inspired leisurewear.

MiniMall *alternative retail space*   `2 C4`

218 Bedford Avenue (at N. 5th St.)
Stores at MiniMall have differing opening times, but most are open between 10 and 7 daily

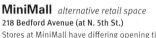

Located on Williamsburg's hippest boulevard *(see p171)*, the MiniMall is one of the best places for shopping and lounging in Brooklyn. This retail space-cum-club house takes up the entire ground floor of a loft building, and houses myriad stores.

Once inside the cavernous entryway (where computers and tables are set up for Internet perusal), you can venture into shops such as **The Girdle Factory,** in which vintage treasures can be found (a $30 Gucci wallet!). **Otte,** on the other hand, sells only what the uptown girl wants: Seven jeans and flirty dresses. **Go Yoga** offers some of the best yoga classes in the city, and the **Tibet Boutique** will help you look the part. One of the most popular stores is the **UVA Wine Shop.** There, you'll find young connoisseurs deliberating over their purchases.

Astroturf *vintage homewares*

 13 B4

290 Smith Street (between Union & Sackett Sts)
718 522 6182 Open 4–7 Thu, noon–5 Sat & Sun

There is something comforting about setting foot into this Cobble Hill homewares and furniture store. It's almost as if you've just stepped into a really groovy grandmother's attic. Astroturf sells everything that was left carelessly behind from the 1950s and 60s: orange plastic bowl sets, curvy lamps, now-prized vintage lunchboxes, turquoise coffee thermoses, and Formica tables. Everything in this store yells – no, screams – kitsch!

If all the fun and funky appeal is too much for the pottery-barn aesthetic you have studiously cultivated in your home, take a sleekly sculpted ashtray or vase to add a dash of *Austin Powers* grooviness to your decor. There are shelves and shelves of knick-knacks, so the choices are practically endless. Best of all, prices are still pretty retro here, so you can afford to have fun with the cheap-and-chic look.

Two Jakes *period furniture* 13 B2

320 Wythe Avenue (between Grand & S. 1st Sts)
718 782 7780
>> www.twojakes.com Open 11–7 Tue–Sun

Head to this industrial-chic area of Williamsburg for used metal cabinets that would be triple the price if they were sold in SoHo. Two Jakes' spacious warehouse offers classic 20th-century chairs, desks, and other furniture in remarkably good condition.

Moon River Chattel *farmhouse furniture* 13 B2

62 Grand Street (between Wythe & Kent Aves) • 718 388 1121
Open noon–7 Tue–Sat, noon–5 Sun

In the urban jungle of Brooklyn sits a store that offers items more befitting a country cottage than a city pad. Light fixtures look as if they were taken from an early 20th-century soda shop, old clocks tick ponderously, wooden tables carry the burden of age, and appliances seem more artistic than purposeful.

art &
architecture

New York is the preeminent
city for Modernist art and
architecture, famously evident in
its towering skyscrapers and in
the unsurpassed collections of the
Guggenheim and the Whitney.
Along with great cultural icons,
such as The Met and Brooklyn
Museum of Art, New York also has
a thriving contemporary art scene,
split between Manhattan's
galleries and a dynamic
community of artists in Brooklyn.

ART & ARCHITECTURE

New York is often described as a modern art town, and the city maintains a proud legacy of championing new artistic movements, from the Art Deco skyscrapers of the 1930s to mid-century Modernism to the graffiti-inspired Postmodern canvases of Jean Michel Basquiat and Andy Warhol. While the city boasts spectacular iconic museums, it is the commercial and independent galleries – now spread far beyond their previous Chelsea and SoHo confines – and New York's own active artists that ensure its vitality today.

Jonathan Schultz

Iconic Skyscrapers

The wedge-shaped **Flatiron Building** *(see p106)* is regarded as New York's first skyscraper, and the two behemoths that capped the city's golden age of building high are the **Empire State** and **Chrysler** buildings *(see pp12 & 105)*. The **Skyscraper Museum** *(see p101)* contains models of these buildings and many others, including the Twin Towers.

Venerable Collections

The Egyptian and Impressionist collections in the **Met** *(see p109)* are perennial favorites, while the **Frick Collection** *(see p108)* offers an intimately scaled alternative for seeing Old Masters and ornate period furniture. Not to be overlooked is the **Brooklyn Museum** *(see p114)*, with its impressive Mesopotamian and early American holdings.

Modern Art Icons

New York is blessed with several wonderful collections of modern art, some housed in museums that are modern icons in their own right. Among them are Frank Lloyd Wright's spiraling **Guggenheim Museum** *(see p110)*; **MoMA** *(see p107)*, redesigned in 2004 by Yoshio Taniguchi; and the **Whitney** *(see p107)*, boldly designed by Marcel Breuer.

choice sights

The Cultural Mix

From pre-Columbian artifacts to contemporary street photography, **El Museo del Barrio** *(see p113)* throws up constant surprises. **Studio Museum in Harlem** *(see p113)* champions the neighborhood's African-American cultural renaissance, and the **Jewish Museum** *(see p111)* explores contributions to painting, music, and literature made by Jews.

Contemporary Art Venues

Some of the best current work can be seen at commercial galleries such as **Gagosian** and **Deitch Projects** *(see p102)*. While in SoHo check out Walter De Maria's **Earth Room** and **Broken Kilometer** *(see p102)*, commissioned in the 1970s by the trailblazing Dia Foundation. And go to Queens for installations and large-scale paintings at **P.S.1** *(see p115)*.

Historical Houses

The **Lower East Side Tenement Museum** *(see p103)* looks increasingly incongruous on rapidly gentrifying Orchard Street. The juxtaposition of old and new is even more striking at the **Merchant's House Museum** *(see p103)*, an 1832 townhouse surrounded by trendy bars. For architectural detailing, stroll along "Block Beautiful" *(see p104)*.

Art & Architecture

U.S. Custom House   *Beaux Arts affair*   `1 D5`
1 Bowling Green (between State & Whitehall Sts)
>> www.nmai.si.edu Open 10–5 daily (to 8 Thu)

New York's grandest example of Beaux Arts architecture has figures representing the four continents incorporated into its facade. They were sculpted by Daniel Chester French, most famous for his work at the Lincoln Memorial in Washington. The National Museum of the American Indian is housed here.

St. Paul's Chapel   *New York's oldest*   `1 D3`
209 Broadway (between Fulton & Vesey Sts)
>> www.saintpaulschapel.org Open 10–6 Mon–Sat, 9–4 Sun

It has served the residents of Lower Manhattan for well over 200 years, but St. Paul's Chapel gained wider public attention in the wake of the 9/11 attack on the World Trade Center, when it acted as a steadfast beacon for New Yorkers.

Modelled on St. Martin-in-the-Fields in London, the church was completed in 1766, making it New York's oldest building in continuous use. George Washington worshipped here during the two-year period (1789–91) when New York served as the nation's capital. His pew is singled out, and above it hangs what is believed to be the first oil painting of the Great Seal of the United States – the image of the bald eagle, with a red-and-white striped shield, thirteen arrows, and an olive branch.

The chapel bore witness to another kind of history on September 11, 2001, as debris from the collapsing North Tower of the World Trade Center rained down, cloaking the building in pale ash. Within hours of the catastrophe, St. Paul's converted into a base for recovery squads. Firefighters, police officers, and medical personnel ate, slept, and grieved here, while volunteers ministered, the city's top chefs cooked, and students from the Julliard School of Music performed impromptu concerts.

The chapel has an exhibition of memorabilia and testimonies from 9/11 survivors called *Out of the Dust: A Year of Ministry at Ground Zero.*

For the very latest on New York go to >> www.realcity.dk.com

Ground Zero *poignant reconstruction site* `1 C3`
Viewing Wall on Church Street (between Liberty & Vesey Sts)
>> www.renewnyc.com

In 2002, the Lower Manhattan Development Corporation – in collaboration with families of victims, local business owners, and politicians – selected a master plan for Ground Zero: site of the former World Trade Center. The design was by Daniel Libeskind, an architect renowned for his ground-breaking Holocaust Museum in Germany. His scheme intended to retain the twin towers' footprints at 30 ft (9 m) below sidewalk level, creating a contemplative space for a memorial. But the most dramatic part of his design was an astonishing 1,776-ft (540-m) skyscraper, the Freedom Tower, its height echoing the date of the signing of the Declaration of Independence – 1776.

Libeskind's designs have undergone significant alterations, however. Until the building is finished, visitors can view the site from a platform. A memorial and museum are due to open in the near future.

Skyscraper Museum *homage to height* `1 D5`
39 Battery Place • 212 968 1961
>> www.skyscraper.org
Open noon–6 Wed–Sun

After seven years bouncing from one office lobby to the next, the Skyscraper Museum finally found a home in 2004. One of the city's most ingeniously designed museums, it honors its soaring subjects through illusion and intriguing details. Freestanding white columns are vertically reflected between stainless steel floors and mirrored ceilings, creating the appearance of infinite height. Throughout this echoing space, architectural fragments from Manhattan's most notable skyscrapers are displayed. The museum contextualizes New York's 100-year-old obsession with building tall in terms of economic cycles, an interesting counterpoint to the apparent brashness of the form. The museum also mounts temporary exhibitions, and future shows are set to redress the current NY bias with more international subjects. **Adm**

Art & Architecture

Woolworth Building *pinnacled tower* `1 D2`

Gothic in style and topped off by a green turret, the Woolworth Building is utterly distinct from its clean-edged, Lower Manhattan neighbors. Erected in 1913 for the houseware-catalogue magnate Frank Woolworth, it was, at 55 stories, the tallest structure in New York until the 1930s, when the Chrysler Building was constructed. The nave-like lobby contains a statue depicting the thrifty Mr. Woolworth counting his dimes.

Broken Kilometer *relative distance* `3 D5`
393 West Broadway (between Spring & Broome Sts)
212 989 5566 (Dia offices)
>> www.brokenkilometer.org Open noon–3 & 3:30–6 Wed–Sun

In five parallel rows, 500 gleaming brass rods lie on a SoHo hardwood floor in Walter De Maria's 1979 installation. Lain end to end, the rods would measure exactly one kilometer. The seemingly straightforward work plays with perspective and is loved by mathematicians.

Earth Room *deep, dark soil* `3 D4`
141 Wooster Street (between Houston & Prince Sts)
212 989 5566 (Dia offices)
>> www.earthroom.org Open noon–3 & 3:30–6 Wed–Sun

Commissioned by the trailblazing Dia Art Foundation, Walter De Maria's *Earth Room* (1977) is a white-walled exhibition space, filled to a depth of about 2 ft (55 cm) with moist, dark soil. The third of De Maria's earth sculptures, it is the only one still in existence.

Contemporary Art Galleries

Some of the hottest galleries in the contemporary art world are grouped in Manhattan. The SoHo nexus, comprising Wooster, Grand, Greene, and Spring streets, boasts the highest concentration of galleries. **Deitch Projects** mounts some of the area's most highly anticipated shows, from paintings inspired by skateboard design to performances. Chelsea has welcomed defecting SoHo dealers for years. **Pace Wildenstein** and **Mary Boone** have Chelsea outposts as well as midtown locations, and **Larry Gagosian's** little empire, extending from Beverly Hills to London, mounts prestigious exhibitions at his large Chelsea space. Elsewhere, Chinatown's **Leo Koenig Gallery** deals in lively work from emerging artists. For individual contact details, *see p229.*

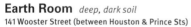

Lower East Side Tenement
Museum *home of NY's early immigrants*
108 Orchard Street (at Delancey St.) • 212 431 0233
» www.tenement.org
Open for guided tours only: see website for days and times

In the heart of the old garment district in the Lower East Side, the Tenement Museum offers an enlightening overview of how pioneering immigrants lived and worked in the late 19th and early 20th centuries. Guided tours explore an 1863 tenement, which was home to some 7,000 immigrants from 20 countries during its 72 years as a residential building.

Engaging tour guides lead visitors through the humble, virtually unchanged units, peppering biographical accounts of former tenants' lives with fascinating facts about the neighborhood's social organizations, businesses, sights, sounds, and smells. It is advisable to book a few days ahead. The museum also arranges historical walking tours of the Lower East Side. **Adm**

Merchant's House
Museum *19th-century opulence*
29 East 4th Street (between Lafayette St. & Bowery)
» www.merchantshouse.com • 212 777 1089
Open noon–5 Thu–Mon (tours: weekdays only)

Between the Bowery's punk-rock bars and Broadway's name-brand shops rises a magnificent Federal-style house of around 1832. It is one of the last vestiges of a prosperous merchant-class suburbia that once thrived in downtown Manhattan. The hardware-importing Tredwell family lived here until 1933, resisting the late-19th century trend among Manhattan's elite to construct estates bordering Central Park.

Opened as a museum in 1936, the Merchant's House provides an unparalleled glimpse into how the high life was lived in mid-19th-century Manhattan. The interior reveals a Greek Revival decorative scheme of Ionic columns, ornate plasterwork, and beautiful marble mantelpieces. The backyard garden contains arbors and 19th-century iron furniture. **Adm**

Art & Architecture

Jefferson Market Courthouse 3 C2

425 Avenue of the Americas (at 10th St.) • 212 243 4334

>> www.nypl.org Open noon–8 Mon & Wed, 10–6 Tue, noon–6 Thu, 1–6 Fri, 10–5 Sat

The fairytale Venetian-Gothic courthouse was saved from demolition when local residents campaigned to have it converted into a public library. The former civic court is now the library's main reading room and the children's reading room occupies the police court.

Forbes Magazine Gallery *toys/games* 3 D2

60 5th Avenue (at W. 12th St.) • 212 206 5548

>> www.forbescollection.com Open 10–4 Tue, Wed, Fri & Sat

The private art estate of publishing magnate Malcolm Forbes is displayed here. Although his unrivaled Fabergé egg collection sold for $100 million in 2004, visitors can still glimpse a frivolous side to the notoriously pragmatic Mr. Forbes in his vintage toy collection and staggering array of boardgames.

Block Beautiful *decorous abodes* 4 E1

Among Manhattan's most picturesque residential blocks is this fanciful melange of Tudor, late-Federal, and brownstone houses. Attractive paint schemes, varied door arch designs, and intricate wrought-iron gates distinguish each home from the next. In fair weather, the block enchants with window-mounted planter boxes brimful of color, and slender trees sprouting acid-green leaves.

Museum at the Fashion Institute of Technology *past and future trends* 5 D4

7th Avenue (at 27th St.) • 212 217 5800

>> www.fitnyc.edu Open noon–8 Tue–Fri, 10–5 Sat

Do Andy Warhol's early footwear sketches bear hints of future greatness? Contemplate this question and scores of other fashion designs at F.I.T.'s free museum. Special exhibitions draw on the school's textile, illustration, and photography collections.

Midtown Deco *classic buildings* `6 F1–6 G2`

Evoking an age of jazz orchestras, limousines, high hems, and cocked fedoras, midtown's Art Deco skyscrapers are quintessential emblems of New York. Beyond the **Empire State Building** *(see p12)* rise equally impressive landmarks. Though the buildings are not open to the public, you can admire the exteriors and nearly always venture into the foyers, which often contain elaborate designs. The **General Electric Building** (570 Lexington Ave.) has a rare, nickel-silver embellished lobby. Look for the **Chanin Building's** intricately carved facade and doorway with gold-plated convector grilles (122 East 42nd St. at Lexington Ave.). Also on 42nd Street, you'll find a huge revolving globe and antiquated weather instrumentation in the lobby of the **New York Daily News Building** (220 East 42nd St.). It's not a hidden gem, but the shimmering **Chrysler Building** (405 Lexington Ave.) is a revelation if you've never seen the lobby's mosaics and whimsical automotive motifs.

Grand Central Terminal `6 F2`
42nd Street & Park Avenue
>> www.grandcentralterminal.com

To enter into the lovingly restored Grand Central – either from the gloomy tracks or from manic 42nd Street – is to be conveyed to an era when train travel evoked glamor and adventure, not mere transportation. Even the most rushed Westchester County commuter, sprinting to make the 6:06pm Harlem Line local, finds the station's artisanal food market, cushy lounges and top-notch restaurants difficult to resist.

The station, a Beaux-Arts building of 1913, is one of the city's greatest architectural achievements. Its cathedral-like windows, the staircase in the Main Concourse (inspired by the Paris Opera House), and the astrological mosaic ceiling are awe-inspiring. For a glimpse of the less obvious architectural and historical details, take a tour led by the Municipal Arts Society (www.mas.org). They depart every Wednesday at 12:30 from the travel information booth.

Art & Architecture

International Center of Photography
`5 D2`

massive photo archive

1133 Avenue of the Americas (at 43rd St.) • 212 857 0000

>> www.icp.org Open 10–6 Tue–Thu, Sat & Sun, 10–8 Fri

Combining a school, an archive, and frequent exhibitions, the ICP is one of the world's biggest centers of photography. The subject of a show here might be historical – a 1920s French avant-gardist, perhaps – or contemporary, such as reportage from Iraq. **Adm**

Whitney Museum of American Art at Altria
`6 F2`

120 Park Avenue (at 42rd St.) • 917 663 2453

>> www.whitney.org Open 11 –6 Mon–Fri (to 7:30 Thu);
sculpture garden 7:30am–9:30pm Mon–Sat, 11am–7pm Sun & hols

The airy, bright lobby of Altria Group, Inc. serves as an exhibition space for cutting-edge contemporary art. There are two spaces, in fact – an intimate gallery and a glass-walled indoor sculpture court. The exhibition program is focused on emerging contemporary artists, such as Mark Bradford, Louis Gispert, and Dario Robleto.

Rose Museum at Carnegie Hall
`7 D5`

musical memorabilia

154 West 57th Street, 2nd Floor (at 7th Ave.) • 212 903 9600

>> www.carnegiehall.org Open 11–4:30 Thu–Tue

This museum gives an insight into the prestigious status of the Carnegie Hall *(see p131)* and is a treasure trove of intriguing memorabilia, from concert programs to vintage costumes. For tours of the concert hall (11:30am, 2pm, and 3pm, Sep–Jun) call 212 903 9765.

Flatiron Building
`6 E5`

NY's first skyscraper

23rd Street, 5th Ave. & Broadway

Immortalized in the moody black-and-white photographs of Alfred Stieglitz and later in the blockbuster Spiderman films, the triangular Flatiron Building was revolutionary in its day. The 21-story structure was completed in 1902 without confirmed tenants, and so was the first building of its stature to be built purely as a speculative venture – a common trend today.

Museum of Modern Art *home at last* `8 E5`
11 West 53rd Street (between 5th & 6th Aves) • 212 708 9400
➤➤ www.moma.org Open 10:30–5:30 Wed–Mon (to 8 Fri)

After leading itinerant lives in cities around the world and in a temporary space in Queens, MoMA's most highly prized holdings have returned to their dramatically revamped six-story gallery back in Manhattan. Reopened in late 2004 after the most ambitious building project of the museum's 75-year history, MoMA has reaffirmed its status as the world's foremost modern art institution.

Yoshio Taniguchi's renovation has doubled the museum's exhibition capacity and restored one of its most beloved attributes, the Abby Aldrich Rockefeller Sculpture Garden. The redesign also incorporates a smart new restaurant. Set off by the refreshed gallery spaces, the collection continues to impress, with such delights as Vincent Van Gogh's *Starry Night*, Picasso's formidable *Les Demoiselles d'Avignon*, and Dalí's seminal *The Persistence of Memory*. **Adm**

Whitney Museum `8 E2`
of American Art *America's finest*
945 Madison Avenue (at E. 75th St.) • 800 Whitney
➤➤ www.whitney.org Open 11–6 Wed, Thu, Sat & Sun, 1–9 Fri

As with Frank Lloyd Wright's Guggenheim building *(see p110)*, Marcel Breuer's cantilevered Whitney is more than just a home for an art collection, it is a statement of radical intent. Built in the mid-1960s, it is distinctive, powerful, and Modernist, reflecting the strongest elements of the exclusively American art it holds. The permanent collection boasts works by Warhol, Pollock, and Jasper Johns, and by abstract sculptors David Smith and Alexander Calder. It also has an extensive collection of paintings by Georgia O'Keeffe and Edward Hopper.

The Whitney's program of temporary exhibitions is excellent, including one-person retrospectives of well-known contemporary artists, themed shows, and film and video works, such as the Andy Warhol Film Project and a series of shorts by John Baldessari. **Adm**

Art & Architecture

Frick Collection *art in a glorious setting*

8 E2

1 East 70th Street (at 5th Ave.) • 212 288 0700
>> www.frick.org Open 10–6 Tue–Sat, 11–5 Sun

The family of steel tycoon Henry Clay Frick bequeathed their Fifth Avenue mansion to the city shortly after Henry's death in 1919. Included in the gift was one of the country's most spectacular collections of fine and decorative arts, spanning more than five centuries, from the Renaissance to the late 19th century.

Henry took incredible care over situating his most prized pieces in specific rooms and halls, a habit not forgotten by the collection's present directors, who may arrange entire floorpans in order to showcase one single piece. The Whistler portraits in the Oval Room, for example, are a mere backdrop to the room's main focal point, Houdon's life-size sculpture

Diana the Huntress . The capacious West Gallery is more egalitarian with its hanging arrangements, granting Old Masters Rembrandt, Velásquez, Van Dyck, and Goya equal wallspace. On the rich, oak-paneled walls of the intimate Living Hall, at the hea of the residence, are major works by Titian, El Greco and Bellini. Elsewhere are Jan van Eyck's *Virgin and Child with Saints and Donor*, El Greco's fearsome *Th Purification of the Temple*, and Holbein's luminous portrait of *Sir Thomas More*.

However, it's the house itself that makes a visit s unforgettable. Furnishings range from Louis XVI opulence to 19th-century English restraint. Plant-fille atriums and a charming outdoor garden, with gracef magnolia trees and views of Central Park, also add extra dimensions to the Frick experience. **Adm**

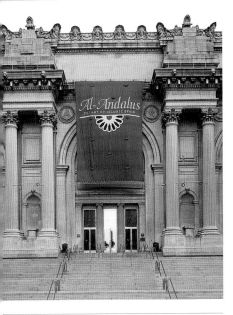

Metropolitan Museum of Art *cultural behemoth*

1000 5th Avenue (between 80th & 83rd Sts) • 212 535 7710
>> www.metmuseum.org
Open 9:30–5:30 Tue–Sun (to 9 Fri & Sat)

The Met's two million objects form one of the world's largest museum collections. Among the myriad galleries are collections of Egyptian artifacts, Islamic art, and European paintings. Among the paintings are works by Botticelli and Leonardo, and canvases by Rembrandt, Cézanne, and Monet.

If the prospect of such a vast museum seems daunting, consider attending an informal gallery talk. More in-depth than the museum highlight tours, they are led by art historians and offer the opportunity to learn more about specific works. Check the Met's website for the talks calendar. Also note the Met's highly varied program of temporary exhibitions, which range from Anglomania (a show on British fashion) to the work of contemporary visual artist Kara Walker. **Adm**

Museum of Television and Radio *classic footage & recordings*

25 West 52nd Street (between 5th & 6th Aves)
212 621 6800
>> www.mtr.org Open noon–6 Tue–Sun (to 8 Thu)

Yearning to revisit a classic *Muppets* episode? This museum exists for just such desires, with its constant stream of classic comedy shows, as well as vintage newsreel and landmark radio broadcasts. **Adm**

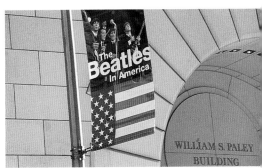

Asia Society *Asian arts*

725 Park Avenue (at 70th St.) • 212 288 6400
>> www.asiasociety.org Open 11–6 Tue–Sun (to 9 Fri)

The superb Asian art collection of American philanthropist John D. Rockefeller III is housed in this bright, modern building. Japanese screens and bronze Buddhist deities are among the exhibits spread throughout a series of galleries. Shows by contemporary Asian and Asian-American artists are often staged, and the building acts as a venue for performances of Asian music and dance. **Adm**

Guggenheim Museum 10 E4

1071 5th Avenue (at 89th St.) • 212 423 3500
» www.guggenheim.org
Open 10–5:45 Sat–Wed, 10–7:45 Fri

With museums now bearing the name in Las Vegas, Venice, Berlin, New York, and Bilbao in Spain, "Guggenheim" has penetrated the world's cultural vocabulary. But in the 1950s, before becoming the art-world juggernaut that it is today, Guggenheim was simply the surname of Solomon, an art lover who wanted to exhibit his collection of abstract art.

In the minds of Guggenheim and his advisor, the painter and curator Hilla Rebay, the collection required a new kind of gallery space – one that complemented the pioneering, iconoclastic form of the paintings in his collection. What resulted was one of the world's most instantly recognizable buildings. Designed by American Modernist architect Frank Lloyd Wright, the building shattered notions of rectilinear exhibition space. Rather than walk through traditional galleries and wings, only to turn around and experience the same art while returning to the

entrance hall, visitors were encouraged to ride elevators to the top of a spiral-shaped tower, the Great Rotunda, and descend via a gently sloping ramp along the spiral's perimeter. Adorning the tower's walls were works by Wassily Kandinsky, Piet Mondrian, and Joan Miró.

This specific vision for the building is no longer upheld, however. Some six years after the building's completion in 1959, the strictly abstract collection was augmented with figurative works by Impressionists Cézanne, Degas, and Renoir, and with paintings by Van Gogh and Picasso. The building was extended, and today the Great Rotunda is used only for temporary exhibitions, while the permanent collection is housed in the adjoining Tower. The Small Rotunda is used to display the "greatest hits" of the Impressionist and Post-Impressionist collection. The museum's temporary shows tend to relate to the Modern Movement, some very obviously, such as the conceptual abstraction of Daniel Buren, others more obliquely, such as art from the Aztec Empire, which influenced some early 20th-century avant-garde painters. **Adm**

Museum of the City of New York *focus on New York* `10 E2`
1250 5th Avenue (at E. 103rd St.) • 212 534 1672
>> www.mcny.org
Open 10–5 Tue–Sun

Dedicated to New York's development, from its past to its present and future, this museum is housed in a handsome Georgian Colonial building, noted for period rooms from actual homes. Donations appreciated.

The Jewish Museum *all things Jewish* `10 E4`
1109 5th Avenue (at 92nd St.) • 212 423 3200
>> www.thejewishmuseum.org
Open 11–5:45 Sun–Wed, 11–8 Thu, 11–3 Fri

The Jewish Museum presents an unparalleled overview of Jewish art and culture. A stunning French Gothic house holds four floors of ceremonial art, photographs, paintings, textiles, sculptures, and video screenings. Each piece in the permanent collection – whether it be a self-portrait by Viennese artist Max Beckmann, a 3,000-year-old ceramic vase, or a vibrant 19th-century quilt from a Jerusalem workshop – encourages the viewer to explore how the object informs, or is informed by, Jewish identity.

Popular temporary exhibitions take place on the ground floor, such as *Kafka's Prague* and *Entertaining America: Jews, Media, and Broadcasting*, as well as retrospectives of individual Jewish artists, such as Marc Chagall and Chaim Soutine. A kosher café in the basement is on hand for refreshments.

Cooper-Hewitt National Design Museum *design classics* `10 E4`
2 East 91st Street (at 5th Ave.) • 212 849 8400
>> www.ndm.si.edu
Open 10–5 Tue–Thu, 10–9 Fri, 10–6 Sat, noon–6 Sun

Housed in the imposing Andrew Carnegie mansion, the Cooper-Hewitt is a shrine to design in all its forms. Exhibits range from a sketch of candelabra by Michelangelo to highly coveted Eames chairs. **Adm**

>> *Access to one of the biggest garden terraces in New York is another highlight of the Cooper-Hewitt*

The Cloisters *portal to the Middle Ages*
Fort Tryon Park • 212 923 3700 • M4 bus or A train to 190th St.
» www.metmuseum.org
Open 9:30–5:15 Tue–Sun (to 4:45 Nov–Feb)

One of New York's most cherished assets seems, paradoxically, about as native to the Manhattan landscape as a Boston Red Sox fan at the Yankee Stadium. The Metropolitan Museum of Art's Cloisters is a neo-medieval composite of stained glass, painstakingly landscaped gardens, cavernous halls, and solemn chapels grafted onto the craggy northern fringes of Manhattan island.

It was the philanthropic might of John D. Rockefeller Jr. that facilitated the building's construction in 1938. The project was undertaken to provide a harmonious context for displaying the Met's superb collection of medieval European art and architecture. It provides a splendid setting for such masterpieces as Robert Campin's *Annunciation* triptych of 1425. It also integrates relics of medieval buildings, such as a 900-year-old apse from a Spanish church, seamlessly woven into a limestone wall. Elsewhere, a unicorn hunt is vibrantly portrayed through a series of 16th-century Dutch tapestries, and scores of ecclesiastical objects from the length and breadth of Europe are scattered throughout the complex. So complete is the illusion of medieval Europe that the Cloisters creates the visitor experiences a sensation of distance, both temporal and geographical. Glimpsing New Jersey's rugged cliffs across the Hudson through a 12th-century portico is positively disorientating.

Turning to more earthly needs, during warm months visitors can stave off hunger at the on-site café in Bonnefort Cloister. But savvy diners take lunch at the nearby New Leaf Café *(see p55)* for moderately priced bistro fare, such as juicy sirloin burgers. **Adm**

El Museo del Barrio *Latin art* `10 E2`
1230 5th Avenue (at 104th St.) • 212 831 7272
www.elmuseo.org Open 11–5 Wed–Sun

Founded in 1969 by artists and activists from Spanish Harlem, El Museo del Barrio was a response to the lack of exhibition space for specifically Puerto Rican art. Since then, the museum has broadened its scope to the whole of the Caribbean and Latin America.

The permanent collection spans two millennia of art production, from Pre-Columbian artifacts to prints, paintings, installations, and film and video works by the latest generation of Latin American artists. Among more than 8,000 objects are wooden *santos* (colorful, often comical, depictions of Catholic saints that incorporate Afro-Caribbean motifs); fascinating documents of the early years of immigration in New York; and films of life in Spanish Harlem from the 1970s to the present day. The adjoining Teatro Heckscher is an enchanting venue for live Caribbean music, film screenings, and book readings. **Adm**

Studio Museum in Harlem `11 D3`
144 West 125th Street (at Lenox Avenue)
212 864 4500
www.studiomuseum.org
Open noon–6 Wed–Sun (from 10am Sat)

The SMH is a contemporary art gallery and resource specializing in African-American culture. As well as a large permanent collection, there are temporary exhibitions, including work by young photographers.

Prospect Park West *beautiful setting* `13 C5`
Between Union and 15th Streets
www.prospectpark.org

This genteel stretch of 19th-century brownstone, brick, and limestone residences borders Prospect Park. Beginning at Grand Army Plaza's majestic Memorial Arch, a southward stroll takes you past the imposing bronze statue of the Marquis de LaFayette at 9th Street, the park's Concert Shell, and beautiful playgrounds.

Prospect Park was landscaped by Olmsted & Vaux, the designers who also laid out Central Park

Art & Architecture

Brooklyn Museum
of Art *world-class repository*

200 Eastern Parkway • 718 638 5000
>> www.brooklynmuseum.org
Open 10–5 Wed–Fri, 11–6 Sat & Sun (to 11pm first Sat of month

13 D◀

The Beaux Arts BMA dates from 1893 and has as diverse and staggering a collection as its larger cross river contemporary, the Metropolitan Museum of Art This is no idle boast – spread over the five floors of the BMA is a collection that embraces Egyptian sarcophagi and mummy cases; statues, masks, and jewelry from Central Africa; Hiroshige's woodblock prints of *One Hundred Famous Views of Edo*; and a vast selection of paintings and sculpture from Europ and America, including works by Rodin, Degas, Pissaro, Matisse, Louise Bourgeois, and Mark Rothko There is also a strong photography collection, with significant prints by Edward Weston and Paul Stranc On the fifth floor, *American Identities* explores the American dream through exhibits that range from Native American totems to Georgia O'Keefe's 1948 meditation *Brooklyn Bridge*.

The BMA's First Saturday events (first Saturday of every month) make for one of the city's best nights out: free admission after 5pm, free concerts and dance performances, and a bar (cash only). **Adm**

Williamsburg Galleries

Priced out of Manhattan's lofts and studios during the late 1980s, frustrated but intrepid artists boarded the L Train and disembarked in Williamsburg, until then a predominantly Polish and Hasidic Jewish working-class neighborhood. There they found vacant industrial warehouses, which were easily converted into studios. Since then, Williamsburg artists have influenced tastes and styles worldwide, from fashion to painting to music. Supporting the neighborhood's visual arts scene from a spectacular c.1867 building is the **Williamsburg Art & Historical Center** (135 Broadway

at Bedford Avenue), which mounts eclectic shows and performances by local artists. **Pierogi 2000** (177 North 9th Street) artists exhibit around the world, but visitors will always see at least one local artist featured at any time. Since 1992, not-for-profit **Momenta Art** (72 Berry Street) has given two artists per exhibition cycle a forum for what is often their first non-group show. The touring **Eyewash** gallery is quintessential Williamsburg: artists exhibit in multiple spaces around the neighborhood. Check **www.freewilliamsburg.com** for the latest exhibition information. For contact details of all the galleries mentioned here, *see p229*.

Brooklyn Historical Society
local culture, historical setting

2 H5

128 Pierrepont Street (at Clinton St.) • 718 222 4111
>> www.brooklynhistory.org
Open noon–5 Wed–Sun

Thousands of Brooklyn-related objects, from slave deeds to Brooklyn Dodgers baseball memorabilia, are housed in a stunning 1880s mansion. The BHS also arranges walking tours and outdoor concerts. **Adm**

Williamsburg Savings Bank Building
opulent interior

13 C4

Hanson Place, corner of Flatbush & Atlantic Avenues

At night, Brooklyn's tallest building is distinguished by the neon red clock face of its 512-ft (156-m) tower. But the greatest highlight of this building (currently a branch of the HSBC bank) is its Neo-Romanesque interior: imposing iron chandeliers, mosaic-covered ceilings, intricately tiled floors, and graceful arches.

P.S.1
cutting-edge contemporary art

22–5 Jackson Avenue (at 46th Ave.) • 718 784 2084
Ⓜ E or V to 23 St./Ely Ave., 7 to 45 Rd./Courthouse Sq.
>> www.ps1.org Open noon–6 Thu–Mon

Modern art aficionados with adventurous tastes and an urge to break from the SoHo and Chelsea scenes need only venture as far as Long Island City to experience one of the world's foremost contemporary art institutions. Housed inside a late-19th-century high school building, P.S.1 consistently presents groundbreaking multimedia, painting, photography, and sculpture exhibitions that challenge conventions and blaze new aesthetic trails.

Featured artists have included the 1980s art star Keith Haring, actor/director/painter Dennis Hopper, and the late Spanish sculptor Juan Muñoz. A 1997 redesign by Frederick Fisher introduced a courtyard. Every summer, artists are selected to create thematic installations in this space for P.S.1's Saturday afternoon party series, Warm Up. **Adm**

>> *P.S.1's alliance with MoMA means that a ticket purchased at either establishment entitles entry to both*

performance

Broadway shows may be the big sellers, but the city's creative heart beats in a host of other artistic venues devoted to music, theater, dance, cinema, poetry, comedy, and literature. The official Music Under New York program promotes talents year-round on the subway and at street level, while the summer months bring superb outdoor entertainments, such as plays and opera in the parks.

PERFORMANCE

New York has plenty of venues for major theater productions, ballet, opera, and concerts, and the performances you'll see at such places as the Lincoln Center and Carnegie Hall are world-class. But the city's performance scene goes way beyond this: it takes in evenings of poetry, comedy, and literature, and live music in New York's many smaller clubs. The quality, again, is extraordinary, and the intimacy of these smaller venues makes a night out all the more special.

Rachel F. Freeman

Classical Venues

For accomplished performances of chamber music in a waterside setting, you can't beat **Barge Music** *(see p136)*. For the best acoustics and programing, head to **Carnegie Hall** *(see p131)* or the **New Jersey Performing Arts Center** *(see p137)*. Alice Tully Hall at the **Lincoln Center** *(see p132)* is a great venue for choral and small ensemble works.

Dance and Performance

Innovative and classical dance is performed regularly at **The Joyce Theater** *(see p126)*, **Brooklyn Academy of Music (BAM)** *(see p135)*, and the New York State Theater at **Lincoln Center** *(see p132)*. BAM also features theater and musical productions and is a hub of activity during the international Next Wave Festival in the fall.

Cutting Edge Shows

If you're searching for something a little offbeat and experimental, try **The Kitchen** *(see p126)*, which also hosts straightforward literary readings, and **The Bowery Poetry Club** *(see p124)*, where poets regularly challenge the minds of the audience. **P.S.122** *(see p126)* offers a variety of performances as well as some thought-provoking artwork.

choice acts

Gig Venues

Embracing the new and experimental as well as established acts, the **Knitting Factory** *(see p120)* offers several on-site venues and a diverse musical line-up. Similarly **Tonic** *(see p123)* showcases a varied roll call of musical acts, while **Mercury Lounge** *(see p122)* is the place to go if you want to check out the latest soon-to-be-signed talent.

Jazz and Blues

One of the best combinations of acoustics, intimacy, and history is found at the famed **Village Vanguard** *(see p122)*. Music is taken equally seriously at nearby **55 Bar** *(see p122)*, while **Lenox Lounge** *(see p135)* harks back to the days when Harlem was *the* place for jazz. **Smoke** *(see p133)* provides quality music nightly and a Monday jam session.

Stand-Up Comedy

For a fresh approach to comedy based on well-executed skits and improvization, get on down to the **Upright Citizen's Brigade** *(see p127)*. More traditional stand-up comedy is found at **The Comic Strip** *(see p131)* and the grittier **Comedy Cellar** *(see p121)*. **Gotham Comedy Club** *(see p127)* is an upscale venue for a mix of the new and the famous.

Performance

Knitting Factory *experimental mecca*

1 D1

74 Leonard Street (between Broadway & Church St.)
212 219 3132
>> www.knittingfactory.com Open 6pm–4am nightly

Arriving here is like entering a funfair attraction; you're not sure which door to go through first. There are three main performance spaces – Main Space, Tap Bar, and Old Office – as well as a free bar area, where late-night jazz jams are often hosted. The media company that runs this venue, and also the Knitting Factory Record label, styles itself "a genre-bending presenter of established avant-garde." The types of music you're most likely to hear are experimental rock, klezmer, and jazz, though there has been a women's choir performance. The Old Office is the most intimate space of the three and sometimes hosts poetry evenings and alternative screenings, as well as regular music slots.This venue has also been used for the June JVC Jazz Festival. Tickets for all events can be ordered from the Knitting Factory website.

Film Forum *independent & vintage films*

3 C4

209 West Houston Street (between 6th & 7th Aves)
212 727 8112
>> www.filmforum.org Box office 12:30–midnight daily

Cineastes can delight in this three-screen venue, each with Dolby Digital Sound. The films shown are widely varied, from old classics such as an Orson Welles season, to the latest underground hit. Director talks, fresh food, and film-related merchandise are offered.

S.O.B.'s *Latin beats*

3 C4

204 Varick Street (at Houston St.) • 212 243 4940
>> www.sobs.com Open 6:30pm–4am Mon–Sat

Shake your body and celebrate the Sounds of Brazil (S.O.B.) – the very best in Latin, French Caribbean, salsa, hip-hop, reggae, and African beats. Live music is performed every night, with musicians coming from around the globe. For a free dance lesson, get here on a Monday or Friday night between 6pm and 8pm.

Blue Note *gold-standard jazz* 3 C3

1 West 3rd Street (between MacDougal & 6th Ave.)
212 475 8592
www.bluenotejazz.com
Open from 7 nightly; to 4am Fri & Sat

Now a franchised chain, with venues in Japan, Korea, and Europe, Blue Note first took root in Greenwich Village. The premise is simple: sophisticated surroundings for seriously good music (not just jazz), with the option of dinner and a classy interior to watch the top-notch performers who come to play. Dizzy Gillespie, Ray Charles, and Sarah Vaughan have lopped the roof off the place in the past, and the club has also witnessed the talents of Oscar Peterson, George Benson, and Tony Bennett.

If it all sounds a little too highfalutin', join New York's poorer musicians, who turn up for the late-night Friday and Saturday jam sessions – it's a mere $5 cover. Blue Note is also known for the Sunday Jazz Brunch and its Saturday afternoon master classes.

The Comedy Cellar *gritty stand-up* 3 C3

117 MacDougal Street (between W. 3rd & Bleecker Sts)
212 254 3480
>> www.comedycellar.com Evening shows nightly

This basement has had comics, famous and infamous, performing nightly for over 20 years. The cramped seating and brick wall backdrop set the tone. The cover charge is normally $10–15, but you can get free passes via the website. Rude heckling isn't tolerated.

Cornelia Street Cafe *eclectic acts* 3 C3

29 Cornelia Street (between W. 4th & Bleecker Sts)
212 989 9319
>> www.corneliastreetcafe.com Evening shows nightly

Performed on a tiny stage in a narrow room beneath a restaurant, acts here have ranged from Inuit poetry to Suzanne Vega. In any week you might encounter one-act plays, comedy, readings, singing, and live Latin, jazz, or samba music. Art on the walls is often for sale.

Performance

Duplex *kitsch & cabaret* 3 B3
61 Christopher Street (at 7th Ave. S.) • 212 255 5438
>> www.theduplex.com Open 4pm–4am nightly

Anything goes in this dual-level space, which features
a piano bar, complete with disco ball, on the first level,
and an intimate-sized cabaret room, with pool table,
upstairs. The monthly schedule is always packed, and
usually includes comedy, cabaret, comedians, and
open mic for singers of varying abilities.

55 Bar *NYC-style jazz/funk/blues* 3 B3
55 Christopher Street (between 7th Ave. S. & Waverly Pl.)
212 929 9883
>> www.55bar.com Open 1:30pm–4am nightly

Soak up the atmosphere that's been brewing in this
West Village stalwart since 1919. The music packs a
punch in a space small enough for the vibes to
resonate off the walls, which are hung with black-and-
white photos of Miles Davis and John Coltrane.

Village Vanguard *amazing acoustics* 3 B2
178 7th Avenue South (at 11th St.) • 212 255 4037
>> www.villagevanguard.com Open from 8pm nightly

One of the world's most famous jazz venues, the
Village Vanguard has hosted singers and musicians of
phenomenal talent since 1935. It continues to take
music very seriously, and socializing during sets is
discouraged. Genres include mainstream jazz (for
popular standards), bebop, fusion, Latin, and funk.

Mercury Lounge *musical excellence* 4 F4
217 East Houston Street (at Essex St.) • 212 260 4700
>> www.mercuryloungenyc.com Open 6pm–4am nightly

The Mercury Lounge hosts a mix of new and established musical talent. You enter a long, narrow room
dominated by a wooden, candle-lit bar. A heavy,
deep-red curtain separates this from the performance
space (with superb sound system), where Lou Reed,
Jeff Buckley, and Tony Bennett have played.

Bowery Ballroom *music in style* `4 E5`
6 Delancey Street (between Bowery & Chrystie St.)
212 533 2111 • Box office 866 468 7619 (noon–7 Mon–Sat)
>> www.boweryballroom.com

This Beaux Arts ballroom, dating from 1929, makes a wonderful setting in which to hear a band and have a drink. Although the venue has been fully updated to accommodate state-of-the-art acoustics and facilities, many of the building's architectural details have been retained. The mezzanine bar is wisely positioned in front of a gorgeous set of arched windows, providing a view of the city lights. The stage can be seen from the wooden ballroom area or the mezzanine. If you'd like a break from the music, you can drink more peacefully in the lower-level cocktail lounge. David Byrne, Beth Orton, Patti Smith, the John Spencer Blues Explosion, and DJ Shadow are among those who have played here. Tickets often sell out, so buy early by phone or at the box office which is at the Mercury Lounge *(see opposite below).*

Tonic *adventurous music* `4 G4`
107 Norfolk Street (between Delancey & Rivington Sts)
212 358 7501
>> www.tonic107.com Open from 7:30pm nightly

From jazz funk to the sounds of "industrial waste percussion" to the whirs of an electronic theremin – the range of music and instruments here often surprises and inspires. The main space is a hip, no-frills venue; downstairs is Subtonic, where DJs spin eclectic beats.

Arlene's Grocery *multi-band options* `4 F4`
95 Stanton Street (between Orchard & Ludlow Sts)
212 995 1652
>> www.arlenesgrocery.net Open 6pm Mon–Fri, 7pm Sat & Sun

It was, indeed, once a grocery store – hence the colorful frontage – and it gets a little crazy when more than four bands are billed in one evening. The music is invariably grunge, indie, pop, and metal. Come on Monday for a rocking Punk Rock Karaoke Night.

Performance

Bowery Poetry Club *literary café* `4 E4`

308 Bowery (at Bleecker St.) • 212 614 0505

>> www.bowerypoetry.com Open 9am–1am Mon–Thu, 9am–3am Fri, 11am–4am Sat, 11am–midnight Sun

First-time visitors with any anti-intellectual angst wi soon feel at ease in this welcoming, unpretentious venue. Even imaginative readings for children are included on the bill.

The main glass doors open to a café with uneven wooden floorboards and mismatched tables, where you can order organic goodies, espresso, juices, an alcoholic drinks. The back of the room widens out tc a high-ceilinged performance area with its own table and chairs, which can pack in 200 word-lovers; there' also a smaller room for intimate readings. A slightly bohemian atmosphere is accentuated by the work of local artists exhibited on one wall, and flyers about events and goods for sale on another. Readings include works by new writers and established poets and authors. Sunday brunch is a good time to come.

Irving Plaza *garish music club* `4 E1`

17 Irving Place (at 15th St.) • 212 777 6800

>> www.irvingplaza.com Box office noon–6:30 Mon–Fri, 1–4 Sat

This former ballroom resembles an old cabaret lounge, with its hanging lamps, gold moldings, and velvet sofas, all saturated in a deep red hue. The acts are a mix of new and old, and performers have included Erasure, Cyndi Lauper, and Gary Numan, as well as some of the U.K.'s latest bands such as The Editors.

Landmark's Sunshine *film theater* `4 E4`

143 East Houston Street (between 1st & 2nd Aves)
212 330 8182

>> www.landmarktheatres.com

Formerly home to a Yiddish Vaudeville Theater, this beautifully renovated film house has five screens, all with Dolby Digital Sound and comfy seats. Foreign and independent films are shown, and there are late-night screenings of cult classics on weekends.

The Public Theater *integrity on stage* `4 E3`

425 Lafayette Street (between E. 4th St. & Astor Pl.)
212 539 8500; 212 539 8750 for Shakespeare in the Park
tickets (free)
>> www.publictheater.org Box office 1–7:30 (to 6 Sun & Mon)

With five theaters, a private rehearsal space, and the recent addition of neighboring performance space/bar Joe's Pub, The Public Theater is a long-established venue for groundbreaking drama. It is where the musical *Hair* had its world premiere in 1967. The main building – formerly the Astor Library – has a grand entrance hall with the theaters leading off, and a small wine and coffee bar in the far corner. Joe's Pub focuses on experimental theater and solo performances of drama and music.

The company operates the summer Shakespeare in the Park season from June to August at Central Park's Delacorte Theater. You can get free tickets from The Public Theater box office or at the park on the day of performance (but there's a line from 7am or earlier).

Nuyorican Poets Cafe *beats & poetry* `4 G3`

236 East 3rd Street (between Aves B & C) • 212 505 8183
>> www.nuyorican.org Events nightly, except Mon

This once "underground" café, founded in 1973, has evolved into a cutting-edge venue for people of all ethnicities to read, slam, rhyme, perform, or play an instrument. The dimly lit, cozy café is a place for contemplative, poetic thought by day and original spoken-word performances by night.

.it *avant-garde basement* `4 E3`

93 Second Ave. (between 5th & 6th Sts) • 212 777 7987
>> www.litloungenyc.com Open 5pm–4am daily

Named for the candlelight that illuminates this no frills basement, Lit prides itself on providing performance space and a supportive community to fledgling bands whose styles elude the mainstream. Fuse Gallery, also located in the club, does for painters what Lit does for musicians (gallery hours: 2–7pm Wed–Sat).

Performance

P.S.122 *innovative performances* 4 F2
150 1st Avenue (at East 9th Street)
Box office 212 477 5288
>> www.ps122.org
Open daily; box office 11–6 daily

This performance space in East Village was once a public school, a shadow of which is seen in the original stairwell, complete with wooden banisters and wrought-iron safety gates. In 1979 a small group of innovative performers began transforming the rooms into spaces for performance workshops, movement classes, and community meetings. The old school gym was converted into a theater in 1986, used by small avant-garde groups and cutting-edge productions. Now a major hub of creative energy, the not-for-profit arts center boasts two theaters and galleries, with a constantly changing program of theatrical, video, musical, and film presentations. Experimental and vibrant in the arts community, P.S.122 has been described as the "petri dish of downtown culture."

The Kitchen *multimedia creations* 3 A1
512 West 19th Street (between 10th & 11th Aves)
212 255 5793
>> www.thekitchen.org Box office 2–6 Tue–Sat

For years, The Kitchen has brought together artists from varied disciplines, taking pride in its innovation. The two black-box theaters serve as backdrops for readings, multimedia installations, dance, and music. Family-friendly presentations feature on Saturdays.

The Joyce Theater *delightful dance* 3 B1
175 8th Avenue (at 19th St.) • 212 242 0800
>> www.joyce.org Box office noon–7 daily (to 6 Sun)

Presenting small- to medium-sized national and international companies, The Joyce Theater is a center of dance, from contemporary to traditional. The auditorium seats 452 in a functional interior that once housed a movie theater. Joyce's satellite space in SoHo (155 Mercer St.) hosts further performances.

Upright Citizen's Brigade *improv* `5 C5`

307 West 26th Street (between 8th & 9th Aves) • 212 366 9176
>> www.ucbtheater.com Performances nightly (cash only)

Step into a world of zany and clever comic sketches and improvization at the UCB Theater. Home-grown Brigade shows and visiting comic troupes are both on the schedule. Ticket prices are very reasonable, and you have the possibility of seeing future stars of the favorite U.S. TV show *Saturday Night Live*.

Jazz Standard *top jazz club* `6 F4`

16 East 27th Street • 212 576 2232
>> www.jazzstandard.com
Open daily; set times 7:30, 9:30, and 11:30pm Fri & Sat

Jazz permeates this club, in the atmosphere and in the impressive line-ups that run from trad jazz to Latin and Brazilian combos and orchestras. Subdued lighting, a casual vibe, comfortable seating, and excellent food contribute further to the club's appeal.

Gotham Comedy Club *funny shows* `6 E5`

208 West 23rd St. (between 7th & 8th Aves) • 212 367 9000
>> www.gothamcomedyclub.com Shows nightly

This comfortable, casual comedy club is given an added air of sophistication by its solid oak bar and shimmering chandelier. The line-up mixes budding comics and surprise guests from the world of TV – comedians who may have appeared on *Conan O'Brien*, *The Tonight Show*, or on the Comedy Central network.

Hammerstein Ballroom *music venue* `5 C3`

311 West 34th Street (at 8th Ave.) • 212 279 7740
>> www.mcstudios.com Check website for upcoming events

Ambience and acoustics rate high at this Art Deco space with a capacity of 2,500. Historic fixtures and a beautiful ceiling mural have been kept, while there's enough rigging to support impressive light and sound equipment for shows by bands such as indie-rockers the Pixies or modern jazzers Medeski, Martin & Wood.

Rodeo Bar *country music crossover* `6 F5`

375 3rd Avenue (at E. 27th St.) • 212 683 6500
>> www.rodeobar.com
Open noon–4am daily (to 2am Sun); live music from 10pm

Mosey along into a world of bluegrass, rockabilly, country music, an amicable atmosphere, drinks served from a converted horse-trailer, and no cover charge for the entertainment! Refreshment is Tex-Mex snacks, peanuts, and powerful Margaritas. Yeeee-haw!

Iridium *upscale jazz* `5 D1`

1650 Broadway (at West 51st Street) • 212 582 2121
>> www.iridiumjazzclub.com
Set times: 8 & 10pm Sun–Thu, 8, 10 & 11:30pm Fri & Sat

Spacious enough for dinner, yet small enough to feel intimate, Iridium has been the venue for many live recordings due to its superior acoustics. Besides top-notch jazz, Iridium prides itself on an award-winning wine list and a sophisticated international clientele.

Roundabout/AA *magical theater space* `5 D2`

227 West 42nd Street (between 7th & 8th Aves)
212 719 1300
>> www.roundabouttheatre.org

This repertory theater company has moved several times and is now based at the beautifully renovated American Airlines Theatre (formerly called the Selwyn) which was built in 1918. The slick productions often feature well-known guest actors.

B.B. King Blues Club *gospel & blues* `5 C2`

237 West 42nd Street (between 8th & 7th Aves) • 212 997 4144
>> www.bbkingblues.com Box office 10am–midnight daily

Legends such as James Brown and, of course, B.B. King himself have played in the club's Showcase Room. It has a tourist vibe, but the aim to entertain prevails, and wins over New Yorkers too. Food is served all day and there's nightly music at Lucille's, the more intimate space, named after B.B. King's favorite guitar.

Swing 46 *jazz & swing dance* `5 C1`
149 West 46th Street (between 8th & 9th Aves) • 212 262 9554
» www.swing46.com Open from 5pm nightly

Try your two-step or lindy between courses at this dinner and dance club, or have drinks up by the bar – away from the frenzy on the floor, but close enough to hear the music. There's no dress code, but a bit of sartorial elegance is encouraged. Bring your tap shoes for the Tap Jam on Sundays between 5 and 8pm!

Don't Tell Mama *piano & cabaret* `5 C1`
343 West 46th Street (between 8th & 9th Aves) • 212 757 0788
» www.donttellmama.com Open from 6pm nightly; cash only

Life is indeed a cabaret, and all believers need to visit this venue at least once, either to listen or to perform. Grab your Liza Minnelli songbook and come on over to the piano bar or one of three intimate theaters, where you can also eat. *The* place to hear the standards, see diva wannabes, and enjoy hilarious musical comedy.

Rainbow Room *vintage sophistication* `6 E1`
0 Rockefeller Plaza, 65th Floor (at W. 49th St.) • 212 632 5100
» www.cipriani.com
Open 7pm–1am Fri; Sunday brunch 11am–3pm

A glorious Art Deco institution with awesome views from the 65th floor to help you forget the $150 per person tab for dinner and dancing. Big band orchestras play for the evening as you sway above the shimmering lights of the city. Black tie is preferred.

City Center *music, drama & dance* `7 D5`
131 West 55th Street (between 6th & 7th Aves) • 212 581 1212
» www.citycenter.org

The colorful tiles and pillars of the beautiful Moorish facade welcome you to the City Center. Inside, the main stage is used for concerts and performances by the Alvin Ailey, American Ballet, Paul Taylor, and Martha Graham dance companies. The Manhattan Theater Club performs in the center's smaller spaces.

Performance

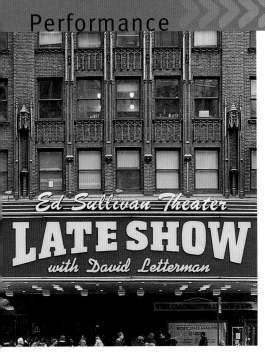

6 E1
NBC Studios/
Ed Sullivan Theater *three seconds of fame?*
>> www.nbc.org
>> www.cbs.org Box office 212 247 6497, from 11am on the day

If you'd like to be in the studio audience for NBC's news and entertainment *Today Show*, which goes out live on weekday mornings, hang around 49th Street between Fifth and Sixth Avenues, between 8:30 and 10am, and join the masses who have the "Hi Mom" signs. You can also try your luck for last-minute studio audience tickets to see *Saturday Night Live* or *Light Night* with Conan O'Brien by lining up outside NBC's main lobby on the 49th Street entrance at 30 Rockefeller Plaza. Both lines often form before 7am (tickets are given out after 9am), but there are no guarantees that you'll get in.

It's easier to obtain standby CBS tickets to see *The Late Show* with David Letterman (Monday to Thursday), staged at the Ed Sullivan Theater at 1697 Broadway between 53rd & 54th Streets (Map 7 D5).

Florence Gould Hall *for Francophiles*
8 F4
55 E. 59th St. (between Park & Madison Aves) • 212 355 6160
>> www.fiaf.org
Box office 11–7 Tue, noon–7 Wed–Fri, noon–4 Sat

The location of interesting lectures and weekly French films, this space is also open for productions ranging from light opera and ballet to various concerts. Acoustics are great in the main 400-person auditorium, while next door's Tinker Auditorium is more intimate.

Tickets for Broadway Theaters
The two main agencies selling theater tickets are **Telecharge** (212 239 6200, www.telecharge.com) and **TicketMaster** (212 307 4100, www.ticketmaster.com). These are convenient but you may be charged up to $9 extra for handling fees. If you want to try your luck at a discount agency on the day of performance, **TKTS** (www.tdf.org/tkts) offers great deals on theater tickets – often 25–50% off the full price – but you will have to line up and you can't use a credit card. The main outlet is on the little island called Duffy Square at 47th and Broadway (Mon–Sat 3–8pm, Sun 11am–7:30pm; for matinees Wed & Sat 10am–2pm). A less crowded outlet is at the South Street Seaport on the corner of John Street and Front Street (Mon–Fri 11am–6pm, Sat 11am–7pm).

The Comic Strip *stand-up showcase* `8 G1`
1568 2nd Avenue (between 81st & 82nd Sts) • 212 861 9386
>> www.comicstriplive.com Shows nightly

Jerry Seinfeld started his career with a regular act here. There's a casual atmosphere, cabaret-style seating, and traditional stand-up. Thursday is "new talent night," while Mondays often feature comics from far and wide auditioning for regular spots. Reserve tickets by phone, and check out discounts on the website.

92nd Street Y *emporium of activity* `10 F4`
1395 Lexington Avenue (at 92nd St.) • 212 415 5500
>> www.92y.org

Established in the 19th century as a men's Hebrew association, the 92nd Street Y has since become a more diverse cultural institution. With a wide-ranging bill of artists, entrepreneurs, and politicians, the Y's two halls have hosted performances and talks by Yo-Yo Ma, Bill Gates, and Kofi Annan.

Carnegie Hall *supreme concert hall* `7 D5`
881 7th Avenue (at 57th St.) • 212 247 7800
>> www.carnegiehall.org Box office 8–8 daily

Tchaikovsky conducted the Carnegie Hall's inaugural concert over a century ago and thus the standard was set. The main hall, the Isaac Stern Auditorium, seats just under 3,000; the Zankel Hall focuses on jazz and contemporary music; the smaller Weill Hall has good acoustics for recitals and chamber music.

Merkin Concert Hall *on-air sound* `7 B3`
129 West 67th Street (between Broadway & Amsterdam Ave.)
212 501 3330 Box office noon–4 Mon–Fri
>> www.elainekaufmancenter.org/merkin.htm

The resonance in this auditorium is wonderful and it is often used for live radio recordings. Performances cover classical, jazz, funk, and other genres. Both the balcony and the orchestra seating provide good views. There is also an art gallery.

Lincoln Center for the Performing Arts
7 B3

rich pickings for culture vultures

Straddling Broadway and Amsterdam
(between 62nd and 66th Streets)
212 875 5456 • Tours 212 875 5350
>> www.lincolncenter.org

One of the world leaders in performing arts since the 1960s, Lincoln Center has 12 resident organizations, including a Chamber Music Society, a Film Society, Jazz at Lincoln Center, The New York City Ballet, Metropolitan Opera, New York City Opera, and the New York Philharmonic.

Formerly the slum area of Lincoln Square, the 15-acre site was first envisaged as an arts complex in the 1950s, the scheme being eventually realized with the support of John D. Rockefeller and President Eisenhower, among others. The **Philharmonic Hall** opened in 1962, and was followed a few years later by the **New York State Theater**, the **Vivian Beaumont Theater**, the **Metropolitan Opera House**, and the **Alice** Tully Hall. Altogether there are nearly 20 performanc spaces and a host of other facilities, including a library and studios for budding musicians and actors Tours of the complex run regularly and last an hour, focusing on history, stories, and architecture.

The central outdoor fountain, designed by America Modernist architect Philip Johnson, is a popular meeting point before a show. It is also close to the spot where the Christmas tree, bedecked in musical instrument ornaments, stands during the holiday period. **Damrosch Park** hosts a free outdoor concert series, usually in August. The **Mostly Mozart Festiva** is a perennial favorite, while **Midsummer Night Swing** features a wide range of dance music.

Renovations are expected to take place over the next few years to give some of the buildings a faceli and to enhance acoustics. The Vivian Beaumont Theater, beyond the reflecting pool and Henry Moor sculpture, has already been refurbished and hosts wonderful theatrical productions.

Makor *culture with hip twist* 7 C3

35 West 67th Street (between Central Park W. & Columbus Ave.)
212 601 1000
>> www.makor.org

Frequented by a 20- to 30-something crowd, Makor –
associated with the 92nd Street Y *(see p131)* – offers
film, discussions, theater, and music, including jazz,
funk, and a cappella. Allow time for a drink in the
café before a show. It has a healthy singles scene too.

Stand-Up NY *heard the one about…?* 7 B1

36 West 78th Street (at Broadway) • 212 595 0850
>> www.standupny.com Shows nightly

Stand-Up is the only comedy club on the Upper West
Side, so it's a popular venue for locals. Get to know
your table neighbors up close and personal as you sit
in on a string of comics delivering their routines. The
standard ranges from decent to hilarious, and past
circuit performers include Robin Williams.

Symphony Space *reggae & throat-singing* 9 B3

2537 Broadway (at W. 95th St.) • 212 864 5400
>> www.symphonyspace.org Box office noon–7 Tue–Sun

This complex offers a vast array of theater, film,
dance, and music. The main Peter Jay Sharp Theatre
– which seats nearly 700 on a gentle slope with
plenty of legroom – is often used by guest musicians
of the World Music Institute. The Leonard Nimoy
Thalia building now includes a café.

Smoke *hot jazz, no tobacco* 9 B2

2751 Broadway (between 105th & 106th St.) • 212 864 6662
>> www.smokejazz.com Open 5pm–4am most nights

Red velvet curtains and low-hanging chandeliers set
the scene in this cozy jazz bar/lounge. If you can't
accessorize with an instrument, then at least bring an
attentive pair of ears, because the live music is taken
seriously here. There's seating for 70, with overflow
accommodated at the bar.

Performance

Apollo Theater *where stars are born*

11 D3

253 West 125th Street (between 7th & 8th Aves)
212 531 5300 • Box office 212 531 5305/4
>> www.apollotheater.com
Box office 10–6 Mon, Tue, Thu & Fri, 10–8:30 Wed, noon–6 Sat

The Apollo – Harlem's top attraction – has made such an important contribution to music history and the cultural life of New York that it was designated a National Landmark in 1983. Originally a burlesque theater, in the 1930s the venue became a showcase for African American musicians, singers, dancers, and comedians, who would perform at the theater's Amateur Night. The careers of many internationally famous musicians and singers were launched here – Ella Fitzgerald and Michael Jackson were among those who were first recognized at the Apollo.

Today, the venue welcomes any talent good enough to withstand the potential boos from the crowd on Wednesday's Amateur Night. Latino music has also been showcased since 2001, and *Showtime at the Apollo* is produced as a syndicated television program.

As well as coming here to see a performance, it is also worth taking a close look around the theater. The lobby Walk of Fame highlights some of the eminent past performers, such as James Brown, Aretha Franklin, and Duke Ellington. The guided backstage tour offers fascinating oral anecdotes and musical history. You'll also get to touch the renowned Tree of Hope – in reality, a wooden stump mounted on an Ionic column. Legendary in the show business world, it is touched by performers before they start their act to bring them good luck.

Lenox Lounge *booze & Billie Holliday* `11 D3`

288 Lenox Avenue (between 124th & 125th Sts)
212 427 0253
>> www.lenoxlounge.com Open 11am–4am daily

Lenox is a leading music club with a solid repertoire of live jazz, DJs, and an open jam session on Monday nights. The front bar is Art Deco in character, and the lounge has been restored to its original plush design, including built-in banquettes and zebra stripes in the back room. Southern-style food is served all day.

A sense of history permeates the proceedings – jazz heroes such as Miles Davis, Billie Holiday, and John Coltrane have played in this space. And Malcolm X is said to have spent many an hour at the Lenox before being galvanized by the political fight. Nowadays, the live music ranges from mainstream jazz through to more esoteric genres. Use the front room for mingling – the clientele includes regulars, locals, and jazz aficionados – and then head to the back for listening and dining pleasure.

Brooklyn Academy of Music *performing arts center* `13 C4`

0 Lafayette Avenue (between Ashland Pl. & St. Felix St.)
18 636 4100
> www.bam.org Box office 10–6 Mon–Fri, noon–6 Sat

ar more than just a music academy, the BAM is a ive of cultural activity, offering live music, opera, ance, film, and theater. The academy's first roduction was in 1861, and the legendary Ellen erry was one of the first actors to perform here.

The main building straddles most of the block and as a grand lobby. The Rose Cinema has four screens nd very comfortable seating. The Howard Gillman)pera House has a capacity of a little over 2,000, vhile the Harvey Lichtenstein Theater holds 874. From hursday to Saturday, you can also catch live perfor-nances in the BAM café, a great place for a drink or ight meal before or after a show. The famed Next Wave estival takes place over three months in the Fall and eatures modern works from around the globe.

>> *For a listing of performance venues by type, see pp230–31*

Performance

Warsaw *pierogi & pro sound* `13 C`
261 Driggs Avenue (between Eckford & Leonard Sts)
718 387 0505
>> www.warsawconcerts.com

A curious collaboration: hip music venue and main ballroom of the Polish National Home. Some nights feature indie and rock groups; others involve Polish festivals and Polka dance. The bistro offers *pierogi* (small pies), and the bar serves strong Polish beer.

Barge Music *classical music on the water* `2 G3`
Fulton Ferry Landing (at Old Fulton St.) • 718 624 4061
>> www.bargemusic.org
Performances Thu–Sun, times vary

This chamber music concert space is absolutely worth the trip for the quality of the performers, the unique setting, and the superb views of the Manhattan skyline and Brooklyn Bridge.

As suggested by the venue's name, performances do, indeed, take place on the water, in a converted barge that features wood paneling and an open fireplace. Seating arrangements cater to a maximum of just 125, which encourages an intimacy and immediacy for the audience and the musicians.

The barge does move gently during performances but there's little danger of sea-sickness.

Unusually for chamber music, there is no regard fo the seasons, and the concert hall is used year-round Highly polished performances of Mozart, Bach, Schubert, Debussy, and Prokofiev might all feature i a typical month, and guest musicians add zest to th program. A fortnight in December each year is given over to Bach's Brandenburg Concertos.

Before a concert, allow time to wander around the revamped ferry landing and enjoy some ice cream at the Brooklyn Ice Cream Factory. Round off the evenin by taking a yellow New York water taxi (718 742 1969 www.nywatertaxi.com) back to Manhattan.

New Jersey Performing
Arts Center (NJPAC) *notable in Newark*
One Center Street, Newark • 888 GO-NJPAC (466-5722)
» www.njpac.org • Train or PATH from Penn Station (New York) to Penn Station (Newark), then LOOP shuttle or walk to NJPAC
Box office open noon–6 Mon–Sat, 10–3 Sun

Newark has never looked so appealing. This stunning, multi-million-dollar arts complex was built in 1997, breathing new life into a downtrodden city and giving Manhattan residents and tourists alike reason enough to cross the water to New Jersey.

The architecture of the main part of the complex – defined by glass and brick, and cubed shapes – was the brainchild of Barton Myers and honors the idea of casual urban living. The two performance spaces,

Prudential Hall (2,730 seats) and Victoria Theater (514 seats) are wonderfully appointed and functional, with first-rate sight lines and excellent acoustics for all seats. The Alvin Ailey American Dance Theater and the New Jersey Symphony Orchestra are regular performers. The complex has also hosted touring productions of musicals (*Les Misérables*, *The Mikado*) and such diverse performers as jazz legends Alice Coltrane and McCoy Tyner, and the Vienna Boys Choir.

Getting to the NJPAC is not too difficult, but does involve either walking five blocks from Newark's Penn Station, or taking the purple-signed LOOP shuttle bus for one dollar. The complex has two restaurants: the Theater Square Grill, which has a lounge bar, and the Calcada restaurant, which offers alfresco dining.

Sports Venues

New York has several capacious sports venues. The **Yankee Stadium** was built for the famous baseball team in 1923, and is fun to visit via the Yankee Clipper ferry. **Shea Stadium** is home to the New York Mets baseball team and lies beneath a flight path to LaGuardia airport. The Beatles famously played here in 1965 and 1966. Part of the Meadowlands complex, **Giants Stadium** is the home of three soccer teams: the New York Giants, New York Jets (both always sold out), and Metrostars. **Madison Square Garden** is home to ice hockey team New York Rangers and basketball teams Knicks and Liberty. The Garden also hosts big-name concerts, monster truck rallies, wrestling, boxing, and top dog and cat shows. For contact details, *see p231.*

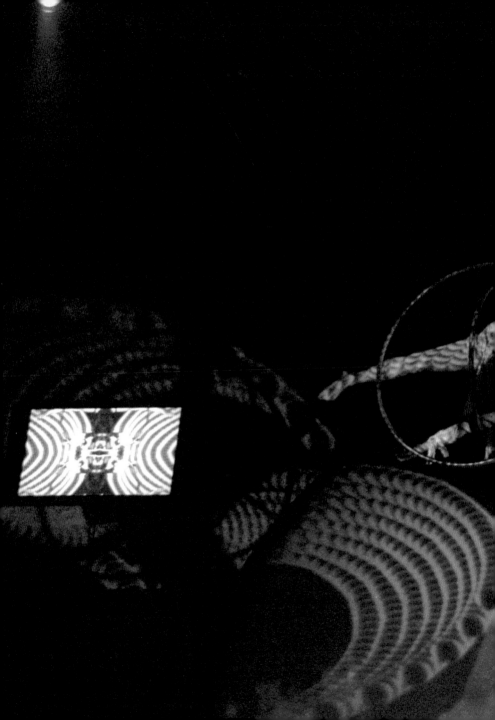

bars & clubs

From super-cool cocktail lounges to dark old ale houses to neighborhood joints with jukeboxes and pool tables, New York has bars to suit everyone. For those in search of an energetic night out, downtown and Chelsea have the most lively DJ bars and clubs, though Brooklyn is catching up fast. More laid-back drinkers may prefer to slip into an easy chair in the cocktail bars of midtown and the Upper East Side.

BARS & CLUBS

The resuscitation of the so-called "Cabaret Law," a 1920s-era regulation criminalizing dancing in many bars, has hardly broken New Yorkers' stride, and turntables are as common a sight as televisions in East Village, Lower East Side, and Chelsea. But if you want a quieter evening of conversation with friends over several perfectly drawn pints, New York has plenty of options in that direction too. Here are some of my fail-proof favorites.

Jonathan Schultz

Genuine Draughts

McSorley's *(see p148)* serves two beers: light and dark. Order one (you'll be handed two), grab a seat, and soak up the olde New York ambience. **Chumley's** *(see p152)*, a favorite writers' hangout of the 1940s and 50s, pours English ales, and Williamsburg's **Spuyten Duyvil** *(see p162)* offers hand-pulled cask-conditioned ales.

The Art of Mixology

NY is the cocktail capital, and **THOM's Bar** *(see p143)* mixes a luscious lychee Martini. Brazilian-style cocktails such as Caipiruvas and Caipirinhas are popular at sleek Chelsea spot **Glass** *(see p156)*, and Grand Central Terminal's **Campbell Apartment** *(see p157)* quells commuters' nerves with lip-smacking Sidecars and bone-dry Martinis.

True Dance Clubs

Nicolas Matar's **Cielo** *(see p154)* has kept a soulful house beat going for over half a decade in the Meatpacking District. Fans of live and DJ'd World music swear by **S.O.B.'s** *(see p120)*. Brooklyn's **Galapagos** *(see p163)* deploys everything from DJ'd garage rock to electro-punk, and the **Sullivan Room** *(see p152)* offers NY's finest minimal techno.

choice nightlife

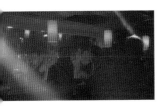

Gay Bars and Clubs

The **Roxy's** *(see p155)* Saturday gay party is the stuff of legend, attracting queens, leather daddies, and everyone in between. The mood is far more casual but equally spirited at West Village's homey, historical **Stonewall** *(see p153)*, just a few blocks from the adorable ladies' hangout **Cubbyhole** *(see p154)*.

Alfresco Drinking

Nothing says summer like hoisting a pint in view of sailboats on the Hudson at the **Boat Basin Café** *(see p161)*. Among Brooklyn's genteel brownstones, the **Gowanus Yacht Club** *(see p161)* serves cheep beers to a youngish crowd, in contrast to the sophistication of **Ava Lounge** *(see p158)*, where Martinis mix with Times Square views on the patio.

DJ Bars

New York's punk/post-punk fascination continues apace at the **Beauty Bar** *(see p150)*, where The Jam, The Ramones, and Stiff Little Fingers are spun on the turntable. In the **TriBeCa Grand Hotel**'s *(see p189)* basement, Europe's top underground DJs make stops, while the mood is laid-back and loungey on week nights at the **Sullivan Room** *(see p152)*.

Bars & Clubs

Pussycat Lounge *trash & banter* `1 D4`

96 Greenwich Street (at Rector St.) • 212 349 4800
» www.pussycatlounge.com Open from 6 Mon–Fri, from 8 Sat

A quiet block near Ground Zero adopts a delectably
sleazy air when the Pussycat Lounge opens up for the
night. Skip the first floor's depressing, 60s-style go-
go strip club, and head upstairs for trashy burlesque
shows, live bands, and ribald weekend dance parties.
Try to wear something a little daring. **Adm**

Winnie's *Chinatown's livelist karaoke bar* `2 E1`

104 Bayard Street (between Baxter & Mulberry Sts)
212 732 2384
Open noon–4am daily

Someone is singing, and probably butchering, your
favorite song here right now. Know before you go:
1. You'll pay $1 per song; 2. Swinging the mic is not
allowed; 3. You'll share any well-known chorus (suc
as in Neil Diamond's *Sweet Caroline*) with the crowd

Antarctica *chilled beer hall* `3 C5`

287 Hudson Street (at Spring St.) • 212 352 1666
» www.antarcticabar.com
Open from 4 Mon–Fri, from 7 Sat

The owners of Antarctica claim that their bar has been
in continuous business since the year in which
Guinness was invented: 1759. You don't have to
believe this, but there is certainly a feeling of age
about the weathered wood floor planks, shining brass
taps, and the picture of 19th-century mustachioed
drinkers on the wall. The overall effect is not of Earth's
last frontier either, though Antarctica's location in the
far reaches of SoHo lends it a certain remoteness
that's appealing.

The bar has received many plaudits for its down-to-
earth appeal in an upscale neighborhood. It has also
won the "Best Bar to Shoot Pool" title from *NY Mag*.
Booth seating and pitchers of beer ensure a merry
crowd. Check the website to see if your first name
qualifies you for free drinks on the night.

HOM's Bar *classy hotel bar* `3 C5`

) Thompson Street (between Broome & Spring Sts)
12 219 2000
www.60thompson.com Open from 5 nightly

he boutique hotel bar craze that swept Manhattan in
he 1990s shows no signs of fatigue at this bar set in
he lobby of the sleek 60 Thompson Hotel.

A sense of occasion starts to build from the
oment you approach the chic SoHo address. The
lass entrance is grandly set back from the curb and
anned by cordial, black-clad doormen. You'll be
irected up to THOM's Bar, which instantly gives the
npression of classic sophistication with its leather
arlor chairs, massive marble fireplace, and lofty
ceilings. Modern touches can be seen in the lacquer-
black bar, gracefully arching chrome lamps, and
strongly geometric purple sofas and banquettes.

A typical weekend night attracts an international,
casually fashionable crowd partial to specialty cocktails. The signature THOM is a blend of the very pure
Skyy citrus vodka, fresh lime, and mint. Sidecars,
lychee Martinis, Tom Collins, and others are deftly
mixed by bartenders who look as if they've stepped
off the pages of hip lifestyle magazine *Wallpaper**.

On particularly crowded nights, patrons have no
compunction about taking their drinks to the adjacent
lobby, where the acid jazz music is quieter than in the
bar, and seating does not come at such a premium.

Bars & Clubs

3 D5

ñ *atmospheric Spanish bar*
33 Crosby Street (between Grand & Broome Sts)
212 219 8856
Open from 5pm nightly (to 4am Fri & Sat); cash only

The labyrinthine lanes of Madrid's old quarter lie a considerable distance from SoHo, but past midnight – especially on Wednesdays – this somewhat desolate stretch of Crosby Street adopts a distinctly *madrileño* mood. As you open the door to ñ (pronounced "enyay"), the insistent, passionate rhythms of flamenco immediately grab you.

An intimate and authentic Spanish tapas bar, ñ is just wide enough to accommodate a few musicians and dancers for its Wednesday flamenco showcase. It compensates for its diminutive size, however, with a genial Iberian atmosphere. An international mix of artists and professionals gathers at the long, gleaming copper bar to choose from a selection of 20 sherries and affordable Spanish wines by the glass. Among the popular tapas plates are savory toasted almonds, addictive, briny olives, and luscious *tetilla con membrillo*: mild, creamy cheese served with a sweet quince paste.

At weekends patrons pack four-deep at the bar, which can result in brusque drink service, but week nights – Wednesdays excepted – are comparatively quiet and easygoing. A homely bar, ñ concedes few points to its style-driven downtown environs. Except, that is, for the one-way glass on the bathroom doors. Fear not, however: the only view afforded is from inside the stall looking out.

Temple Bar *for lounging lovers*

4 E4

332 Lafayette Street (between Houston & Bleecker Sts)
>> www.templebarnyc.com • 212 925 4242
Open 5pm–1am daily (to 2am Sat & Sun)

Exuding luxury and romance from every dimmed Deco wall lamp, Temple Bar is a favorite destination among amorous SoHo couples. Discreet servers bring Martinis to the table, while the sultry crooning drifting from the speakers raises the seduction ante.

ravda *Russian speakeasy* `4 E4`

1 Lafayette Street (between Houston & Prince Sts)
2 226 4944
www.pravdany.com Open from 5pm Mon–Sat, from 6pm
n (closed Sun in Jul & Aug)

een eyes are indispensable for locating this
ibterranean SoHo destination, indicated by a lone
d lamp atop an iron banister. At the entrance,
imson velvet curtains part to reveal a sprawling
unge painted terra cotta and furnished with
urgundy parlor chairs, candlelit cocktail tables, and
aded glass wall lamps. Combined with the Cyrillic
iaracters stenciled on low ceiling arches, the scene

evokes the gritty romance of a Moscow train station,
circa 1929. Statuesque, black-clad servers weave
between throngs of chic patrons, balancing cocktail
trays laden with generous vodka shots, single-malt
Scotches, and house specialties such as the Nolita:
chilled mango-infused vodka, apricot liqueur, and
lime juice. In true vodka-room style, Pravda also
offers an appealing menu of European finger foods,
from garlicky mussels to smoked-fish plates and caviar.

Upstairs, a tiny lounge, with no more than one
couch and a bar, is a prime spot for amorous couples
– that is, if they can ignore the constant parade of
drinkers traipsing up to use Pravda's bathrooms.

ansky Lounge *discreet cocktail bar* `4 G4`

4 Norfolk Street (between Delancey & Rivington Sts)
2 677 9489
www.lanskylounge.com Open from 6pm nightly

spacious, modern bar, named after one of the
eighborhood's most notorious sons, Jewish gangster
eyer Lansky. Join the uptown crowd through the
speakeasy" entrance for excellent classic cocktails.
s spin hip-hop on Wednesdays and weekends.

Bars & Clubs

Welcome to the Johnson's *the real dive bar*

4 F4

123 Rivington Street (between Norfolk & Essex Sts)
212 420 9911
Open 3pm–4am Mon–Fri, 1pm–4am Sat & Sun

While some New York bars may classify themselves as "dives," a close inspection often reveals that the shabby decor has been painstakingly cultivated, the jukebox song catalog caters only to esoteric tastes, the place is full of elitist poseurs, and the beer is $7 a glass. Whereas the genuine requirements of an American dive bar are cheap beer, anthemic rock music, decrepit furniture, and graffitied bathrooms nothing else will do.

Fortunately, there is a Lower East Side bar that delivers the requisite attributes with just the right touch of self-assured, devil-may-care attitude: Welcome to the Johnson's – or, as it's known to the regulars, The Johnson's.

Though it opens late morning, the fun really begins from around 6pm, as the neighborhood's young musicians, professionals, and students make themselves comfortable on thrift-shop sofas. The favorite beer, Pabst Blue Ribbon, is absurdly cheap. Diversions involve playing pool on a warped billiard table, waging intergalactic warfare on the vintage video game machine, and feeding dollar bills into the hard-rocking juke.

A word of caution: The Johnson's gets very crowded after 10pm. Also, the bathroom stalls are not for the squeamish. Consider yourself informed.

Barramundi *backpackers' hangout*

4 F4

167 Clinton Street (between Stanton & Rivington Sts)
212 529 6900
≫ www.chezessaada.com Open 6pm–4am daily

Young travelers feel at home at this funky, Australian-owned Lower East Side bar. An international crowd sips reasonably priced beverages on the back room's couches while gesturing at the otherworldly wall sculptures. Daily "happy hour" from 6 to 9pm.

Slipper Room *lively entertainment*
4 F4

167 Orchard Street (at Stanton St.) • 212 253 7246
>> www.slipperroom.com Open from 8pm nightly

Five dollars is usually all that's required to experience anything from burlesque and classic vaudeville theater to cash-prize trivia nights at this inviting Lower East Side lounge. The crowd changes according to the event schedule, but patrons invariably arrive equipped with sharp wits and playful attitudes.

Parkside Lounge *easygoing joint*
4 G4

317 East Houston Street (between Aves A & B) • 212 673 6270
>> www.parksidelounge.com Open from 1pm daily

Cheap beers, generous cocktails, and zero attitude draw neighborhood residents young and old to the Parkside. In the afternoon, the affable crowd's banter mixes with the jukebox's classic country. Nighttime arrivals head straight to the back room, where bluegrass bands and burlesque troupes perform.

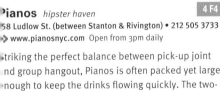

Pianos *hipster haven*
4 F4

158 Ludlow St. (between Stanton & Rivington) • 212 505 3733
>> www.pianosnyc.com Open from 3pm daily

Striking the perfect balance between pick-up joint and group hangout, Pianos is often packed yet large enough to keep the drinks flowing quickly. The two-level bar consists of a room for live bands and an upstairs room where DJs spin dance music. Check the website for nightly events.

2A *rocking bar & upstairs lounge*
4 F3

25 Avenue A (between 1st & 2nd Sts) • 212 505 2466
Open 4pm–4am daily

For better or worse, 2A has become an easy place to spot a hip celebrity. New Wave and punk music from the 70s set the tone at the street-level bar. The couch-filled upstairs lounge is cozier, with a more flirtatious atmosphere. Though most of the clientele drinks beer, 2A's red wine selection should not be overlooked.

KGB *vodka & old Russia* `4 E3`

85 East 4th St. (between 2nd Ave. & Bowery) • 212 505 3360
≫ www.kgbbar.com Open from 6pm nightly

Detached from the frenetic barhopping of nearby
2nd Avenue is this Bolshevik-red, dimly-lit den of
Soviet nostalgia. Staff keep glasses full of vodka or
Central European imported pilsners, while bookish
patrons turn up for occasional readings by guest
novelists. Vintage Leninist posters adorn the walls.

Swift *Celtic vibe* `4 E3`

34 East 4th Street (between Bowery & Lafayette St.)
212 260 3600
≫ www.swiftbarnyc.com Open noon–4am daily

A mural of Irish satirist Jonathan Swift raising a pint of
Guinness welcomes Irish expats, NYU students, and
everyone else to this spacious pub. Come for the
wide draft beer selection, hearty pub food, sharp-
witted bartenders, weekly live Irish music, and cheer.

McSorley's *historic ale house* `4 E3`

15 East 7th Street (between 2nd & 3rd Aves) • 212 473 9148
Open from 11am Mon–Sat, from 1pm Sun

Reputedly New York's oldest bar, McSorley's hasn't
changed much since Civil War president Abraham
Lincoln hoisted his tankard here. You'll still find
sawdust littering the wooden floor, drinkers from
around the globe crowding the rustic booths, and
robust dark and pale ales on draft.

Angel's Share *cocktails with a Tokyo flavor* `4 E2`

8 Stuyvesant Street (at 3rd Ave.) • 212 777 5415
Open from 7pm nightly

Standing is not allowed, nor are groups exceeding
four people, but with these criteria met, Angel's Share
is a wonderful place for cocktails. In fact, you might
not find better classic mixes anywhere downtown.
There's an extensive sake selection and delicate
Japanese bar snacks too. Service is exemplary.

Nevada Smith's *soccer-oriented bar* `4 E2`

74 3rd Avenue (between 11th & 12th Sts) • 212 982 2591
≫ www.nevadasmiths.net Open 11am–4am daily

Diehard soccer fans, behold your Manhattan head-
quarters. Upstairs, jersey-wearing Europeans and a
dusting of Americans sip pints while watching their
favorite teams on TV. Downstairs, the scene is different, with dim lighting, polished wooden furnishings,
and, on Thursdays, stand-up comedy.

B-Bar & Grill *East-West Village crossover* `4 E3`

0 East 4th Street (between Bowery & Lafayette St.)

12 475 2220

>> www.bbarandgrill.net

Open 11:30am–2am Sun–Thu, 10:30am–4am Fri & Sat

Barring an electrical blackout, one cannot miss the B-Bar: a neon red sign protrudes from the facade, and towering trees sparkle under a multicolored blanket of festive lights. Aside from its location between New York's East and West Villages, this former petrol station has other attributes that place it on the nocturnal crossroads of the East/West divide. The fabulous outdoor patio – with its nicely spaced tables and bar – draws equal numbers of conservative West Villagers and their counterculture-embracing neighbors to the East. Inside the handsome dining room and at the bar, retro vinyl booths, wood-beamed ceilings, and mammoth framed photographs suggest a hip, East Side sensibility; yet this is executed with a polish befitting a refined West 4th Street bistro.

Neighborhood allegiances aside, everybody unites in their love for B-Bar's cocktails. Take note, however: the pretty hues of apple, lychee, and watermelon Martinis belie their explosive potency. Regarding the "Grill" portion of the name, B-Bar offers a varied, if somewhat uneven, American diner menu. But the crowd-pleasing, busy, prix-fixe brunch on the weekend brings the nighttime vibe into day: chatty crowds, outside seating in good weather, and an unlimited supply of Mimosas and Bloody Marys.

Bars & Clubs

Bar Veloce *Italian-style wine bar* `4 E2`
175 2nd Avenue (between 11th & 12th Sts) • 212 260 3200
>> www.barveloce.com Open from 5pm nightly

This comfortable, sleek little wine bar would not look
out of place on the elegant streets of Florence.
A smart menu of Italian snacks, from toasted panini
to Nutella and fruit plates, gives peckish drinkers
something to nibble while choosing a wine. Glasses
are priced under $10, bottles up to $80.

Beauty Bar *intimate theme bar* `4 E2`
231 East 14th Street (between 2nd & 3rd Aves) • 212 539 1389
>> www.beautybar.com
Open 5pm–4am nightly (from 7pm Sat, Sun)

This place is swathed in retro beauty-salon kitsch.
East Village rockers and graduate students sip potent
cocktails, while 70s glam rock and punk blare out.
Check out the "happy hour" until 9pm weekdays for
deals on drinks. Manicures are on offer too.

Lotus `3 A2`
409 West 14th Street (between 9th & 10th Aves)
212 243 4420
>> www.lotusnewyork.com Open 10pm–4am Tue–Sun

It's been several years since this sleek, sexy club
opened its black lacquer doors in a neighborhood
best known for wholesale meat butchers, rumbling
garbage trucks, and transvestite prostitutes. In so
doing, Lotus helped blaze the trail that converted the
Meatpacking District into a hotbed of nightlife.

Imitated throughout the city, Lotus's design is still
the best, with three distinct areas for lounging upstairs,
pan-Asian dining on the ground floor, and dancing
below. The place exudes a subtle Eastern warmth,
with a mix of blonde and cherry woods, rusty-red
walls, and half-moon banquettes. The cocktail menu
features signature blackberry Caipirinhas. Friday's
house party GBH pulls in a serious dance crowd, while
Saturday's blend of 80s pop and contemporary hip-
hop draws a more mainstream, uptown element. **Adm**

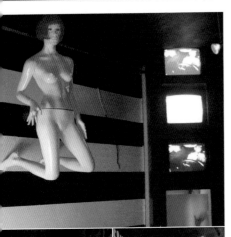

Korova Milk Bar *homage to a cult film* `4 F2`
200 Avenue A (between 12th & 13th Sts) • 212 254 8838
>> www.korovamilkbar.com Open 7pm–4am nightly

From the rounded, swooping white script above the doorway to the geometric zebra stripes lining the entrance hall, visitors to Korova know a distinctive visual experience awaits them. The entire place is a homage to Stanley Kubrick's 1971 film about brutality and youth, *A Clockwork Orange*; indeed, the bar takes its name from the film (it was the haunt of Malcolm Macdowell's band of miscreants). Once inside, film buffs will immediately recognize many references, such as the stark white, wigged, and lipsticked mannequins protruding from the walls. The cinematic homage continues with wall-mounted video monitors and curvaceous, matching black and white recliners swathed in vinyl and velvet, perched on a platform opposite the exceptionally long bar. Korova is a final destination on the East Village/Alphabet City barhopping circuit, so before midnight the spacious floor has room to spare.

After midnight, 70s punk and glam blares, while a throwback bunch of mods, punks, and stragglers recounts the night's wanderings over cheap beer, Jack Daniel's shots, and wicked vodka gimlets. For those who possess the stomach for it at such an hour, Korova's series of signature cocktails, Molokos (of course), should not be missed. The Moloko is an ice cream-based concoction, mixed with any number of liqueurs and flavorings, served in a Martini glass and kept cool in an ice-filled miniature fishbowl.

Rue B *Gallic-style retreat* `4 G2`
188 Avenue B • 212 358 1700
Open noon–4am Mon–Fri, 11am–4am Sat & Sun

Rue B's seductive air renders any intention of East Village barhopping pointless. The Parisian-style bar is decked out with comfy banquettes and offers respectable French wine, bistro menus, and – its *coup de grâce* – hosts live jazz with no cover charge. With all that on offer, there's no need to go anywhere else.

>>> >>>

Uncle Ming's *cozy, crazy lounge* `4 G2`

225 Avenue B, 2nd Floor (between 13th & 14th Sts)
212 979 8506

>> www.unclemings.com Open 8pm–4am Wed–Sat

Discreetly plying its trade above a liquor store, this unmarked lounge feels like a party that's strictly for the in-crowd. Deep purple and pink lighting, old chandeliers, strong cocktails, and DJs spinning electro beats inspire a flirtatious vibe.

Sullivan Room *relaxed clubbing* `3 C3`

218 Sullivan Street (between Bleecker & W. 3rd Sts)
212 252 2151

>> www.sullivanroom.com Open from 10pm Thu–Sun

This modest, subterranean West Village jewel is one of those rare spaces in which you can feel comfortable whether you've come to dance to soulful house, lounge with friends, or chat at the bar. A refreshing lack of attitude comes with the territory. **Adm**

Vol de Nuit *Belgian beer & cheer* `3 C3`

148 West 4th Street (at 6th Ave.) • 212 982 3388
Open from 5pm nightly

Behind an inconspicuous door on West 4th, Vol de Nuit counts eight Belgian brews on draft – each served in its appropriate style of glass – and dozens of others in bottles. Snacks are wonderful: Belgian fries served in paper cones, and mussels paired with irresistible sauces. There's an outdoor courtyard too.

Chumley's *former speakeasy* `3 B3`

86 Bedford Street (between Grove & Barrow Sts)
212 675 4449 Open from 5pm nightly

"Eighty-sixed," the American bartender's code for denying service to a particularly inebriated patron, evolved from the address of this institution in the 1920s Prohibition era. Booth seating and yellowing portraits of famed writers who once sipped their pints here round out the warm, convivial pub atmosphere.

Stonewall *famous & still fabulous* `3 B3`
3 Christopher Street (at 7th Avenue South) • 212 463 0950
Open from 2:30pm daily

When this bar's predominantly gay male clientele resisted a police raid in 1969, the ensuing riot touched off NYC's gay activist movement. Stonewall demands reverence, but it's also a fun place. Campy 60s pop music and multicolored lighting dominate the main bar, and drag queens strut their stuff nightly.

Blind Tiger Ale House *serious beers* `3 B3`
518 Hudson Street (at W. 10th St.) • 212 675 3848
>> www.blindtigeralehouse.com Open noon–4am Mon–Fri,
(from 1pm Sat & Sun)

West Village beer connoisseurs hoist their pints at the convivial Blind Tiger. No fewer than 24 microbrews chill on draft. It's one of New York's most friendly, casual places for mid-week beer drinking. Go on Wednesday evening for free cheese pairings.

White Horse Tavern *writers' haunt* `3 B3`
567 Hudson Street (between Perry & W. 11th St.)
212 243 9260
Open from 11am daily

Few New York bars shelter as many literary ghosts as the White Horse Tavern. Before the West Village became a gentrified expanse of French bistros and NYU dormitories, this circa-1880 bar was a favorite spot for the neighborhood's bohemian writers to brood over 20-cent ales. But the address attained infamy in 1953, when – as legend has it – the Welsh poet and dramatist Dylan Thomas dropped dead outside, the victim of undiagnosed diabetes and untold whiskeys. Fittingly, posters from Thomas's theatrical productions line the dark wood walls. Grandfather clocks, porcelain horses, a pressed tin ceiling – even the bartenders' amiable rapport with afternoon regulars – evoke a bygone era. But it's decidedly 21st-century after work and at weekends, when crowds fill the bar and adjoining dining rooms.

Bars & Clubs

Cubbyhole *one for the girls*   `3 B2`
281 West 12th Street (between W. 4th St. & Greenwich Ave.)
212 243 9041
Open 4pm–4am Mon–Fri (from 2pm Sat & Sun)

If the suspended goldfish figurines, Chinese lanterns, and whimsical bar stools at this lesbian bar don't charm you, perhaps this will: half-price drinks until 7pm, all-you-can-drink specials on Saturday nights, and notoriously huge Martinis. Very friendly and casual.

Level V *underground excess*   `3 A2`
675 Hudson Street (at 14th Street)
212 699 2410 Open from 8pm nightly

The dark basement beneath Italian eatery Vento has certainly cleaned up since its days as a gay sex club in the 1980s. The current tone provides a discreet backdrop for the beautiful young crowd that gathers here to drink cocktails, served by sexy barstaff who are mostly dressed in short skirts and high boots.

Cielo *award-winning dance club*   `3 A2`
18 Little West 12th Street (between 9th Ave. & Washington St
212 645 5700
» www.cieloclub.com Open 10pm–4am Wed–Sat

Soulful house with Latin grooves leave patrons little choice but to abandon their suede banquettes and storm the sunken dance floor. Co-owned by DJ Nicola Matar (well known on the Ibiza scene), Cielo attracts clubbers and top DJs from around the world. **Adm**

Daytime Bars
When a thirst for something stronger than bottled water strikes you during midtown sightseeing, these bars make welcome stops. The daytime crowd at **Rudy's Bar & Grill** in Hell's Kitchen is as friendly as any you'll find, and Miles Davis on the jukebox makes a welcome change from the classic rock barrage of neighboring bars. Murray Hill's campy

Cabin Club at Pinetree Lodge has a huge back patio where potent fruit slushes are dispensed to a fun, flirty crowd. Afternoon sophistication abounds at the rooftop **Mica Bar**, within blocks of the United Nations. A parlor atmosphere pervades the Hudson Hotel's **Library Bar**, where chessboards, architecture books, and a purple-felt billiard table are all at guests' disposal. For full addresses, *see p232.*

For the very latest on New York go to » www.realcity.dk.com

Roxy *perennially popular nightclub* `3 A1`
515 West 18th Street (between 10th & 11th Aves)
212 645 5157
» www.roxynyc.com Open Wed, Fri & Sat nights

Friday-night house, salsa, and hip-hop tend to mean this most massive of Chelsea clubs is overrun by a young crowd. By contrast, Wednesday Roller Skating nights offer a fun, if bruising reminder of disco's last days. Saturday brings NYC's biggest gay party. **Adm**

Avalon *Chelsea club with attitude* `3 C1`
47 West 20th Street (at 6th Ave.) • 212 807 7780
» www.nyavalon.com Check website for club nights

Avalon occupies hallowed ground on two counts: it's housed in a Gothic church and is the former address of Limelight, a legendary 1980s club that engendered near-religious devotion among its regulars. These days, a mixed gay and straight crowd comes to lounge and dance to the sounds of the world's top DJs. **Adm**

Eugene *upscale schmoozing post* `6 E5`
27 West 24th Street (between 5th & 6th Aves) • 212 462 0999
» www.eugenenyc.com Open 5pm–4am Thu–Sat

Realized in Art Deco retro, Eugene is a spacious supper club designed with big spending in mind. Well-dressed Flatiron professionals nibble tuna tartare in the cream-hued dining room, then settle themselves onto burgundy banquettes and ottomans in the adjacent lounge. There's dancing on weekends.

Serena *soft pink lounge* `5 C5`
Chelsea Hotel, 222 West 23rd Street (between 7th & 8th Aves)
212 255 4646
» www.serenanyc.com Open from 6pm Tue–Fri, from 7pm Sat

It's had a makeover to meet fire-safety standards, but the home of pop culture personalities hasn't lost its touch. The Chelsea's subterranean Serena lounge delights with its velvet couches and pink walls up front, and Moroccan motifs in the adjacent rooms.

Hiro *hotel lounge with a Japanese theme* `3 A1`
363 West 16th Street (at 9th Ave.) • 212 727 0212
>> www.themaritimehotel.com Open from 10pm Thu–Sun

The lounge at the Maritime Hotel is Chelsea's brooding-celebrity scene of the moment. Fashion models and rock stars sip sake, while, behind a luminescent rice paper wall, more energized guests move to 80s pop, rock remixes, and electro in Hiro's sizeable ballroom. Not famous? Try a weeknight.

Glass *receptacle for the beautiful people* `5 B5`
287 10th Avenue (at 26th & 27th Sts) • 212 904 1580
Open Tue–Sat 8pm–4am

An ultra-cool design and Brazilian electro rhythms draw Chelsea's gallery set to Glass like magnets. In summer, the bamboo-filled patio is the site for one of Manhattan's most exclusive people-watching scenes. Models, artists, and curators mingle over *Caipiruva* cocktails, made from cachaça rum and crushed grapes.

Bungalow 8 *West Coast seduction* `5 B4`
515 West 27th Street (between 10th & 11th Sts) • 212 629 3333
Open from 10pm nightly

Nightlife impresario Amy Sacco delivers a cozy, albeit exclusive, Hollywood Hills-inspired lounge to Chelsea's young style mavens. Strike your most unaffected L.A. pose – $30 glass of champagne in hand – amid swimming pool murals, quirky designer furniture, and potted palms. A digital "sunset wall" stands in for that most essential of Californian ingredients – the sun setting on the ocean.

Spirit *holistic nightlife* `5 B4`
530 West 27th Street (between 10th & 11th Sts) • 212 268 9477
>> www.spiritnewyork.com
Open from 10pm Fri & Sat (Wed, Thu & Sun occasionally)

Eastern and Native American religions have inspired this "wellness club." Spirit has three zones: Mind, a holistic spa with massage rooms; Body, an immense dance space, with superstar DJs; and Soul, an organic restaurant, overlooking the dance floor. **Adm**

Copacabana *salsa, meréngue & samba* `5 B3`
560 West 34th Street (between 10th & 11th Aves)
>> www.copacabanany.com • 212 239 2672
Open from 6pm Tue & Thu, from 10pm Fri–Sun

With its plush banquettes and Art Deco palm-frond motifs, the Copa evokes the glamor of a 1940s supper club in Havana. Massive dance floors and a stage that can accommodate huge ensembles make for unforgettable evenings. Dress strictly to impress. **Adm**

The Ginger Man *distinguished ale house* `6 E3`
11 East 36th Street (between Madison & 5th Aves)
212 532 3740
>> www.gingerman-ny.com Open from 11:30am daily

This handsome bar includes all the accoutrements of a classic pub: lustrous woods, booth seating, and hearty food. Despite the vintage Guinness signage, it is Belgian ales and single-malt Scotches that fill the glasses of most regulars and visitors.

Campbell Apartment *pricey cocktails* `6 F2`
15 Vanderbilt Ave., Southwest Balcony, Grand Central Terminal
>> www.hospitalityholdings.com • 212 953 0409
Open 3pm–1am Mon–Sat, 3–11 Sun

For all its restored Beaux Arts splendor, Grand Central Station can still be a hassle. But the sting of crowds and late trains can be swiftly soothed by the divine cocktails at Campbell Apartment. Formerly the office of 1920s railroad tycoon John W. Campbell, it looks every bit the inner sanctum of a prosperous American industrialist, with dark wood paneling, monstrous stone fireplace, and intricate, leaded glass windows.

Suited midtown professionals unwind on comfy parlor furniture or on high bar stools, tapping feet to swing and calypso rhythms. The deceptively potent libations include Prohibition Punch – a mix of passion fruit juice, cognac, Grand Marnier, and champagne. A small balcony provides more privacy for latter-day John W.s to discuss mergers and acquisitions. Note: no sneakers, jeans, or baseball caps are allowed.

Bars & Clubs

Métrazur *Grand Central splendor*   `6 F2`
East Balcony, Grand Central Terminal • 212 687 4600
» www.charliepalmer.com/metrazur
Open 11:30am–3pm Mon–Fri, 5–10:30pm Mon–Sat, 2–8pm Su

Métrazur packs enough panache to lure rail travelers and non-commuters alike to Grand Central's East Balcony. Smart professionals relish Charlie Palmer's beautifully crafted cocktails, such as the Riviera: Dubonnet, Grand Marnier, blood orange, and lime juice

Single Room Occupancy *discreet bar*   `7 C5`
360 West 53rd Street (between 8th & 9th Aves) • 212 765 629
Open 7:30pm–4am Mon–Sat

This Theater District cubbyhole might be midtown's best-kept secret. Ring the outdoor buzzer, and a member of staff will show you into a dark bar, where chic patrons sip Malbecs and full-bodied Brooklyn Monster Ale served in elegant glassware. House music pounds from the stereo.

Ava Lounge *modernist vision at the Majestic*   `7 D5`
Top of Majestic Hotel, 210 West 55th Street (between Broadway & 7th Ave.) • 212 956 7020
» www.avaloungenyc.com Open from 6pm nightly

The 1950s Golden Age of cocktail culture is evoked here through gorgeous linear furnishings, geometric patterns on the bar, designer Martinis, and jazzy house music. The outdoor patio comes into its own in summer – you'll be mesmerized by nearby Times Square.

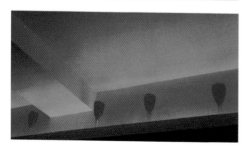

Flûte *Theater District champagne lounge*   `7 D5`
205 West 54th Street (between Broadway & 7th Ave.)
212 265 5169
» www.flutebar.com Open from 5pm nightly (live jazz Wed)

Velvet couches, Belle Époque poster art, discreet alcoves, and cuddling couples create a cozy, romanti mood. Choose your bubbly from 100 bottles (18 are available by the flute), and snack on smoked salmon tuna tartare, and foie gras. DJs play Thu–Sat.

Russian Vodka Room *for connoisseurs* `7 C5`
265 West 52nd Street (between Broadway & 8th Ave.)
212 307 5835
Open from 4pm daily

Gloss, glamour, and rampant pretension are the usual hallmarks of Manhattan lounges with extensive vodka selections. Fortunately, the Russian Vodka Room dodges this unsavory trend. The block's boisterous theater crowds rarely even notice RVR's black awning amid the twinkling lights, which means that proceedings inside the windowless lounge are intimate and relaxed. East Europeans, young and old, sit at the crescent-shaped wood bar or alcove tables, talking animatedly over music from a resident pianist.

No fewer than 50 kinds of the potent spirit fill the shelves. The large glass jars you may notice above the coat rack hold home-made vodka infusions – try a bracing shot of horseradish, tangy cranberry, or mellow pear. An extensive menu of Russian delicacies, from borscht to caviar, is also available.

Baraonda *Italo-Latin festivity* `8 G2`

439 2nd Avenue (at 75th St.) • 212 288 8555
www.baraondany.com Open from 5:30pm Mon–Sun

Baraonda single-handedly proves that staid Upper East Siders can, in fact, party. Around midnight, the restaurant transforms into a Latin American dance house, with samba, techno, and *rock en español* compelling revelers to gulp down sangría and dance on the tables. (Skip the middling, overpriced food.)

Bemelmans Bar *cabaret & cocktails* `8 E1`
Carlyle Hotel, 35 East 76th Street (at Madison Ave.)
212 744 1600
>> www.thecarlyle.com Open noon–12:30am (to 1:30 Fri & Sat)

Ludwig Bemelmans, creator of the *Madeline* children's book series, painted the exquisite zoological mural in this superb uptown piano lounge. Top cabaret acts, subdued lighting, and peerless classic cocktails set the tone for romantic evenings. Attire can be casual.

The Auction House *uptown elegance* `10 G4`
300 East 89th Street (between 1st & 2nd Aves)
212 427 4458 Open from 7:30pm nightly

Apartment space in New York can be scarce, but this cozy living room-like bar serves as a home away from home for neighborhood dwellers. Complete with a fireplace and mahogany bar, the ambience of the Auction House is warm and laid-back – very much like its friendly clientele.

Frank's Lounge *DJ bar* `13 B4`
660 Fulton Street (between Lafayette & S. Elliot Sts)
718 625 9339
>> www.frankscocktaillounge.com Open from 5pm nightly

New York's best classic 60s soul and R&B jukebox sets the weeknight mood for nights of bonhomie among the clientele and bar staff. Weekends are when DJs play hip-hop and soulful house, and the dance floor is jam-packed with Brooklyn's urban elite.

Zombie Hut *surprisingly refined lounge* `13 B4`
273 Smith Street (between Sackett & Degraw Sts)
718 875 3433
Open 5:30pm–2am Mon–Thu, 5pm–4am Fri & Sat

The cartoonish name suggests tiki bar clichés such as plastic palms and grass skirts, but this intimate cocktail lounge on Brooklyn's restaurant row is a dreamier, plusher evocation of Polynesia. Young couples share potent Mai Tais by the stone fireplace while jazzy electronic music plays. The ambience is friendly but probably not for those who are looking for a quiet couple of beers.

Ultra-colorful cocktails such as the Tiki Torch, Singapore Sling, and Scorpion Bowl are quite reasonably priced but pack a punch and (warning!) may have a tiny palm tree or a monkey floating in them. Try a pink and powerful Frozen Zombie with orange juice, rum, and grenadine (to name a few of its poisons), just to kick off and you'll probably not remember much more of the evening.

Gowanus Yacht Club *local gem* `13 B4`
323 Smith Street (at President St.) • 718 246 1321
Open May–Oct: from mid-afternoon daily

Summer in Carroll Gardens means strolls in the park and beers at the Yacht Club. Nautical only in name, this tiny outdoor bar feels as convivial as a suburban backyard. Patio furniture, sizzling burgers and festive lights keep a hip crowd lingering long after their cheap domestic beers have been drained.

Great Lakes *graduates' gathering* `13 C4`
284 5th Avenue (at 1st St.) • 718 499 3710
Open from 6pm nightly

This spacious Park Slope favorite, with its worn couches, young, amiable crowd, and cracking indie-rock jukebox, suggests a college dormitory lounge for grown-ups. Defend your thesis anew over a Brooklyn Lager while making friends at the bar or out on the sidewalk with the banished smokers.

Bars with Views

For all the millions of dollars sunk into New York's myriad theme bars and luxe lounges, a bar with appealing views will have endless allure. **Sky Bar**, atop the Herald Square outpost of the La Quinta Inn chain, offers ample proof. The 14th-floor terrace compensates for the diminutive size of its split outdoor/indoor patio and undistinguished drinks by providing spectacular views of the Empire State Building, which literally towers above you. It's a popular gathering spot for the neighborhood's young after-work crowd.

The **Boat Basin Café** presents as rarified a setting for drinking beer and chomping on burgers as any in New York: a quirky, spacious complex, with limestone archways in its outdoor courtyard that are reminiscent of a Moorish grotto. Watch sailboats ply the Hudson from your shaded, riverfront patio table along with sociable Upper West Side couples and families. The preferred retreat among young, cosmopolitan travelers keen on seeing and being seen is the new Hotel Gansevoort's aptly named **Plunge Bar**, adjacent to the hotel's rooftop pool. Sleek patio furniture and an unfaltering ly beautiful clientele are formidable distractions from the 360-degree views.

The View, on the 47th floor of the Marriott Marquis Hotel, underwent a renovation in 2004 that removed the dance floor, but the bar still slowly revolves over Times Square. Comfy chairs and a famed mixologist make this a great spot to unwind (**www.nymarriottmarquis.com/hotel/view**).

As a counterpoint to all this refinement, nothing matches the gritty charm of hoisting your plastic beer cup at the weathered bar of **Ruby's** at Coney Island, where salty breezes and the boardwalk's colorful, wonderful spirit can be enjoyed free of charge. For full addresses, *see p232*.

» *Another café-bar with a superb view over Central Park is The Met's Roof Garden Café (see p178)*

Bars & Clubs

Buttermilk Bar *Brooklynite classic* `13 C5`
577 5th Avenue (at 16th St.) • 718 788 6297
Open from 6pm nightly

Operated by the same people as Great Lakes *(see p161)*, Buttermilk is remote by Park Slope standards, but worth seeking out for its hip young atmosphere. There's an excellent indie-rock jukebox, ample booth seating, and Brooklyn Brewery beers on tap. A locals' local, Buttermilk's a place to chat with Brooklynites.

Larry Lawrence *easy-going lounge* `13 C2`
295 Grand Street (between Roebling & Havermeyer Sts)
718 218 7866
Open from 6pm nightly

This bi-level Williamsburg space flaunts all the sophistication of a Manhattan lounge, without the pretension. Below, neighborhood professionals and artists sip reasonably priced Martinis and wines by the glass. Above, smokers enjoy the views from an atrium.

Black Betty *Trashablanca* `13 C2`
366 Metropolitan Ave (at Havermeyer St.) • 718 599 0243
Open 6:30pm–4am nightly

Williamsburg hipsters flock to this intimate bar-lounge featuring Middle Eastern decor and food in the adjacent restaurant. Think dive bar meets Arabian bordello, with pumpkin-colored walls, sofas, red velvet and beaded curtains, and tapestries. Music can be either a live band, a DJ, or from the jukebox.

Trash *gay & lesbian bar* `13 C`
256 Grand Street (between Driggs & Roebling)
718 599 1000
>> www.thetrashbar.com Open 5pm–4am nightly

Trash (formerly Luxx, then Toybox) has established itself as the bar of choice for Williamsburg boys and girls who like to rock. Glittery vinyl booths fill with young singles nightly, and it's jam-packed on Friday and Saturdays, when there's backroom dancing.

Spuyten Duyvil *Belgian beers/wicked fun* `13 C`
359 Metropolitan Avenue • 718 963 4140
Open from 5pm nightly

A hundred different bottled beers and six rotating cask ales await beer connoisseurs at this cozy Williamsburg bar. The bright red facade hints at merriment. Inside, you'll find locals sampling rare Belgian brews, snacking on hot *soppressata* (spicy salami) sandwiches, and sharing group toasts.

For the very latest on New York go to >> www.realcity.dk.com

Galapagos *playhouse for the arty* `13 B2`
0 North 6th Street (between Wythe & Kent)
18 782 5188
www.galapagosartspace.com Open from 6pm nightly

lmost every New York neighborhood boasts a space
where the values, styles, and habits of its residents
use into something emblematic. For Williamsburg –
Brooklyn's much-hyped bastion of artistic activity – it
s Galapagos. Anchoring North 6th Street's minimally
ppointed bistros, cutting-edge boutiques, and few
emaining vacant warehouses, the venue gives voice
 o musicians, wall space to film-makers and painters,
nd a great excuse for visitors to visit Williamsburg.

A soft magenta spotlight points out the door,
eyond which sits a huge reflecting pool and, above

it, a projection screen suspended in the air. Behind
this theatrical entrance, the performance and bar
area fills up with the neighborhood's hip young
members of Brooklyn's arts and music scene. Lushly
illuminated with ingenious spotlighting, the intimate
stage hosts everything from avant-garde rock bands
to risqué burlesque troupes – usually enthusiastically
supported by friends in the audience.

Ocularis, a weekly film series, features domestic
and international cinema. A film's director or one of
its actors is often invited along for a post-screening
discussion. Weekends bring DJs spinning electro, rock
'n' roll, soul, breakbeats, and more.

Some nights carry a cover charge, so check the
website for information about scheduled events.

streetlife

Away from the well-known tourist destinations are neighborhoods where New Yorkers shop, eat, and just hang out. To experience the variety and energy of authentic NY life, you need to visit places frequented by recent immigrants as well as born-and-bred New Yorkers. This chapter is the insider's view of where things happen for the locals – snapshots of street culture in a bubbling, bustling metropolis.

Streetlife

Lunchtime on Wall Street   *Finance District frenzy*

For a quintessential New York phenomenon, head to Wall Street between noon and 2pm on a weekday, and join the fast-paced business crowd for lunch. There are numerous delis and sandwich shops, including **Cosi**, **Pret a Manger**, the **Green Market**, and the **Amish Fine Food Market**. Be warned, though: ordering a sandwich in this high-powered financial district is not for the timid. Decide in advance what you want and be prepared to bark your order to an impatient server who will yell "next" if you show any hesitation.

Once you've got through this experience, sit on the steps of **Federal Hall**, opposite the **Stock Exchange**. This is a good place for gazing along the concrete canyons. Alternatively, find a space in **Bowling Green Park** (south end of Broadway) or by the river in **Battery Park**. For a little calm after the lunchtime storm, **Trinity Church** (Map 1 D4) offers daily tours at 2pm, and Thursday afternoon music concerts at 1pm.

Canal Street   *chopsticks & bargains*

A visit to New York isn't complete without a walk along the main thoroughfare of Chinatown. Canal Street is always crowded with cars and people: a jumble of languages making themselves heard within the din.

Street vendors peddle NYC T-shirts, counterfeit Rolex watches, and all manner of cheap knick-knacks. Ignore these and focus instead on the fresh produce, red bean buns, and Chinese paraphernalia in the stores on Canal Street and the quieter side streets of Bayard, Pell, and Mott. **The Chinatown Ice Cream Factory** on Bayard (No. 65) is an essential stop in summer; **HSF** on Bowery (No. 46) is fantastic for dim sum. **Great NY Noodle Town** on Bowery (No. 28½) also has good food.

For an insight into the local culture and history, visit the **Museum of Chinese in the Americas**, at the intersection of Mulberry and Bayard. The **Mahayana Buddhist Temple** on Canal St. (No. 133) is another Sino-American establishment that's worth a look; with a bright yellow facade it's impossible to miss.

West 4th Street Courts
on 6th Avenue *sport on the streets*   `3 C3`

A simple area of asphalt by West 4th Street has become so popular for basketball that it has been officially recognized by the NYC Parks Department. Casual "pick-up" games occur year-round, and a summer tournament draws semi-pro players from around the world. Get in on the action: grab a hotdog from a street vendor, and cheer the players.

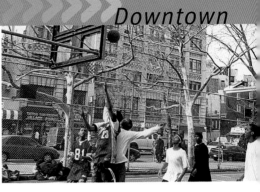

Meatpacking District *gentrified area*   `3 A2`

This historic district in the westernmost pocket of West Village, just below 14th Street, is undergoing rapid change. In its 19th-century heyday, the area housed over 200 slaughterhouses and meatpacking plants. A handful of these remain, but most of the meat business has moved up to the Bronx or out of the city altogether. The former meat storage facilities – many of them listed as landmarks – are being reborn as cafés, restaurants, galleries, bars, and chic stores, and the Meatpacking District is now the hang-out of models and celebrities. A shiny limousine is more often spotted than a side of beef these days. Remnants of the past can be seen, however, in architectural details. The curious metal awnings over the roads, for example, would have protected the meat as it was being moved off the trucks.

Cobbled **Gansevoort Street** was once a notorious spot for transvestite and she-male prostitutes. Diner/bistro **Florent** *(see p42)* opened on this street in 1985, pioneering the area's path to gentrification. Other established venues include **Cielo** *(see p154)*, a club where dancing is taken seriously, and French bistro **Pastis** *(see p225)*. High-end fashion boutiques **Stella McCartney** *(see p77)*, **Alexander McQueen** *(see p227)*, and **Jeffrey** *(see p78)* are steps away at 14th Street, while designer furniture is available at **Karkula Gallery** and **Vitra** *(see p228 for both)*. The former Gansevoort Docks now form part of the **Hudson River Park**. A waterside path is used by pedestrians, runners, cyclists, and roller-bladers, and leads past some scenic piers.

Streetlife

Tompkins Square Park Dog Run *canine romps*

4 G2

If Fluffy isn't wearing the latest Burberry sweater, that's okay, so long as he's behaving and not sporting a spiked, pronged, or pinched collar. Toys aren't allowed either because "toys cause fights." These are some of the many rules, carefully displayed at the entrance to the dog run at Tompkins Square Park. This singular spot is the culmination of the American obsession with regulations and the New Yorker's need to give his or her dog room to promenade and socialize.

Once the preserve of drug users and prostitutes, the park is decidedly bourgeois now – the orderly dog run and its prim owners are a testament to that. Once you have gazed at the dog-walking spectacle over the fence (no people without dogs allowed in, and vice versa), stroll along 9th Street and avenues A and B. In contrast to the dog run, these roads have a funkier vibe. Notable cafés include **Itzocan** (438 East 9th St.), and **Rue B** and **DT–UT** on Avenue B (Nos. 188 & 41, respectively).

Chelsea Flea Market & Union Square Markets *deals for steals*

3 D1

Outdoor Market open 8–5 Sat & Sun • Union Square Green Market open 8–6 Mon, Wed, Fri & Sat • Holiday Market open from day after Thanksgiving until Christmas Eve

Chelsea's weekend flea and antiques markets are prime for finding anything from belt buckles and old buttons to botanical drawings, maps, vintage clothing, axes, and lace. The **Outdoor Market** on the northwest corner of 24th Street and 6th Avenue is a mélange of curios and furniture. **Antiques Garage** and **Antiques Annex** are geared more toward antique treasures, but also harbor a fair share of junk. Both are worth a browse; there's a $1 admission to get into the Annex. A few blocks further south, **Union Square Green market** showcases farmers' stalls offering fruit, vegetables, fish, meat, and baked goods. During winter, the **Holiday Market** takes over – a mine of handmade jewelry, T-shirts, candles, massage oil, paintings, and hats.

Subway Passages: Grand Central to Times Square *underground music* `6 F2`

Grand Central Station and Times Square are connected by an underground Shuttle train, and the subway passages at either end of the short route are abuzz with New York energy, as bustling workers swarm through the passageways on their way to and from work. In these tunnels you'll also find excellent musicians, their performances good enough to make even the most determined commuter slow down to catch a few bars. While you may come across the occasional "rogue" performer – who'll set up and play wherever there's space – most are part of the MTA's Music Under New York program. The scheme promotes a variety of music, including jazz, Cajun, African, classical, Asian, and bluegrass. A stringent audition process held each year ensures that a high standard is maintained. Look for the authorized performers, who display an orange and black "Music Under New York" banner.

125th Street *gateway to Harlem* `11 D3`

One of the main roads in Harlem, 125th Street came to prominence during the Harlem Renaissance of the 1920s, when it became synonymous with dancing and jazz clubs. Since then the street has been the main commercial center for Harlem's predominantly black community and, over time, has provided the backdrop to civil rights activism and a creative flourishing of music, painting, literature, and drama.

Having gone through a prolonged period of economic depression and attendant crime problems, 125th street is back to being a vibrant thoroughfare again, with a mix of gentrified boutiques, mainstream chains, and street vendors. Some would argue that the soul of Harlem has moved to smaller side streets, but 125th remains the hub. For tours of Harlem, check out www.harlemspirituals.com or www.bigapplejazz.com. See if you can catch a gospel service at the Lenox Lounge *(see p135)* or some Southern-style cooking at **Amy Ruth's** *(see p224)*.

Brooklyn Heights
Promenade *sublime views of Manhattan*   13 A4

This is one of the best vantage points for a panorama of Manhattan. It's also a great place to enjoy a stroll – alone, hand in hand with a lover, or lead in hand with your dog. Grab an espresso at **Connecticut Muffin** at 115 Montague (the main commercial street) and head towards the water to get onto the walkway.

A favorite spot for both locals and visitors, the promenade offers a mix of calm (despite the fact that it overlooks the Brooklyn to Queens expressway), and excitement – a thrill instilled by the awesome view of Manhattan that confronts you every time you look across the water.

The strip isn't very long, but you can combine the stroll with a perusal of Brooklyn Heights and its beautifully maintained brownstones. Back on Montague Street, there are several decent places to eat, such as **Teresa's** restaurant (No. 80), which offers tasty and authentic Polish fare alongside grilled cheese and hamburgers. Retail stores include **Heights Books** (No. 109), which specializes in second-hand books.

Alternatively, you can take a different route from the promenade and walk along Columbia Heights to the Fulton Ferry landing, where you can buy an ice cream at the **Brooklyn Ice Cream Factory** before catching a water taxi over to Manhattan. To extend your walk further, cross via the Brooklyn Bridge.

Red Hook Food Stalls *spice & soccer*   13 B5
Corner of Bay and Clinton Streets
Sat & Sun (end of Apr to first weekend in Oct)

Weekends in Red Hook's playing fields are dedicated to soccer, socializing, soaking up rays, and working one's way through as much delicious, home-cooked Latin American food as possible. Mexico, Honduras, Guatemala, and Colombia are all well represented. Try out your Spanish, and be willing to experiment.

Bedford Avenue *Williamsburg's heart* `13 C2`

Williamsburg is a compact area in north Brooklyn, packed with the accessories of bourgeois bohemia – funky cafés, hip bars, renovated lofts, fashion boutiques, and a few more trendy cafés. And Bedford Avenue is at its pulsating heart. This is an area that has changed dramatically in the last ten years, and some bemoan the arrival of Brooklyn's hip young things, who have pitched camp, placed their laptops on the counters of every café and bar in sight, and by their very presence have raised the rents. However, others are grateful for the attention the neighborhood is receiving and are happy to see some of the disused factories converted into apartments, stores, and clubs.

It is true that some of the grit may have been replaced by something funkier, lighter, and more affluent, but it is possible to find an earthy feel to the neighborhood once you look beyond the iPods and messenger bags (which you can pick up for a snip at **Brooklyn Industries**, No. 162). This is an eclectic locale, incorporating a Hasidic community in South Williamsburg, a profusion of artists, and a Polish contingent that has spilled over from Greenpoint. The Polish influence can be seen and tasted in places such as **Cukiernia** (a Polish bakery at No. 223) and **S & B Polish Restaurant** (No. 194).

The Bedford Avenue strip is most lively between North 6th and 10th streets. For a cool coffee stop, try **Verb Café** (No. 218), and watch the locals sitting at rickety wooden tables, indulging in java, listening to off-beat music, and playing checkers. The Verb is connected to a mini-mall that houses a variety of establishments, including an Internet café, the famed **Bedford Cheese Shop**, a vintage clothing store, and the bookstore **Spoonbill and Sugartown** *(see p92)*. Try **Bliss Café** (No. 191) for veggie delights, or a slice of superb pizza at **Anna Maria's** (No. 179). Noteworthy stops are **Metaphors** (No. 195) for women's clothing and **Mini Minimarket** *(see p92)* for girly fashions. Check out the **Brooklyn Lager Brewery** (79 North 11th Street), and take a free tour on Saturday (1–4pm) or indulge in Friday Night's Happy Hour (6–11pm).

>> *For the art scene in Williamsburg, see p114*

171

Brighton Beach
Boardwalk *sea, sand, and snacks*

Ⓜ B, Q to Brighton Beach; F, D, Q to Coney Island/Stillwell Ave.

The Russian enclave of Brighton Beach at the southern tip of Brooklyn, also known as "Little Odessa," has much to offer for a day trip from Manhattan. The Brighton Beach Boardwalk is alive with Slavic languages, chess games, the smell of the ocean, and a whiff of borscht wafting from one of the boardwalk cafés. For the area's best food and prices, however, go off the boardwalk and eat "inland" at **Café Glechik** (3159 Coney Island Avenue) or **Café Arbat** (306 Brighton Beach Avenue). Try the *vareniki* (similar to *pierogi* or ravioli) and drink a wholesome fruit compote. If you want to pick up snacks to take back to the waterfront, **M & I International Food Market**

(249 Brighton Beach Avenue) has an impressive selection of Eastern European delicacies.

The boardwalk provides a vantage point for a lovely beach and water view. If you walk all the way along it, you'll reach Coney Island, where you can't miss the **New York Aquarium** (www.nyaquarium.com) and **Astroland** (www.astroland.com). This amusement park has the famed and rickety-looking Cyclone roller-coaster, which now has National Landmark status.

For the full Brighton Beach/Coney Island experience, have a **Nathan's Hotdog** from the original outpost on the corner of Surf and Stillwell. This is where the July 4th Hotdog Eating Championships take place. If you visit in mid- to late June, check **www.coneyisland.com** to find out when New York's aquatic version of Mardi Gras, the Mermaid Parade, struts down Surf Avenue.

Roosevelt Avenue *vibrancy and spice*

Ⓜ Roosevelt Avenue subway station is served by the E, F, V, G, and R trains

Roosevelt Avenue is one of the main thoroughfares in the Queens neighborhood of Jackson Heights, and is a veritable smorgasbord of cultures and food, including Colombian, Chinese, Indian, Pakistani, Korean, and Mexican. As soon as you leave the subway station, your olfactory sense starts working overtime to decipher the wafts of exotic ingredients that are being mixed in various kitchens. The area may lack aesthetic appeal, but it compensates in variety and vitality.

Along the adjacent 74th Street, you'll find stores full of phonecards, toys, food, and confections. For a meal try **Jackson Diner** (No. 37), or visit **Patel Brothers Market** (Nos. 27–37) to see myriad fresh and dried Asian spices and vegetables. Also on 74th Street, you'll find dazzlingly intricate jewelry as well as colorful saris and beautiful silk cloth in **Sahil Sari Palace** (Nos. 37–55).

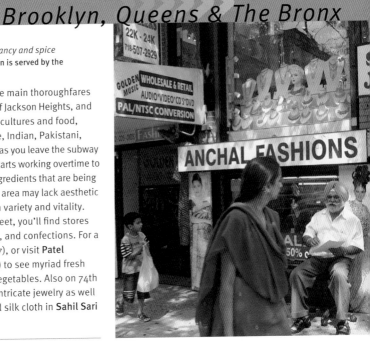

Arthur Avenue *a mini Little Italy*

Ⓜ 4 or D subway train to Fordham Rd, then bus No. 12 east; 2 or 5 subway train to Pelham Parkway, then bus No. 12 west

≫ www.arthuravenuebronx.com

Another testament to the New York patchwork of ethnic communities, Arthur Avenue, in the north Bronx, is suffused with southern Italian traditions. The strip offering the best in Italian produce is between 187th Street and Crescent Avenue. Here you can find some of the freshest and tastiest Italian food on this side of the Atlantic. The **Egidio Pastry Shop** (622 East 187th Street) sells scrumptious chocolate cakes and excellent *cannoli* (deep-fried tubes of pastry with a sweetened ricotta filling), along with superb espresso. You can buy the best home-made pasta and ravioli (rolled out and cut right in front of you) from **Borgatti's** (632 East 187th Street). Shops and stalls tease the senses with an array of salamis, parmigianos, pastas, and seafood. Italian is spoken widely on the street and there's a relaxed, family-oriented vibe. *Mangia!*

≫ Combine a visit to Arthur Avenue with a trip to the Botanical Gardens or Wave Hill (see p181)

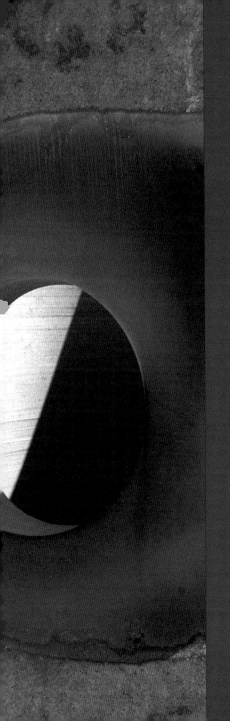

havens

In New York, there's no need to leave the city limits in order to find a piece of Nirvana. Along with parks and gardens, there are yoga centers, spas, churches, and tea rooms to retreat to. Vantage points at the tops of the city's towers provide inspirational views. And out at its farthest reaches – whether at Wave Hill in the Bronx or in the marshlands of Jamaica Bay – you may well discover an unexpected "wild" side to New York.

Havens

The River Project *waterside pleasures*

1 B1

Pier 26, off West St. (at N. Moore St.) • 212 233 3030
>> www.riverproject.org Open 11–5 daily

Just a few steps from Tribeca, this "estuarium" and research center is a perfect place to come for a deep breath or to confess to the marine gods for having jus eaten sushi at neighboring Nobu *(see p42)*. Watch the boats and learn a bit about the local marine life from informative displays and the friendly volunteer staff.

Bliss SoHo *top-notch spa*

3 D4

568 Broadway, 2nd Floor (at Prince St.) • 212 219 8970
>> www.blissworld.com Open 9:30–8:30 Mon–Fri (12:30–8:30 alternate Weds), 9:30–6:30 Sat

Forget about the outside world for a couple of hours, slip on a soft robe and slippers, and indulge in home made brownies, apples, and fresh juices while you wait for your chosen treatment. Bliss has three locations in New York, but the SoHo spot – the Bliss flagship – is the one to seek out. Both men and women are pampered here, in a space reminiscent o a ship's interior. Treatments cater for the whole body from head to toes, but the Bliss forte is facials. The trademarked Triple Oxygen Treatment and Fully Loaded facials are extremely popular with beauty-conscious New Yorkers. Alternatively, book a basic facial and add on treatments from an amazing à-la-carte menu, which offers masks, lip plumping, and capillary zapping. The changing rooms have saunas, steam rooms, and showers for further relaxation.

Angel Feet *divine foot relief*

3 B3

77 Perry Street (between Bleecker & W. 4th Sts) • 212 924 3576
>> www.angelfeet.com Open 10–9 Mon–Fri, 10–8 Sat & Sun

As the name of this jewel-box sized basement room suggests, a reflexology session here is truly heavenly. The treatment rids feet of soreness and is given while you sit in one of two plush chairs that take up most of the intimate space. Relaxing music, candles, and a fragrant water mist for the feet add to the experience.

Jivamukti Yoga
Center *for body and spirit*
404 Lafayette Street, 3rd floor (between Astor Pl. & E. 4th St.)
212 353 0214
> www.jivamuktiyoga.com
Open 11:30–8 Mon–Fri, 9–6:30 Sat & Sun

Calm your senses and align your posture with one of a vast selection of hatha yoga classes, offered throughout the day. Jivamukti, with two Manhattan locations, has made yoga accessible to New York's masses. You can simply drop in for a class or join an open meditation session, but it's generally worth calling ahead to check that space is available.

Throughout the building, the aroma of fragrant oils, mellow music, mood lighting, and a soothing waterfall help the process of relaxation. Massage treatments, workshops, lectures, and yoga demos are held regularly. Take note: the etiquette at the center dictates that shoes are to be taken off before you enter the clean, loft-like studio areas and changing rooms.

Wild Lily Tea Room *zen relaxation*
511a West 22nd Street (between 10th & 11th Aves)
212 691 2258
>> www.wildlilytearoom.com Open 11–10 Tue–Sun

Take time out from shopping, gallery hopping, and sightseeing at a place that takes tea very seriously. There's no need to be stressed out by the range of teas available; if you'd like to venture away from a regular teabag, staff will guide you through a wide selection of loose black tea blends, and jasmine, ginseng, green, barley, and berry teas.

With a maximum capacity of 32 people, Wild Lily isn't big, but the high ceilings and tiny goldfish pond in the front create a fresh, airy, and Zen-like ambience. As you sip, enjoy the simplicity of the Japanese decor, and the neat bento boxes, trays, and tea sets. The food is fresh, inventive, and tasty; there's traditional British fare, such as scones with clotted cream, as well as intriguing concoctions, such as pea and yogurt soup, and green-tea cake. Sake is also available.

>> *For a selection of other fine tea rooms, see p35*

Havens

The Spa at the Mandarin Oriental
luxurious respite

80 Columbus Circle (at 60th St.), 35th Floor • 212 805 8800
>> www.mandarinoriental.com Open 9am–9pm Mon–Sun

It's not cheap, but this spa is worth the expense! Splurge on wonderful body treatments, including exotically named massages such as Life Dance and Balinese Body. Herbal infusions are prepared daily by a chef (and are free), and almonds and dried fruits are offered in the Tea Lounge, which has stunning views of the Hudson River and the West Side of Manhattan. The decor is inspired by crisp Asian simplicity, elegance, and style: tiny candles line the carefully appointed hallway, and orchid buds decorate surface tops. Be sure to take advantage of the many amenities available as part of a visit to the spa, such as the Vitality Pool, the amethyst-crystal steam room (where eucalyptus oil is available to soften the skin) and the "rainforest experience" shower. Round it all off with some quality time in the Relaxing Room.

Top of the Tower @ Beekman Tower Hotel
6 G1
26th-floor calm

3 Mitchell Place (at 49th St. & 1st Ave.) • 212 355 7300
>> www.topofthetowernyc.com Open 5pm–1am daily

A jewel of a space with wonderful views and a full cocktail menu. The calm atmosphere, unhurried service, and superb vantage point take you far away from the street-level clamor. Get a table by the window, from where the roof slopes vertiginously downward.

The Iris and B. Gerald Cantor Roof Garden
8 E1
art & leisure

The Metropolitan Museum of Art, 1000 5th Avenue (at 82nd St.)
>> www.metmuseum.org • 212 535 7710
Open May–late Fall: 10–4:30 Tue–Thu & Sun, 10–8:30 Fri & Sa.

Gorgeous views, sculpture in the foreground, and wine or cappuccino to lift your spirits. The joys of an elevated outdoor space are combined with art from the Met collection and the whole of Central Park as a backdrop.

Conservatory Gardens at Central Park *floral sanctuary*

`10 E2`

Entrance on 5th Avenue and 105th Street • 212 360 2766
» www.centralparknyc.org Open 8am–dusk daily

Wildflowers, pruned rare roses, trimmed hedges, trees, and a thousand other floral delights are carefully arranged within these six acres, the most studiously tended area in Central Park. It's no wonder that New York brides scramble for permits for wedding ceremonies within these garden walls, or that school teachers are keen to bring classes for story-time sessions.

The central fountain is glorious in spring, when the wisteria that surrounds it bursts with purple, violet, pink, and white blossoms. Two more fountains are set closer to Fifth Avenue, one encircled by concentric rings of flowers. The fragrance, peace, and quiet of this garden is perfect for sitting on a bench, writing postcards, and taking time to reflect. There are free tours (rain or shine) on Saturdays from April to October; meet at Vanderbilt Gate on Fifth and 105th Street at 11am.

The Ramble at Central Park *green mazes*

`7 D2`

Enter via 5th Avenue or Central Park W. between 72nd & 80th Sts
» www.centralparknyc.org

The Ramble is the perfect place to get lost in a web of winding paths which cross 36 acres of wonderfully dense wooded areas, encompassing ponds, small bridges, and rocky outcrops. The wilderness factor in this pocket of Central Park is so great that the National Audubon Society has ranked the Ramble as one of the top 15 bird-watching sites in the whole of the U.S., putting it among National Parks such as Yosemite and geographical regions like the Everglades. If you visit early in the morning, you'll see die-hard birders at their regular spots, sporting binoculars and sipping cups of coffee or hot chocolate. The rest of the day brings a more diverse crowd, most of them with a more leisurely interest in a lunchtime stroll or a rendezvous. Note that the Central Park website refers to The Ramble within the Great Lawn section of the park.

The Ramble is a great place for a wander after visiting the Met (see p109)

The Rotunda
at The Pierre *traditional tea* `8 E4`
The Pierre Hotel, 2 East 61st Street • 212 838 8000
Afternoon tea served 3–5:30 daily

This is New York's best spot for afternoon tea. The atmosphere is gracious and welcoming, with a high, domed ceiling above, and linen and fresh flowers at your table. Choose a three- or five-course tea, depending on your appetite for sandwiches and cakes.

The Cathedral Church of
St. John the Divine *glorious peace* `9 B1`
1047 Amsterdam Avenue at 112th Street • 212 316 7490
≫ www.stjohndivine.org Open 7am–6pm daily (to 7pm Sun)

Begun in 1892 but still unfinished, St. John's will be one of the largest cathedrals in the world when completed. However, its size and huge vaulted ceilings do not intimidate; rather, the church envelops you, and encourages a sense of well-being. Smaller chapels are reserved for prayer during the day, and services are held in the nave on Sunday at 11am and 6pm, with the Cathedral Choir in full voice. The organ, however, was damaged in a fire in 2001, and is awaiting repair once sufficient funds are raised.

Stained glass, intricately carved altars, and fine stonework is found throughout the cathedral, alongside modern interpretations of religious icons. These include a three-paneled, white and gold-leaf altarpiece by the late graphic designer and artist Keith Haring. As you walk down the central aisle, look up at the stunning Great Rose Window, an extraordinary creation made from over 10,000 pieces of stained glass in patterns dominated by hues of vibrant royal blue and calming indigo.

Next to the cathedral is a **Children's Sculpture Garden**, which exhibits a selection of bronze animal sculptures created by school children aged between 5 and 18. After your visit, head to the **Hungarian Pastry Shop** across the street on Amsterdam Avenue. (1030). There you can have a snack, and mingle with the erudite Columbia University set.

Upper West Side, The Bronx & Brooklyn

Wave Hill *escape to an estate*
Independence Ave. at 249th St. • **718 549 3200** • Ⓜ Riverdale
» **www.wavehill.org** Open Spring & Summer: 9–5:30 Tue–Sun
(to 9 Wed); Fall & Winter: 9–4:30 Tue–Sun

It's hard to believe that you're still within NYC limits
(the Bronx no less) when you visit the well-situated
and beautifully laid out garden and cultural center of
Wave Hill. Part of Wave Hill's mission is to connect
people with nature; to this end it presents impressive
horticultural and art exhibits, and offers an array of
environmental workshops, and musical and literary
performances. Regular events include storytelling,
poetry readings, and chamber music and jazz
concerts. T'ai chi is taught in the grounds too.

The café at Wave Hill House is a great spot, partly
for the sustenance it offers, but mostly for the exceptional views. For another great view, walk along one
of the paths through the white-columned pergola
covered in flowering plants, and look downriver to the
suspension cables of the George Washington Bridge.

Prospect Park *the lungs of Brooklyn* `13 D5`
Wollman Rink: **718 287 6215**; Prospect Park Zoo: **718 399
7339**; Kensington Stables: **718 972 4588**
» **www.prospectpark.org**

Designed by the dynamic duo of landscape design
Olmstead and Vaux (the planners of Central Park),
Prospect Park is a lesser-known but equally enjoyable
green playground for New Yorkers – Brooklynites in
particular. It's a place to cycle, run, stroll, picnic, bird-
watch, and skate, and every season has something to
offer. Winter is the time for ice-skating at the
Wollman Rink; summer brings colorful local festivals
and concerts at the Bandshell. Prospect Park Zoo is a
year-round family favorite, and other perennial
attractions include horse-back riding on a track by
Kensington Stables, and birding at the beautiful
Audubon Center (www.prospectparkaudubon.org).
Locals often use the park drive, also known as the
loop, for bike riding, roller-blading, and running.
Check the website for a list of seasonal events.

Havens

Brooklyn Botanic Garden *paradise* 13 D4
1000 Washington Avenue • 718 623 7200
>> www.bbg.org Open 8–6 Tue–Fri, 10–6 Sat & Sun & hols;
closes at 4:30 Oct–Mar

Your olfactory and visual senses will be sharpened in
the wonderfully maintained BBG. A visit here may be
rewarded by bluebells in late spring or the scent of
roses in summer, while May's Cherry Blossom Festival
will transport you to the orchards of Asia *(see p16)*.

Jamaica Bay Wildlife
Refuge *an antidote to city life*
Crossbay Boulevard, Broad Channel • 718 318 4340
Ⓜ A train to Broad Channel Open 8:30–5 daily

This wild habitat in the huge bay south of JFK airport
is where New Yorkers go to escape the intensity of the
city and delight instead in tranquillity, bird-watching,
and walking. The train takes an hour from Manhattan,
allowing you to adjust to a different pace and prepare
for another world. The journey is interesting as well:
before the train reaches Broad Channel stop, it travels
along a stretch of track surrounded by marsh and water
on either side, which heightens a sense of remoteness.

   Walking to the refuge from the stop is straightforward. Go along Noel Road until you reach

Crossbay Boulevard and turn right; the refuge
entrance will be on your left after 10–15 minutes.
On the way, you'll pass waterfront houses on stilts
and wooden platforms.

   The visitor center has a small but informative
interpretive area explaining the history and features
of the refuge, including the abundant wildflowers.
Jamaica Bay is a regular rest stop for migrating birds,
and teems with airborne life as thousands of shore,
land, and water birds flock to its wetlands; over 320
species have been spotted. Benches along the main
path allow you to sit, observe, and listen to bird
songs. Particularly captivating, though, is the contrast
of freshwater ponds, marshes, and wildlife set
against the distant skyline of Manhattan.

Noguchi Sculpture
Museum *intimacy, solitude, design*
32–7 Vernon Boulevard, Long Island City (entrance on 33rd Rd)
718 204 7088 • Ⓜ N & W trains to Broadway
≫ www.noguchi.org Open all year 10–5 Wed–Fri, 11–6 Sat & Sun

Several million dollars-worth of renovation work
has been put into this museum, ensuring that it
continues to provide inspiration for visitors. It has an
intimacy that's not often found in art spaces; the
renovations have not contributed to a "blockbuster
experience" in the manner of the recent downtown
museum revamps, but rather have attempted to
refine the concrete and wood space.

This museum is a tribute to the Japanese-American
sculptor, landscaper, and set designer Isamu Noguchi,
who established a studio in this Queens neighborhood in 1961. Noguchi created beautiful pieces made
of materials such as wood, marble, basalt, and metal,
and his sculptures are in a multitude of shapes and
textures. The museum is designed to eliminate

distractions while you contemplate the work, allowing
the art of Noguchi to be the sole focus of attention.
The space – its aesthetic a refined, pared-back
Modernism – contains several galleries; some are
exposed to the elements, others are fully enclosed.
There is also a garden, with a majestic, fully grown
Katsura tree and a subtle fountain sculpture. At its
center is what appears to be a bottomless pool.

The park is a place to reflect, to relax, and to
appreciate art without having to fight a crowd or have
museum attendants hovering over your shoulder.
There's an on-site café for light snacks, and a store
that stocks a wide range of design books and
Noguchi's trademark rice-paper lamps.

While in the Long Island City area, it's also
worth dropping by the **Socrates Sculpture Park**
(www.socratessculpturepark.org), a little further
north on Vernon Boulevard. On the bank of the East
River, the park exhibits temporary installations of
sculpture by international contemporary artists.

hotels

The independent hotel scene is stronger in New York than in any other major city. More than half the hotels are not affiliated to a national or international chain, which means that they are particularly good at providing individuality, character, and style. Rooms don't come cheap, but there are deals to be had with a little planning. Check hotel and reservation agency websites to get the best deals.

HOTELS

Getting a room in NYC is possibly the costliest part of your trip because real estate for tourist and local alike is *expensive*. With good timing and research on hotel and agency websites superb deals can still be had. But the best advice for getting good value regardless of when you book is to be bold and stay outside of Manhattan's midtown area – you'll have a good incentive to walk and use the subway more often (the best ways of exploring New York).

Rachel F. Freeman

Romantic Hideaways

Cozy up with a partner in front of your own fireplace at **1871 House** *(see p194)*, or if you want a fabulous view, book the top-floor room at the **Bed & Breakfast on the Park** *(see p197)* – there you can look out on the Manhattan skyline from a roomy four-poster bed. **Soho House** *(see p190)* offers a rooftop pool and the fun of their private "playrooms."

Gastronomic Hotels

Despite the thrill of finding an undiscovered eatery, it's also good to know that you can depend on quality cooking at your hotel. **Hotel Wales** *(see p196)* offers wholesome breakfasts at Sarabeth's Kitchen, **The Mark** *(see p195)* provides refined dining, and **60 Thompson** *(see p188)* is home to one of the trendiest and tastiest Thai kitchens, Kittichai.

Live Like a Local

Nothing beats authentic and personable hospitality, and the best B&Bs give you a taste of what it's like to "go native." The **Harlem Flophouse** *(see p196)* revels in a jazzy vibe; the **Union St B&B** *(see p197)* provides a family feel; **Bevy's SoHo Loft** *(see p188)* offers sanctuary in SoHo; while **Akwaaba Mansion** *(see p197)* has found a tranquil spot in Brooklyn.

choice stays

Best of the Bargains

Clean, comfortable, and conveniently located, these establishments offer superb deals. At **Chelsea Lodge** *(see p191)* you'll have to share toilets, but the hotel is well decorated and appointed; **Chelsea Inn** *(see p191)* has handy kitchenettes; and **Abingdon Guest House** *(see p189)* provides individually decorated rooms in the West Village.

Style Statements

For chic furnishings and an emphasis on design, you can't go wrong with the Ian Schrager/Philippe Starck partnership that created the **Hudson Hotel** *(see p193)*. **Morgans** *(see p193)*, one of NYC's original boutique hotels, hangs original Mapplethorpe prints in the rooms, and the **Mercer Hotel** *(see p188)* provides a cool, minimalist aesthetic.

Great Location

Some of the best-located hotels are in areas that have a distinct neighborhood feel, and such is the case with the **Washington Square Hotel** *(see p189)* in Greenwich Village. The **W Union Square** *(see p191)* is within a short walk of Chelsea and the East and West Villages, while the **Four Seasons** *(see p194)* is handy for Upper East Side shopping sorties.

Bevy's SoHo Loft *three great rooms* `3 D5`

70 Mercer Street (between Spring & Broome Sts)
212 431 8214
>> www.sohobevy.com

Bevy – known to many as the "SoHo Mom" – is a real character, who relishes conversation with her guests. Her loft is a funky, renovated industrial space filled with paintings and colorful fabrics. There are just three rooms, but they're spacious. Great location. **Cheap**

SoHo Grand Hotel *pet-friendly place* `3 D5`

310 Broadway (between Grand & Canal Sts)
800 965 3000
>> www.sohogrand.com

Pets are made welcome here – indeed, if you haven't brought your own, you'll be offered a fish as a room mate. A selection of CDs is also provided; you can buy them and the fish. As for the 367 rooms: some are small, but all the beds are big and comfy. **Moderate**

Mercer Hotel *minimalist finesse* `3 D4`

147 Mercer Street (at Prince St.) • 212 966 6060
>> www.mercerhotel.com

In a solid 1890 building near the Village, the Mercer focuses on style and service. The 62 rooms are light and minimally furnished, and the bathrooms come with large soaking tubs and Swedish Face Stockholm cosmetics. The Mercer Kitchen restaurant is worth a visit, and is a fine spot for celebrity spotting. **Expensive**

60 Thompson *SoHo taste* `3 C5`

60 Thompson Street (between Spring & Broome Sts)
877 431 0400
>> www.60thompson.com

There are 100 rooms and suites, all with music and DVD systems. The setting is modern, with a sleek interior design, plush bedding, and marble bathrooms. Check out the high-backed chairs, designed for the hotel by Thomas O'Brien of Aero Studios. **Expensive**

Tribeca Grand Hotel *hip & stylish* `3 C5`
2 Avenue of the Americas (at Canal St.) • 800 965 3000
>> www.tribecagrand.com

Built in 2000, this hotel attracts a cool clientele. All rooms lead off from the Church Lounge, the hub of its atrium-style layout. The guest rooms match simple, modern design with top technology in the form of great sound systems and high-speed Internet access. The hotel offers the same deal on fish and CDs as its older sister, the SoHo Grand *(see opposite)*. **Expensive**

Washington Square Hotel *location, location* `3 C3` ✓
03 Waverly Place (at Macdougal St.) • 800 222 0418
>> www.wshotel.com

This budget option is in a prime Village location, close to many attractions by foot or subway. The rooms are a little floral and frilly, but the lobby has a smart, Art Deco style. Complimentary continental breakfast makes this even better value for downtown. **Cheap**

Abingdon Guest House *Village comfort* `3 B2` ✓
13 8th Ave. (bet. W. 12th & Jane Sts) • 212 243 5384
>> www.abingdonguesthouse.com

Two landmark townhouses in West Village have been converted into a guest house with nine rooms. Each room has its own style, as suggested by the names – "Martinique," "Ambassador," and so on. Prices vary according to size and decor. Light breakfasts and lunches are served at its Brewbar café. **Cheap**

Old Establishments

The **Carlyle** on Madison Avenue has been appreciated since the 1930s for its understated elegance, superb service, and striking Art Deco design. The hotel's Café Carlyle is popular with a well-heeled Upper East Side crowd. No stranger to scandal and creativity, the **Hotel Chelsea** has a thousand stories to tell. Each room and apartment is different, and much of the building is occupied by long-stay residents. A great slice of bohemia, the Chelsea has welcomed writers and musicians from Mark Twain and Tennessee Williams to Bob Dylan and Sid Vicious. At the foot of Central Park, the **Plaza Hotel** was a New York institution. Sadly it has recently been sold and is being converted into apartments. For individual hotel details, *see p233.*

Soho House

3 A2

New York *chic hotel in the Meatpacking District*
29–35 9th Avenue (at W. 13th St.) • 212 627 9800
» www.sohohouse.com

Blink and you'll miss the entrance to Soho House –
a level of discretion you'd expect of a hotel that
doubles as a private members' club. Staying at the
hotel gives you access to the club facilities, which
include a fitness room, private screening room,
restaurant and bar, drawing room and library, a
games room with pool table and pinball, and an
elegantly comfortable club room. The Cowshed Spa
offers a variety of healthy treatments and a soothing
environment. The "Cowshed" products are made by
hand in the UK (home of the original London Soho
House). The prime facility, however, is the rooftop

pool. Although not a place for serious laps, the pool
is great for a quick dip, and the deck around it has
chaise longues, umbrellas, tables, chairs, and a full
bar with light snacks. The roof area is open year
round, with a heated marquee in winter.

The 24 comfortable guest rooms are classified
according to size and labeled (in ascending order)
playpen, playroom, playhouse, and playground.
Mini-bars are stocked with all sorts of temptations,
including Ben & Jerry's ice cream in the freezer, and
chilled Martini glasses. The decor is an eclectic mix,
with touches of luxury such as freestanding, egg-
shaped bathtubs. Bedrooms have state-of-the-art
gadgets, such as surround-sound entertainment
systems, and there is wireless Internet access
throughout the whole building. **Expensive**

Maritime Hotel *nautical swank* `3 A1`

363 West 16th Street (at 9th Ave.) • 212 242 4300
>> www.themaritimehotel.com

The rooms here have a maritime theme, complete
with porthole windows and an appealing blue-and-
white color scheme for the bedding. Rates are
reasonable, and the location is great for Chelsea and
the Meatpacking District. There's 24-hour room
service, a roof terrace, and a sushi bar. **Moderate**

Chelsea Lodge *fresh, clean & friendly* `3 B1`

318 W. 20th St. (between 8th & 9th Aves) • 800 373 1116
>> www.chelsealodge.com

Toilets are shared at this low-priced lodge, but each
of the 22 refurbished rooms has wooden floors and
high ceilings, and is well appointed, with a shower
stall, sink, TV, and double bed. You also have the
option to pay extra for a suite with more amenities.
The place is bright and on a quiet side street. **Cheap**

Chelsea Inn *affordable charm* `3 C1`

46 West 17th St. (bet. 5th & 6th Aves) • 800 640 6469
>> www.chelseainn.com

Ask for a quiet room at the back of this renovated
19th-century townhouse in a great downtown
location. The budget-priced rooms all have
kitchenettes and TVs, and the shared bathrooms are
decorated with charming, colorful painted murals.
Continental breakfast is included in the price. **Cheap**

W New York, Union Square *stylish* `3 D1`

201 Park Avenue South (at E. 17th St.) • 212 253 9119
>> www.whotels.com

The signature style of the "W" hotel chain involves
subdued lighting and touches of purple in an otherwise minimalist white interior. Rooms are sleek, with
comfy feather beds, and the service is impeccable.
The dramatic lobby has a soaring staircase and
areas of sand, grass, and marble. **Moderate**

>> *The price categories used are based on a hotel's rack rate, but discount deals are frequently available*

Hotels

Affinia Shelburne *old glamor*

6 F3

303 Lexington Avenue (at 37th Street) • 212 689 5200
» www.affinia.com

A hotel since the 1920s, the Shelburne maintains the elegant simplicity of a bygone era. In summer the Rooftop Garden offers views of midtown's skyline, including the Empire State and Chrysler buildings. The stylish Rare Bar & Grill on the ground floor is famous for its gourmet hamburgers. **Moderate**

Royalton *theatrical style*

6 E2

44 West 44th Street (between 5th & 6th Aves) • 800 606 6090
» www.royaltonhotel.com

In the heart of the Theater District, this Ian Schrager hotel *(see also Morgans, opposite)* has a stunning lobby that's almost like a runway. Sit on the chairs at the side and socialize, or slip into the Round Bar for cocktails and people-watching. For the best views, try to get a deal on a deluxe room or suite. **Moderate**

St. Regis *Beaux Arts beauty*

8 E5

2 East 55th Street (at 5th Ave.) • 800 625 5144
» www.stregis.com

Built in 1904 by John Jacob Astor IV, this luxurious hotel is meant to be a home away from home. The rooms even have doorbells. Original details are mixed with modern amenities, including flat-screen TVs in the bathrooms and high-speed Internet access. The hallways are wonderfully airy and bright. **Expensive**

The Peninsula *discriminating modernity*

8 E5

700 5th Avenue (at 55th St.) • 800 262 9467
» www.peninsula.com

The 1905 landmark building and deluxe, spacious rooms are as much a draw here as the ultra-modern facilities, which include Internet connections and "silent fax machines" in all the boldly colored rooms. Remote controls in the bathrooms can be used to operate speaker phones, TVs, or radios. **Expensive**

Morgans *understated sophistication* `6 E3`

237 Madison Avenue (at E. 37th St.) • 800 606 6090
\>\> www.ianschragerhotels.com

The concept of the "boutique hotel" originated at Morgans. Defined not by size (as with the grand hotels of the past) but by a unique sense of style and coolness, the hotel was an instant hit with fashion-conscious travelers. Morgans, designed in the late 1980s, recreates the ambience of an apartment house. The lobby is functional, with a small side office for the helpful and knowledgeable concierge. Decorative themes include the black-and-white checkerboard motif, reminiscent of old New York cabs, seen subtly in the elevator, in the pattern of the hallway carpets, and in the sleek stainless steel and glass bathrooms (which are also adorned with fresh flowers).

Renowned designer Andrée Putman planned the interiors, mixing materials such as raw silk, corduroy, maplewood, and formica. All rooms have grey, white, and beige color schemes, and feature banquettes and original Robert Mapplethorpe photographs – which have had to be bolted to the wall. Communal spaces include the "living room," with free computer access, and a welcoming area conducive to playing scrabble, reading, or writing.

The famed restaurant Asia de Cuba is where breakfast is served (included in the price), and Morgans Bar has a lively night scene and superb cocktails. Owner Ian Schrager has replicated his hotel philosophy with other New York establishments, including the Hudson (*below*) and the Royalton (*opposite*). **Moderate**

Hudson *cosmopolitan, affordable & urbane* `7 C4`

356 W. 58th St. (bet. 8th & 9th Aves) • 212 554 6000
\>\> www.hudsonhotel.com

One thousand rooms are priced at various scales so that the surfer dude can mix with the film producer in the swanky Hudson Bar. Note that the rooms tend to be very small – the concept at this Ian Schrager hotel is that you'll spend most of your time in the beautiful and funky communal spaces. **Moderate**

Hotels

Four Seasons *contemporary panache* 8 E5

57 East 57th Street (between Park & Madison Aves)
212 758 5700
>> www.fourseasons.com

There's nothing understated about the Four Seasons
– just look at the immense lobby with its cathedral-
like ceiling, marble floors, and floral arrangements as
large as refrigerators. The hotel was built with the
savvy customer in mind; even the most modest rooms
have generous dimensions – 500 sq ft (47 sq m) rival
the floorspace of many New York studio apartments.
Rooms on the top floors offer great city views,
including the sweep of Central Park. The windows
open to let in fresh air, and curtains can be opened
from the bed with a switch. All bathrooms have
Bulgari products, a glass-enclosed shower, and a
deep, fast-filling tub. Other gadgets include a flat
screen TV in the bathroom, and a top-quality CD
player/radio. The on-site spa and fitness center offer
a "sensory escape," perfect for jetlag. **Expensive**

1871 House *country-style feel* 8 F4

130 East 62nd St. (between Park & Lexington Aves)
212 756 8823
>> www.1871house.com

This beautifully renovated brownstone building is
close to Central Park and an upscale shopping zone,
but the quiet, leafy street makes you forget you're in
the city at all. There's no common area for guests,
but the spacious, high-ceilinged rooms, suites, and
studios are ideal for lounging, and most have working
fireplaces – quite a treat for a New York property.
The keepers even provide duraflame logs to burn.

So long as you don't require 24-hour room service,
these cozy, relaxing accommodations are a good
option. The whole place is furnished with antiques
and the decor is warm and homey. If you are
traveling in a group of four or more, reserve the Great
Room and Cottage combination; both have access to
a lovely garden. Some rooms have kitchenettes.
A four-night minimum is usually expected. **Cheap**

194 ✓ *Good value* >> www.realcity.dk.com

The Lowell *intimate retreat* `8 F4`

8 East 63rd Street (between Madison & Park Aves)
212 838 1400
» www.lowellhotel.com

With 21 rooms and 47 suites, The Lowell focuses more
on comfort than numbers. High-profile guests stay
here to escape the paparazzi. The suites offer options
such as wood-burning fireplaces, terraces, and
kitchenettes. There's a fitness room too. **Expensive**

Hotel Surrey *a home from home* `8 E1`

20 East 76th Street (at Madison) • 212 288 3700
» www.affinia.com

Situated on Madison Avenue, one of NY's premier
shopping streets, Hotel Surrey seeks to accommodate
both long- and short-stay guests, with pet- and family-
friendly suites that feature either a kitchen or
kitchenette and dining table. A nice touch is the menu
from which guests choose their pillows. **Moderate**

The Pierre *New York landmark* `8 E4`

5th Avenue (at 61st St.) • 212 838 8000
» www.fourseasons.com

A top hotel since 1930, The Pierre is a bastion of
gentility, and is the perfect place to return to after a
shopping spree at neighboring Bergdorf's. Attentive
staff perform to a backdrop of chandeliers and Art
Deco details. The **Rotunda** *(see p180)* is on hand for
afternoon tea; Café Pierre offers full meals. **Expensive**

The Mark *Upper East Side elegance* `8 E1`

25 East 77th Street (between Madison & 5th Aves)
212 744 4300
» www.themarkhotel.com

An air of sophistication permeates the generously
sized rooms of this hotel, part of the Mandarin group.
Inspiration for the Neoclassical interior is said to have
come from the work of 19th-century English architect
Sir John Soane. Service is professional. **Expensive**

Hotel Wales *classic & fresh*   `10 E4`

1295 Madison Avenue (at 92nd St.) • 866 925 3746
>> www.waleshotel.com

This Upper East Side boutique hotel has an intimate
feel. Aveda products and fresh flowers feature in the
comfortable rooms, and free coffee is available and
night. The roof deck is a great place from which to watch
the buzzing city, and adjacent Sarabeth's Kitchen
whips up fantastic omelets and soups. **Moderate**

Harlem Flophouse *jazz-related fun*   `11 D4`

242 W. 123rd St. (bet. 7th & 8th Aves) • 212 662 0678
>> www.harlemflophouse.com

A small brass plaque is the only thing that sets the
Flophouse apart from the other residences on this
quiet, tree-lined brownstone block. The first thing you'll
notice upon entering is the sound of jazz, drifting softly
from the mantelpiece radio in the charming front room.
It has been a B&B since 2000, and the owner has
worked on various parts of the house to restore original
details, including patterned tin ceilings, wooden
moldings, and a downstairs dining room for parties.

A touch of faded glory and fresh renovation add to
the appeal and charm of the four guest rooms. Each
has a sink, but bathrooms are shared – a claw-foot
tub in one is nicely set right under a sky light. All
beds are firm, with good mattresses, and the rooms
are named after notable people with either jazz or
Harlem connections – often both. There are no TVs,
but alarm clocks are provided. There's a smoking room
in the basement, and guests have access to a garden
for summer barbecues, relaxation, and reflection.
Hearty and delicious breakfasts of eggs, grits,
sausage, and yogurt are available at an extra charge.

The Flop House is conveniently located for subway
trains and buses (the M60 can bring you right here
from LaGuardia airport), and is close to the Apollo
Theater *(see p134)*, Lenox Lounge *(see p135)*, and the
Studio Museum in Harlem *(see p113)*. The Flophouse
also hosts occasional art exhibitions in the common
area on the main floor. **Cheap**

Akwaaba Mansion *African tranquility*

347 MacDonough St. • Ⓜ Last car of A train to Utica Ave, then walk 4 blocks along Stuyvesant Ave. • 718 455 5958
>> www.akwaaba.com

An Italianate villa tucked away on a tree-lined street in historic Stuyvesant Heights. African motifs and antiques create a unique style. Some rooms include a Jacuzzi. Spend a lazy afternoon in the garden or sipping lemonade on the sun porch. **Cheap**

Union St B&B *bohemian charm* `13 B4`

405 Union St. (at Hoyt), Brooklyn • 718 852 8406
>> www.unionstbrooklynbandb.com

Floral wallpaper, wooden floors, and music boxes in each of the six rooms create a charming, warm, and homey atmosphere. The continental-style breakfast includes good strong coffee. The owners provide a well-stocked shelf of books on local history for your perusal. **Cheap**

Bed & Breakfast on the Park `13 C5`

113 Prospect Park West (between 6th & 7th Sts)
718 499 6115
>> www.bbnyc.com

The fixtures here have been lovingly restored to maintain an ambience of Victorian gentility. Reserve the Lady Liberty Room for a four-poster bed, great city views, and exclusive access to the roof garden. Breakfast includes home-made pastries. **Moderate**

Accommodations Agencies

Hotel rates can be rather mysterious: the officially quoted "rack rate" may say one thing, but certain packages, the time of year, and discounts found on the web can give a completely different price. If you get the timing right, you can slice a lot of money off your room price. At weekends in off-peak seasons, for example, hotels often offer rooms at discounted rates. Accommodations agencies with websites to try include: **www.simply-newyork.com**, **www.a1-discount-hotels.com**, and **www.hotels.com**.

Also, if you're interested in longer stays – a duration of seven days or more – and are thinking about subletting an apartment, try **www.subletinthecity.com**, **www.citysublets.com**, and **www.newyorkhabitat.com**.

New York Street Finder

Almost every listing in this guide includes a (boxed) page and grid reference to the maps in this section. The few entries that fall outside the area covered by these maps give transport details instead. Maps 1 to 12 cover the whole of Manhattam, while Brooklyn is shown on Map 13. An index of the streets names follows on *pages 213–15*.

The Outer Boroughs

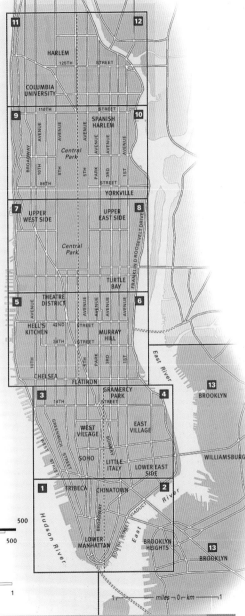

Key to Street Finder

Sight/public building		⊗	Post office
M	Subway station	P	Railway line
R	Railway station	===	Pedestrian street
Ferry terminal			Motorway
Bus terminal			Expressway
Heliport			
Aerial tramway			
❶	Tourist information office		
✚	Hospital with casualty unit		
⊙	Police station		
✚	Church		
✡	Synagogue		

Scale of maps 1–12

0 meters   500

0 yards   500

Scale of map 13

0 kilometers   1

0 miles   1

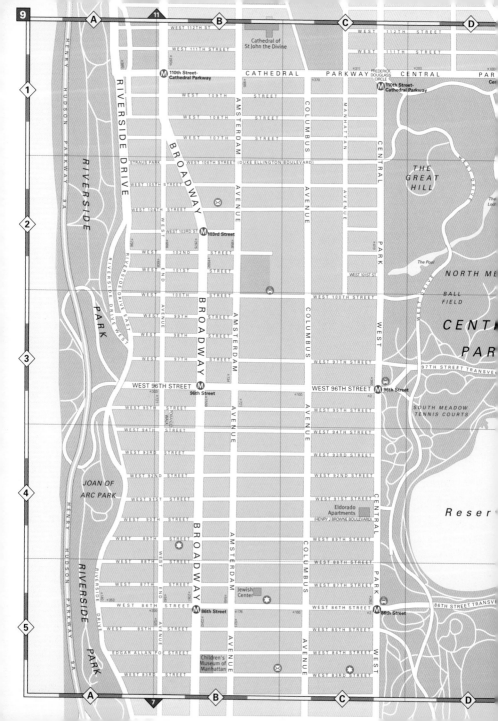

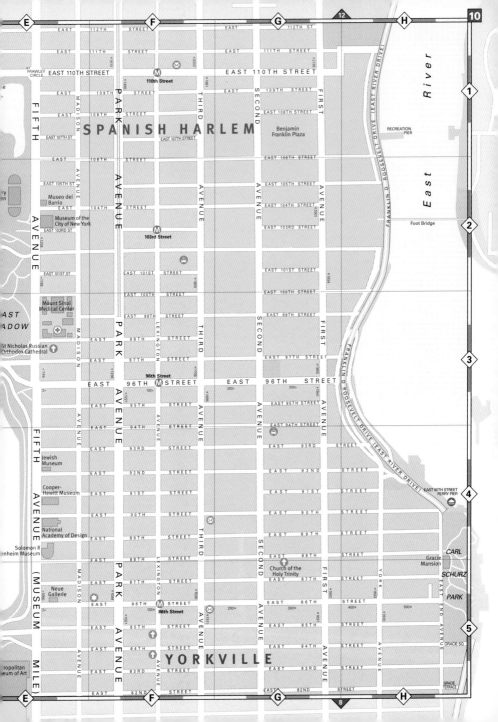

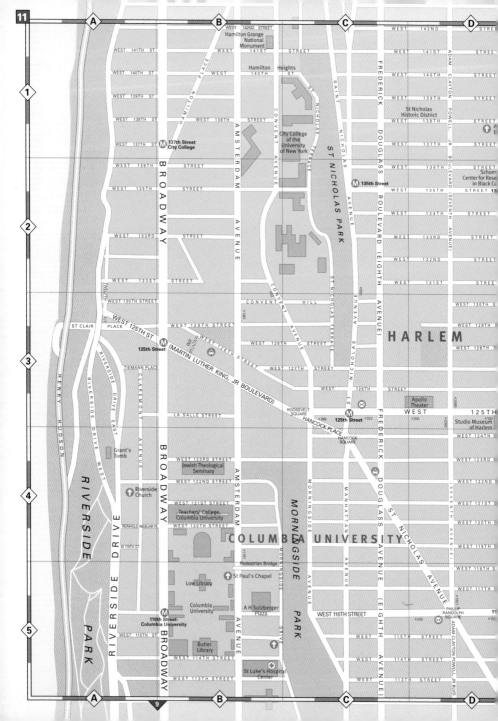

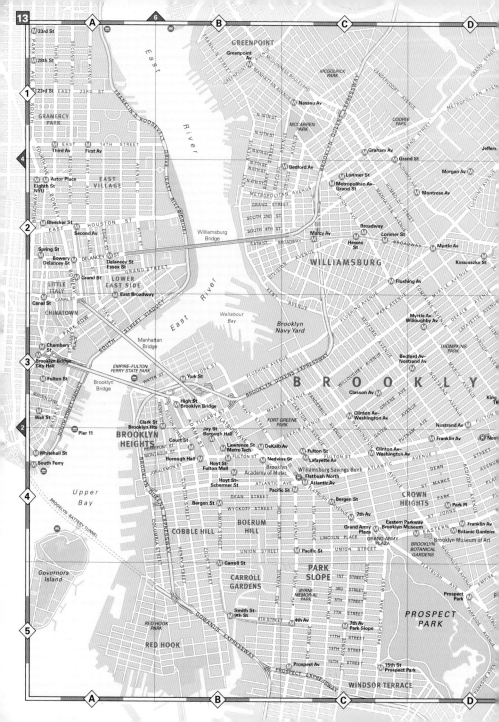

Street Finder Index

Street Finder Index

Index by Area

Downtown

Restaurants

Chinatown

Golden Unicorn (p28) $
18 East Broadway (Map 2 F1)
Chinese

Peking Duck House (p29) $$
28 Mott Street (Map 2 E1)
Chinese

HSF (p166) $$
46 Bowery (Map 2 E1)
Chinese

**Chinatown Ice Cream
Factory** (p166) $
65 Bayard Street (Map 2 E1)
Ice Cream Parlor

Great NY Noodle Town (p166) $
28½ Bowery at Bayard Street
(Map 2 E1)
Chinese

East Village

Angelica Kitchen (p36) $
300 East 12th St (Map 4 E2)
Vegetarian

Bao (p33) $
111 Avenue C (Map 4 G3)
Vietnamese

Crif Dogs (p40) $
113 St. Mark's Place (Map 4 F3)
American

DT—UT (p168) $
41 Avenue B (Map 4 G2)
Café

The Elephant (p31) $$
58 East 1st Street
(Map 4 F4)
French/Thai

Freemans (p34) $
Freeman Alley (Map 4 E4)
American

Mermaid Inn (p35) $$
96 2nd Avenue (Map 4 E3)
Seafood

Mud Spot (p35) $
307 East 9th Street (Map 4 E2)
www.themudtruck.com
Café

Paul's Palace (p35) $
131 2nd Avenue (Map 4 E3)
American

Pommes Frites (p40) $
123 2nd Avenue (Map 4 E3)
Belgian

Pylos (p34) $$
128 East 7th Street (Map 4 F3)
Greek

Rue B (p168) $
188 Avenue B (Map 4 G2)
Café

Sobaya (p36) $
229 East 9th St. (Map 4 E2)
Japanese

Le Souk (p33) $$
47 Avenue B (Map 4 G3)
North African

Le Tableau (p33) $$
511 East 5th Street (Map 4 F3)
French

Yaffa Cafe (p34) $
97 St. Mark's Place (Map 4 F3)
Middle Eastern

Lower East Side

Alias (p32) $$
76 Clinton Street (Map 4 G4)
American

Bereket (p31) $
187 East Houston St (Map 4 F4)
Turkish

Cube 63 (p32) $$
63 Clinton Street (Map 4 G4)
Japanese

Fried Dumpling (p40) $
99 Allen Street (Map 4 F4)
Chinese

'inoteca (p32) $$
98 Rivington Street (Map 4 F4)
Italian

WD-50 (p32) $$$
50 Clinton Street (Map 4 G4)
American

Lower Manhattan

Amish Fine Food Market (p166) $
17 Battery Place (Map 1 D5)
Deli

Cosi Downtown (p166) $
55 Broad Street (Map 1 D4)
Deli/Sandwich Shop

Pret a Manger (p166) $
60 Broad Street (Map 1 D4)
Deli/Sandwich Shop

Meatpacking District

Bonsignour (p76) $
35 Jane Street (Map 3 B2)
Bakery

Florent (pp42 & 167) $$
69 Gansevoort Street (Map 3 A2)
American/European

Pastis (p167) $$
9 Ninth Avenue (Map 3 A2)
French

Nolita

Cafe Gitane (p31) $
242 Mott Street (Map 4 E4)
North African

Cafe Habana (p31) $
17 Prince St (Map 4 E4)
Cuban/Mexican

SoHo

Balthazar (p29) $$
80 Spring Street (Map 3 D5)
French

Blue Ribbon Sushi (p37) $$$
119 Sullivan Street (Map 3 C4)
Japanese

Dean & DeLuca (p69) $
560 Broadway (Map 3 D4)
Bakery/Deli

L'Ecole (p30) $$
462 Broadway (Map 3 D5)
French

Mercer Kitchen (p28) $$
99 Prince Street (Map 3 D5)
French/American

The Spotted Pig (p37) $
314 West 11th St. (Map 3 C2)
British

Tribeca

66 (p28) $$$
241 Church Street (Map 1 D1)
Chinese

Acappella (p28) $$$
1 Hudson Street (Map 1 C2)
Italian

Chanterelle (p42) $$$
2 Harrison Street (Map 1 C1)
www.chanterellenyc.com
French

Montrachet (p28) $$$
239 West Broadway (Map 1 D1)
European

Nobu (p42) $$$
105 Hudson Street (Map 1 C1)
212 219 0500, www.myriad
restaurantgroup.com
Japanese

West Village

Babbo (p38) $$$
110 Waverly Place (Map 3 C3)
Northern Italian

BB Sandwich Bar (p40) $
120 West 3rd Street (Map 3 C3)
Deli

**Blue Ribbon
Bakery** (p37) $$$
33 Downing Street (Map 3 C4)
European

Cones (p40) $
272 Bleecker St. (Map 3 C3)
Ice Cream Parlor

Jane (p30) $$
100 W. Houston St. (Map 3 D4)
American

Joe (p35) $
141 Waverly Place
212 924 6750 (Map 3 C3)
Café

**John's of
Bleecker Street** (p39) $$
278 Bleecker Street (Map 3 C3)
Pizzeria

Magnolia Bakery (p75) $
401 Bleeker Street (Map 3 B3)
Downtown/West Village

Mamoun's (p40) $
119 MacDougal St. (Map 3 C3)
Middle Eastern

Mary's Fish Camp (p41) $$
64 Charles Street (Map 3 B3)
Seafood

Mud Truck (p35) $
14th Street and Broadway
(Map 3 D2)
www.themudtruck.com
Café

NY Dosas (p41) $
West 4th Street & Sullivan
Street (Map 3 C3)
Vegetarian

Otto Enoteca & Pizzeria $
(p36)
1 5th Avenue (Map 3 D3)
Italian

La Palapa Rockola (p38) $$
359 6th Avenue (Map 3 C3)
Mexican

Pepe Rosso's (p40)
149 Sullivan Street (Map 3 C4)
Italian

Sumile (p42) $$$
154 West 13th Street
(Map 3 C2)
Japanese

Tartine (p42) $
253 West 11th Street
(Map 3 B2)
French

Tea & Sympathy (p35) $
108 Greenwich Avenue
(Map 3 C2)
British

Tomoe Sushi (p37) $$
172 Thompson Street
(Map 3 C4)
Japanese

Wallsé (p41) $$$
344 West 11th Street
(Map 3 A3)
Austrian

Shopping

East Village

Kiehl's (p81)
109 3rd Avenue (Map 4 E2)
Health & Beauty

St. Mark's Sounds (p82)
16 St. Mark's Place (Map 4 E3)
Music

The Strand (p81)
828 Broadway (Map 3 D2)
Books

Little Italy

The Apartment (p70)
101 Crosby Street (Map 3 D4)
Interiors

Calypso (p71)
280 Mott Street (Map 4 E4)
Fashion

Hable Construction (p68)
230 Elizabeth St. (Map 4 E4)
Interiors

INA (p71)
21 Prince Street (Map 4 E4)
Fashion

Malia Mills (p65)
199 Mulberry St. (Map 4 E5)
Fashion

Mayle (p72)
242 Elizabeth St. (Map 4 E4)
Fashion

Rescue Beauty Lounge (p70)
21 Cleveland Place (Map 4 E5)
Health & Beauty

Lower East Side

ALife Rivington Club (p73)
158 Rivington St. (Map 4 F4)
Shoes & Accessories

Shop (p74)
105 Stanton Street (Map 4 F4)
Fashion

Teany (p74)
90 Rivington St. (Map 4 F4)
Food

TG-170 (p73)
170 Ludlow St. (Map 4 F4)
Fashion

Lower Manhattan

Century 21 (p64)
22 Cortlandt Street
(Map 1 D3)
Fashion

Green Market (p166)
Farmer's market at Bowling
Green Park (Map 1 D4)
Food Market

Amish Market Downtown
(p166)
17 Battery Place (Map 1 D4)
Food Market

Meatpacking District

Alexander McQueen (p167)
417 West 14th St. (Map 3 A2)
Fashion

Bonsignour (p76)
35 Jane Street (Map 3 B2)
Food

Jeffrey (pp78 & 167)
449 West 14th St. (Map 3 A2)
Department Store

MXYPLYZYK (p77)
125 Greenwich Ave (Map 3 B2)
Interiors

Stella McCartney (p77)
429 West 14th Street (Map 3 A2)
Fashion

Vitra (p167)
29 9th Avenue (Map 3 A2)
Interiors

Nolita

Bond 07 by Selima (p72)
7 Bond Street (Map 3 D3)
Shoes & Accessories

LAFCO (p73)
285 Lafayette St. (Map 4 E4)
Health & Beauty

Rafe (p72)
1 Bleecker Street (Map 4 E4)
Shoes & Accessories

SoHo

A.P.C. (p66)
131 Mercer Street (Map 3 D4)
Fashion

Barney's Co-Op (p66)
116 Wooster Street (Map 3 D4)
Fashion

Clio (p67)
92 Thompson Street
(Map 3 C4)
Interiors

Le Corset by Selima (p66)
80 Thompson Street
(Map 3 C5)
Lingerie

Costume National (p67)
108 Wooster Street
(Map 3 D4)
Fashion

Dean & DeLuca (p69)
560 Broadway
(Map 3 D4)
Food

Hotel Venus by Patricia Field
(p64)
382 West Broadway
(Map 3 D5)
Fashion

Kate Spade Travel (p64)
59 Thompson Street
(Map 3 C5)
Shoes & Accessories

Kate's Paperie (p70)
561 Broadway
(Map 3 D4)
Stationery

Kirna Zabete (p67)
96 Greene St. (Map 3 D4)
Fashion

Miu Miu (p63)
100 Prince St. (Map 3 D4)
Fashion

Moss (p68)
146 Greene St. (Map 3 D4)
Interiors

Pearl River Mart (p65)
477 Broadway (Map 3 D5)
Department Store

Prada (p68)
575 Broadway (Map 3 D4)
Fashion

SCO (p71)
584 Broadway (Map 3 D4)
Health and Beauty

Scoop (p69)
532 Broadway (Map 3 D4)
Fashion

West Village

Fat Beats (p75)
406 6th Avenue (Map 3 C2)
Music

Flight 001 (p76)
96 Greenwich Ave.
(Map 3 B2)
Shoes & Accessories

Fresh (p75)
388 Bleecker Street
(Map 3 B3)
Health & Beauty

Index by Area

Downtown

Shopping *continued*

Magnolia Bakery (p75)
401 Bleecker St. (Map 3 B3)
Food

Marc by Marc Jacobs (p76)
403–5 Bleecker St. (Map 3 B4)
Fashion

Marc Jacobs (p68)
163 Mercer Street (Map 3 B4)
Fashion

Subterranean Records (p155)
5 Cornelia Street (Map 3 C3)
Music

Art & Architecture

Chinatown

Leo Koenig (p102)
249 Centre Street (Map 2 E2)
212 334 9255
Art Gallery

Mahayana Buddhist Temple (p166)
133 Canal Street (Map 2 E1)
Temple

Museum of Chinese in the Americas (p166)
70 Mulberry Street, 2nd Floor (Map 2 E1)
Museum

Lower Manhattan

Federal Hall (p166)
26 Wall Street (Map 1 D4)
Historic Building

Ground Zero (p101)
(Map 1 C3)
Modern Architecture

Skyscraper Museum (p101)
39 Battery Place (Map 1 D5)
Museum

St. Paul's Chapel (p100)
209 Broadway between Fulton & Vesey streets (Map 1 D3)
Church

Trinity Church (p166)
Broadway at Wall Street (Map 1 D4)
Church

U.S. Custom House (p100)
1 Bowling Green (Map 1 D5)
Historic Building

Woolworth Building (p102)
233 Broadway at Barclay Street (Map 1 D2)
Historic Building

Lower East Side

Lower East Side Tenement Museum (p103)
90 Orchard Street (Map 4 F5)
Museum

Meatpacking District

Karkula Gallery (p167)
68 Gansevoort St. (Map 3 A2)
Interiors

Nolita

Merchant's House Museum (p103)
29 East 4th Street (Map 4 E3)
Museum

SoHo

Broken Kilometer (p102)
393 West Broadway (Map 3 D5)
Installation

Deitch Projects (p102)
18 Wooster Street (Map 3 D5)
Art Gallery

Earth Room (p102)
141 Wooster Street (Map 3 D4)
Installation

West Village

Forbes Magazine Gallery (p104)
60 5th Avenue at West 12th Street (Map 3 D2)
Art Gallery

Jefferson Market Courthouse (p104)
425 6th Avenue (Map 3 C2)
Historic Building

Performance

East Village

Bowery Poetry Club (p124)
308 Bowery (Map 4 E4)
Music/Poetry Venue

Landmark's Sunshine Theater (p124)
143 East Houston Street (Map 4 E4)
Film Theater

Lit (p125)
93 2nd Ave. (Map 4 E3)
Music Venue

Nuyorican Poet's Cafe (p125)
236 East 3rd Street (Map 4 G3)
Poetry

P.S.122 (p126)
150 1st Avenue (Map 4 F2)
Combined Arts Center

Lower East Side

Arlene's Grocery (p123)
95 Stanton Street (Map 4 F4)
Music Venue

Bowery Ballroom (p123)
6 Delancey Street (Map 4 E5)
Music Venue

Mercury Lounge (p122)
217 East Houston Street (Map 4 F4)
Music Venue

Tonic (p123)
107 Norfolk Street (Map 4 G4)
Music Venue

Nolita

The Public Theater (p125)
425 Lafayette Street (Map 4 E3)
Theater

SoHo

Film Forum (p120)
209 West Houston Street (Map 3 C4)
Film Theater

S.O.B's (p120)
204 Varick Street (Map 3 C4)
Music Venue

Tribeca

Knitting Factory (p120)
74 Leonard Street (Map 1 D1)
Music Venue

Union Square (p124)
17 Irving Place (Map 4 E1)
Music Venue

West Village

55 Bar (p122)
55 Christopher St. (Map 3 C3)
Jazz Venue

Blue Note (p121)
131 West 3rd Street (Map 3 C3)
Jazz Venue

The Comedy Cellar (p121)
117 MacDougal St. (Map 3 C3)
Comedy

Cornelia Street Cafe (p121)
29 Cornelia St. (Map 3 C3)
Music/Poetry Venue

Duplex (p122)
61 Christopher St. (Map 3 B3)
Cabaret

Village Vanguard (p122)
178 7th Ave. South (Map 3 B2)
Jazz Venue

Bars & Clubs

Chinatown

Winnie's (p142)
104 Bayard Street (Map 2 E1)
Bar

East Village

2A (p147)
25 Avenue A (Map 4 F3)
Bar

Angel's Share (p148)
8 Stuyvesant St. (Map 4 E2)
Cocktail Lounge

Bar Veloce (p150)
175 2nd Avenue (Map 4 E2)
Bar

Beauty Bar (p150)
231 East 14th St. (Map 4 E2)
DJ Bar

KGB (p148)
85 East 4th Street (Map 4 E3)
Bar

Korova Milk Bar (p151)
200 Avenue A (Map 4 F2)
Bar

Lansky Lounge (p145)
104 Norfolk Street (Map 4 G4)
Cocktail Lounge/DJ Bar

McSorley's (p148)
15 East 7th Street (Map 4 E3)
Ale House

Nevada Smith's (p148)
74 3rd Avenue (Map 4 E2)
Bar

Parkside Lounge (p147)
317 East Houston St. (Map 4 G4)
Bar

Rue B (p151)
188 Avenue B (Map 4 G2)
Bar

Swift (p148)
34 East 4th St. (Map 4 E3)
Ale House

Uncle Ming's (p152)
225 Ave. B, 2nd Flr. (Map 4 G2)
DJ Bar

Little Italy

ñ (p144)
33 Crosby Street (Map 3 D5)
Bar

Lower East Side

Arlene's Grocery (p123)
95 Stanton Street (Map 4 F4)
Bar & Music Venue

Barramundi (p146)
67 Clinton Street (Map 4 F4)
Bar

Pianos (p147)
158 Ludlow Street (Map 4 F4)
Bar

Slipper Room (p147)
167 Orchard Street (Map 4 F4)
Bar

Welcome to the Johnson's
(p146)
123 Rivington Street (Map 4 F4)
Bar

Lower Manhattan

Pussycat Lounge (p142)
96 Greenwich St. (Map 1 D4)
Bar

Meatpacking District

Cielo (pp154 & 167)
18 Little W. 12th St. (Map 3 A2)
Club

Cubbyhole (p154)
281 West 12th Street (Map 3 B2)
Bar

Level V (p154)
675 Hudson Street (Map 3 A2)
Cocktail Lounge

Nolita

B-Bar & Grill (p149)
40 East 4th Street (Map 4 E3)
Bar

Pravda (p145)
281 Lafayette Street (Map 4 E4)
Cocktail Lounge

Temple Bar (p144)
332 Lafayette Street (Map 4 E4)
Cocktail Lounge

SoHo

Antarctica (p142)
287 Hudson Street (Map 3 C5)
Bar

THOM's Bar (p140)
60 Thompson Street
(Map 3 C5)
Cocktail Lounge

West Village

Blind Tiger Ale House (p153)
518 Hudson Street
(Map 3 B3)
Ale House

Chumley's (p152)
86 Bedford Street (Map 3 B3)
Bar

Lotus (p150)
409 West 14th Street
(Map 3 A2)
DJ Bar

Stonewall (p152)
53 Christopher St. (Map 3 B3)
Bar

Sullivan Room (p152)
218 Sullivan Street (Map 3 C3)
DJ Bar

Vol de Nuit (p152)
148 West 4th Street (Map 3 C3)
Ale House

White Horse Tavern (p153)
567 Hudson Street (Map 3 B3)
Ale House

Havens: Parks & Gardens

Lower Manhattan

Battery Park (p166)
Battery Place & State Street
(Map 1 D4) www.bpcparks.org

Havens: Spas & Treatments

SoHo

Angel Feet (p176)
77 Perry Street (Map 3 B3)

Bliss SoHo (p176)
568 Broadway (Map 3 D4)

Jivamukti Yoga Center (p177)
404 Lafayette Street
(Map 4 E3)

Hotels

Meatpacking District

Abingdon $
Guest House (p189)
13 8th Avenue (Map 3 B2)

Soho House $$$
New York (p190)
29–35 9th Avenue (Map 3 A2)

SoHo

Bevy's SoHo Loft (p188) $
70 Mercer Street
(Map 3 D5)

60 Thompson (p188) $$$
60 Thompson Street (3 C5)

Mercer Hotel (p188) $$$
147 Mercer Street (Map 3 D4)

SoHo Grand $$
Hotel (p188)
310 West Broadway
(Map 3 D5)

Tribeca

Tribeca Grand Hotel (p189) $$$
Two Avenue of the Americas
(Map 3 C5)

West Village

Washington Square $
Hotel (p189)
103 Waverly Place (Map 3 C3)

Midtown

Restaurants

Chelsea

Biltmore Room (p44) $$$
290 8th Avenue (Map 5 C5)
International

City Bakery (p43) $
3 West 18th Street (Map 3 C1)
Bakery

Grand Sichuan $
International (p43)
229 9th Avenue (Map 5 C5)
Chinese

Red Cat (p43) $$
227 10th Avenue (Map 5 B5)
International

Wild Lily Tea Room (p177) $
511a West 22nd Street
(Map 5 B5)
Tea Room

Flatiron

Tamarind (p45) $$
41–3 East 22nd St. (Map 6 F5)
Indian

Bolo (p44) $$$
23 East 22nd Street
(Map 6 E5)
Spanish

Tabla (p44) $$$
11 Madison Avenue
(Map 6 E5)
Indian

Mandoo Bar (p46) $
2 West 32nd Street
(Map 6 E4)
Korean

Gramercy

Artisanal (p46) $$
2 Park Avenue (Map 6 F4)
European

Blue Smoke (p45) $$
116 East 27th Street (Map 6 F4)
American

Dos Caminos (p45) $$
373 Park Avenue South
(Map 6 F5)
Mexican

Index by Area

Midtown

Restaurants *continued*

Gramercy Tavern (p42)
42 East 20th Street
(Map 4 E1) 212 477 0077
American

i Trulli (p46) $$$
122 East 27th Street
(Map 6 F4)
Italian

Lady Mendl's Tea Room (p35)
56 Irving Place (Map 4 E1)
Tea Room

Union Square Café (p43) $$$
21 East 16th Street (Map 3 D1)
American

Hell's Kitchen

Sandwich Planet (p47) $
534 9th Avenue (Map 5 C2)
Deli

Murray Hill

Cho Dang Gol (p47) $
55 West 35th Street (Map 6 E3)
Korean

Ess-a-Bagel (p48) $
831 3rd Avenue (Map 6 F1)
Bagel Shop

Theater District

Acqua Pazza (p49) $$$
36 West 52nd St. (Map 8 E5)
Italian

Aquavit (p49) $$$
65 East 55th Street (Map 8 E5)
Swedish

**Churrascaria
Plataforma** (p48) $$$
316 West 49th Street
(Map 5 C1)
South American

Four Seasons (p42) $$$
99 East 52nd Street
(Map 7 D5)
American

Genki Sushi (p48) $
9 East 46th Street (Map 6 E1)
Japanese

Mi Nidito (p47) $$
852 8th Avenue (Map 5 C1)
Mexican

Norma's (p50) $$
Le Parker Meridien Hotel, 118
W. 57th Street (Map 7 D5)
Breakfast/Brunch

Palm Court Tea Room (p35)
Plaza Hotel, 5th Ave. (Map 8 E4)
Tea Room

Town (p50) $$$
Chambers Hotel, 15 West 56th
Street (Map 8 E5)
International

Shopping

Chelsea

La Cafetiere (p78)
160 9th Avenue (Map 3 A1)
Interiors

Chelsea Flea Market (p168)
North West corner of 24th St.
& 6th Ave. (Map 5 D5)
Market

Gap (p74)
60 West 34th Street (Map 5 D3)
Music

Jazz Record Center (p82)
236 West 26th Street,
8th floor (Map 5 C5)
Music

Macy's (p80)
151 West 34th St. (Map 5 D3)
Department Store

Gramercy

ABC Carpet and Home (p79)
888 Broadway (Map 3 D1)
Interiors

Paragon Sporting Goods (p80)
867 Broadway (Map 3 D1)
Sporting Goods

**Union Square
Green Market** (p168)
Union Square (Map 3 D1)
Market

Theater District

Bergdorf Goodman (p85)
754 5th Avenue (Map 8 E4)
Department Store

Felissimo (p84)
10 West 56th Street (Map 8 E5)
Interiors

Henri Bendel (p80)
712 West 5th Ave. (Map 8 E5)
Department Store

Jimmy Choo (p82)
645 5th Avenue (Map 8 E5)
Shoes & Accessories

Manolo Blahnik (p82)
31 West 54th St. (Map 8 E5)
Shoes & Accessories

Niketown (p84)
6 East 57th Street (Map 8 E5)
Shoes & Accessories

Sak's Fifth Avenue (p80)
611 5th Avenue (Map 5 C5)
Department Store

Takashimaya (p83)
693 5th Avenue (Map 8 E5)
Department Store

Art & Architecture

Chelsea

Gagosian (p99)
555 West 24th Street (Map 5 B5)
www.gagosian.com
Art Gallery

Mary Boone (p102)
541 West 24th Street (Map 5 B5)
www.maryboone.com
Art Gallery

**Museum at the Fashion
Institute of Technology** (p104)
7th Ave. at 27th St. (Map 5 D4)
Museum

Pace Wildenstein (p102)
534 West 25th Street (Map 5 B5)
Art Gallery

Flatiron

Flatiron Building (p106)
23rd St., 5th Ave. & Broadway
(Map 6 E5)
Historic Building

Gramercy

Block Beautiful (p102)
East 19th St., between Irving
Place & 3rd Ave. (Map 4 E1)
Historic Building

Murray Hill

Chanin Building (p105)
122 East 42nd Street at
Lexington Avenue (Map 6 F2)
Modern Architecture

Chrysler Building (p105)
405 Lexington Ave. (Map 6 F2)
Modern Architecture

Daily News Building (p105)
220 East 42nd Street (Map 6 G2)
Modern Architecture

Empire State Bldg (pp12 & 105)
350 5th Avenue (Map 6 E3)
Modern Architecture

General Electric Bldg. (p105)
570 Lexington Avenue at 51st
Street (Map 6 F1)
Modern Architecture

Grand Central Terminal (p105)
42nd St. & Park Ave. (Map 6 F2)
Historic Building

**Whitney Museum of American
Art at Altria** (p106)
120 Park Avenue at 42nd
Street (Map 6 F2)
Museum

Theater District

**International Center of
Photography** (p106)
1133 Ave. of the Americas
(Map 5 D2)
Art Gallery

Museum of Modern Art (p107)
11 West 53rd Street (Map 8 E5)
Museum

**Museum of Television
and Radio** (p109)
25 West 52nd Street (Map 8 E5)
Museum

**Rose Museum at
Carnegie Hall** (p106)
154 West 57th Street, 2nd
Floor (Map 7 D5)
Museum

Performance

Chelsea

Hammerstein Ballroom (p127)
311 West 34th Street (Map 5 C3)
Music Venue

For the very latest on New York go to ≫ www.realcity.dk.com

The Joyce Theater (p126)
175 8th Avenue (Map 3 B1)
Dance

The Kitchen (p126)
512 West 19th Street (Map 3 A1)
Combined Arts Center

Upright Citizen's Brigade (p127)
307 West 26th Street (Map 5 C5)
Comedy

Flatiron

Gotham Comedy Club (p127)
34 West 22nd Street (Map 6 E5)
Comedy

Madison Square Garden
(p137)
(Map 6 E5)
Sports Arena

Gramercy

Jazz Standard (p127)
116 East 27th St. (Map 6 F4)
Jazz Club

Rodeo Bar (p128)
375 3rd Avenue (Map 6 F5)
Music Venue

Theater District

B.B. King Blues Club (p128)
237 West 42nd St. (Map 5 C2)
Jazz & Blues Venue

Carnegie Hall (p131)
881 7th Avenue at 57th Street
(Map 7 D5)
Concert Hall

City Center (p129)
131 West 55th Street (Map 7 D5)
Combined Arts Center

Don't Tell Mama (p129)
343 West 46th Street (Map 5 C1)
Cabaret

Ed Sullivan Theater (p130)
51 West 52nd Street (Map 7 D5)
TV Studio

Iridium (p128)
1650 Broadway (Map 5 D1)
Jazz & Blues Venue

NBC Studios (p130)
Main Lobby, 49th St. between
5th and 7th Aves (Map 6 E1)
TV Studio

Rainbow Room (p129)
30 Rockefeller Plaza,
65th Floor (Map 6 E1)
Ballroom

Roundabout/
AA Theatre (p128)
227 West 42nd St.
(Map 5 D2)
Theater

Swing 46 (p129)
349 West 46th Street (Map 5 C1)
Ballroom

Bars and Clubs

Chelsea

Avalon (p155)
47 West 20th Street (Map 3 C1)
DJ Bar

Bungalow 8 (p156)
515 West 27th Street (Map 5 B4)
Bar

Copacabana (p157)
560 West 34th Street (Map 5 B3)
Ball Room

Glass (p156)
287 10th Avenue (Map 5 B5)
Bar

Hiro (p156)
366 West 17th Street
(Map 3 A1)
Bar

Plunge Bar (p161)
18 9th Avenue (Map 3 A1)
Bar

Roxy (p155)
515 West 18th Street
(Map 3 A1)
Club

Serena (p155)
Chelsea Hotel, 222 West 23rd
Street (Map 5 C5)
Bar

Spirit (p156)
530 West 27th Street (Map 5 B4)
Bar

Flatiron

Eugene (p155)
27 West 24th Street
(Map 6 E5)
Club

Sky Bar (p161)
27 West 24th St. (Map 6 E5)
Club

Hell's Kitchen

Rudy's Bar & Grill (p154)
627 9th Avenue (Map 5 C1)
Bar

Murray Hill

Campbell Apartment (p157)
15 Vanderbilt Ave., SW Balcony,
Grand Central Terminal
(Map 6 F2)
Bar

The Ginger Man (p157)
11 East 36th Street (Map 6 E3)
Bar

Métrazur (p158)
East Balcony, Grand Central
Station (Map 6 F2)
Cocktail Lounge

Theater District

Ava Lounge (p158)
210 West 55th Street (Map 7 D5)
Bar

Flûte (p158)
205 West 54th Street (Map 7 D5)
DJ Bar

Russian Vodka Room (p159)
265 West 52nd Street (Map 7 C5)
Bar

Single Room Occupancy (p158)
360 West 53rd Street (Map 7 C5)
Bar

Turtle Bay

Mica Bar (p154)
252 East 51st Street (Map 6 F1)
Bar

Top of the Tower @
Beekman Tower Hotel (p178)
3 Mitchell Place at 49th Street
& First Avenue (Map 6 G1)
Bar

Havens:
Spas & Treatments

Flatiron

Oasis Day Spa (p79)
108 East 16th St. (Map 3 C1)

Theater District

The Spa at the Mandarin
Oriental (p172)
80 Columbus Circle
at 60th Street, 35th Floor (Map
7 C4)

Hotels

Chelsea

Chelsea Inn (p191) $
46 West 17th Street
(Map 3 C1)

Chelsea Lodge (p191) $
318 West 20th Street
(Map 3 B1)

Hotel Chelsea (p189) $$
222 West 23rd Street
(Map 5 C5)

Maritime Hotel (p191) $$
363 West 16th Street
(Map 3 A1)

Gramercy

W Union Square (p191) $$
201 Park Avenue S (Map 3D1)

Murray Hill

Affinia Shelburne (p192) $$
303 Lexington Ave.
(Map 6 F3)

Morgans (p187) $$
237 Madison Avenue
(Map 6 E3)

Theater District

Four Seasons (p194) $$$
57 East 57th Street
(Map 8 E5)

The Peninsula (p192) $$$
700 5th Avenue at 55th Street
(Map 8 E5)

The Plaza (p189) $$$
5th Avenue at Central Park
South (Map 8 E4)

Royalton (p192) $$
44 West 44th Street
(Map 6 E2)

St. Regis (p192) $$$
2 East 55th Street
(Map 8 E5)

Index by Area

Upper East Side

Restaurants

Annie's (p51) $
1381 3rd Avenue (Map 8 F1)
American

Atlantic Grill (p52) $$
1341 3rd Avenue (Map 8 F1)
Seafood

Candle 79 (p52) $$
154 East 79th Street (Map 8 F1)
Vegetarian/Vegan

Geisha (p50) $$
33 East 61st Street (Map 8 E4)
Japanese

March (p51) $$$
405 East 58th Street (Map 8 H4)
Asian

Mezzaluna (p51) $$
1295 3rd Avenue (Map 8 H4)
Italian

Rotunda at the Pierre (p180)
The Pierre Hotel, 2 East 61st
Street (Map 8 E4)
Tea Room

Serendipity 3 (p51) $$$
225 East 60th Street (Map 8 F4)
American

Sushi of Gari (p53) $$$
402 East 78th Street
(Map 8 G1)
Japanese

Via Quadronno (p35) $
25 East 73rd Street (Map 8 F2)
www.viaquadronno.com
Italian

Shopping

ABH Designs (p88)
401 East 76th Street (Map 8 H1)
Interiors

Anik (p87)
1122 Madison Ave. (Map 8 E2)
Fashion

Barney's New York (p86)
660 Madison Avenue
(Map 8 E4)
Department Store

Bloomingdale's (p80)
1000 3rd Avenue (Map 8 F4)
Department Store

Bra Smyth (p86)
905 Madison Avenue
(Map 8 E2)
Lingerie

Christian Louboutin (p87)
941 Madison Avenue
(Map 8 E2)
Shoes & Accessories

Clyde's (p87)
926 Madison Avenue
(Map 8 E2)
Heath & Beauty

Diane B (p87)
1414 3rd Avenue
(Map 8 F2)
Fashion

Dylan's Candy Bar (p8)
1011 3rd Avenue
(Map 8 F4)
Food

La Perla (p8)
803 Madison Avenue
(Map 8 E3)
Lingerie

Searle (p8)
1124 Madison Avenue
(Map 10 E5)
Fashion

Art & Architecture

Asia Society (p10)
725 Park Avenue
at 70th Street (Map 8 F2)
Gallery

**Cooper-Hewitt National
Design Museum** (p111)
2 East 91st Street (Map 10 E4)
Museum

Frick Collection (p10)
1 East 70th St. (Map 8 E2)
Museum

Guggenheim Museum (p1)
1071 5th Avenue at 89th Street
(Map 10 E4)
Museum

The Jewish Museum (p111)
1109 5th Avenue at 92nd
Street (Map 10 E4)
Museum

Metropolitan Museum of Art
(p109)
1000 5th Avenue
(Map 8 E1)
Museum

El Museo del Barrio (p113)
1230 5th Ave. at 104th St.
(Map 10 E2)
Museum

**Whitney Museum
of American Art** (p107)
945 Madison Avenue
(Map 8 E2)
Museum

Performance

92nd Street Y (p131)
1395 Lexington Avenue
(Map 10 F4)
Combined Arts Center

The Comic Strip (p131)
1568 2nd Avenue
(Map 8 G1)
Comedy

Florence Gould Hall (p130)
55 East 59th Street
(Map 8 F4)
Combined Arts Center

Bars

The Auction House (p160)
300 East 89th St.
(Map 10 G4)
Bar

Baraonda (p159)
1439 2nd Avenue
(Map 8 G2)
Bar

Bemelmans Bar (p159)
Carlyle Hotel, 35 East 76th
Street (Map 8 E1)
Bar

Havens: Parks & Gardens

**Conservatory Gardens at
Central Park** (p179)
5th Avenue at 110th Street
(Map 10 E2)

**The Iris and B. Gerald Cantor
Roof Garden** (p178)
Metropolitan Museum of Art,
1000 5th Avenue
(Map 8 E1)

Ramble at Central Park (p179)
5th Avenue between 72nd and
80th streets (Map 7 D2)

Hotels

1871 House (p194) $
130 East 62nd St. (Map 8 F4)

The Carlyle (p189) $$$
Madison Avenue at 76th Street
www.thecarlyle.com
(Map 8 E1)

Hotel Surrey (p195) $$
20 East 76th St. (Map 8 E1)

Hotel Wales (p196) $$
1295 Madison Ave. (Map 10 E4)

The Lowell (p195) $$$
28 East 63rd St. (Map 8 F4)

The Mark (p195) $$$
25 East 77th St. (Map 8 E1)

The Pierre (p195) $$$
5th Avenue at 61st Street (Map
8 E4)

Upper West Side

Restaurants

Aix (p55) $$$
2398 Broadway (Map 9 B5)
French

El Malecón II (p54) $
764 Amsterdam Avenue (9 B3)
Caribbean

Ouest (p53) $$$
2315 Broadway (Map 9 B5)
American

Pasha (p54) $$
70 West 71st Street (Map 7 C2)
Turkish

Picholine (p54) $$$
35 West 64th St. (Map 7 C3)
European

Tavern on the Green (p42) $
Central Park West between
66th and 67th Sts. (Map 7 C3)
212 873 3000
www.tavernonthegreen.com
American

Shopping

Blades Board & Skate (p88)
120 West 72nd St. (Map 7 B2)
Sporting Goods

Housing Works Thrift Shop (p89)
306 Columbus Ave. (Map 7 C2)
Thrift Store

Intermix (p88)
210 Columbus Ave. (Map 7 C3)
Fashion

Super Runners (p89)
360 Amsterdam Ave. (Map 7 B1)
Sporting Goods

Zabar's (p89)
2245 Broadway (Map 7 B1)
Food

Art & Architecture

Cathedral Church of St. John Divine (p180)
1047 Amsterdam Ave. (Map 9 B1)
Church

Performance

Lincoln Center for the Performing Arts (p132)
Broadway & Amsterdam btwn 62nd & 66th Sts (Map 7 B3)
Performing Arts Center

Makor (p133)
35 West 67th Street (Map 7 C3)
Combined Arts Center

Merkin Concert Hall (p131)
129 West 67th Street (Map 7 B3)
Concert Hall

Smoke (p133)
2751 Broadway (Map 9 B2)
Jazz Venue

Stand-Up NY (p133)
236 West 78th St. (Map 7 B2)
Comedy

Symphony Space (p133)
2537 Broadway (Map 9 B3)
Combined Arts Center

Bars & Clubs

Boat Basin Café (p161)
West 79th St. at Henry Hudson Parkway (Map 7 A1)
Bar

Library Bar (p154)
Hudson Hotel, 356 West 58th Street (Map 7 B4)
Bar

Hotels

Hudson Hotel (p193) $$
356 West 58th Street (Map 7 C4)

Above Central Park

Restaurants

Columbia University

Symposium (p55) $$
544 West 113th St. (Map 11 B5)
Greek

Fort Tryon

New Leaf Café (p55) $$
Fort Tryon Park
American

Harlem

Amy Ruth's (p169) $
113 West 116th St.
(Map 11 D5) 212 280 8779
American

Shopping

Harlem

Demolition Depot (p90)
216 East 125th St.
(Map 12 G3)
Interiors

Xukuma (p90)
183 Lenox Avenue (11 D4)
Fashion/Interiors

Art & Architecture

Fort Tryon

The Cloisters (p112)
Fort Tryon Park
Museum

Harlem

Studio Museum in Harlem (p113)
144 West 125th St. (Map 11 D3)
Museum

Performance

Harlem

Apollo Theater (p134)
253 West 125th St. (Map 11 D3)
Music/Combined Arts Venue

Lenox Lounge (p135)
288 Lenox Avenue between 124th & 125th (Map 11 D3)
Jazz Venue

Hotels

Harlem

Harlem Flophouse (p196) $
242 West 123rd St. (Map 11 D4)

Brooklyn

Restaurants

Boerum Hill

Stan's Place (p58) $
411 Avenue (Map 13 C3)
American

Brooklyn Heights

Brooklyn Ice Cream Factory (p170) $
Fulton Ferry Landing
(Map 13 A4)
Ice Cream Parlor

Connecticut Muffin (p170) $
115 Montague Street
(Map 13 A4)
Bakery

Noodle Pudding (p55) $$
38 Henry Street
(Map 13 A3)
Italian

The River Café (p56) $$$
1 Water Street (Map 13 A3)
International

Teresa's (p170) $$
80 Montague St. (Map 13 A4)
Polish

Carroll Gardens

The Grocery (p56) $$
288 Smith Street
(Map 13 B4)
American

Joya (p56) $
215 Court Street
(Map 13 B4)
Thai

Coney Island

Café Arbat (p172) $
306 Brighton Beach Avenue
Eastern European

Café Glechik (p172) $
3159 Coney Island Avenue
Eastern European

Nathan's Famous Hotdogs (p172) $
Corner of Surf & Stillwell Aves
American

Fort Greene

i-Sheebeen Madiba (p58) $$
195 DeKalb Avenue
(Map 13 C3)
South African

LouLou (p57) $$
222 DeKalb Avenue
(Map 13 C3)
French

Park Slope

Convivium Osteria (p57) $$
68 5th Avenue
(Map 13 C4)
Italian

Park Slope Chip Shop (p57) $
383 5th Avenue
(Map 13 C5)
British

Shopping

Calliope (p94)
135 Grand St. (Map 13 B2)
Fashion

Darr (p93)
369 Atlantic Ave.
(Map 13 B4)
Interiors

Nom de Guerre (p93)
88 North 6th St. (Map 13 B2)
Fashion

Hotel

Akwaaba Mansion (p197) $
347 McDonough St.
(Utica Ave. Stn.)

Restaurants

Verb Café (p171) $
218 Bedford Avenue
(Map 13 C2)
www.verbcafe.com
Brooklyn/Williamsburg

Via Quadronno (p35) $
25 East 73rd Street
212 650 9880
(Map 8 F2)
Upper East Side

Caribbean

El Malecón II (p54) $
764 Amsterdam Avenue
(Map 9 B3)
Upper West Side

Chinese

66 (p28) $$$
241 Church Street
(Map 1 D1)
Downtown/Tribeca

Fried Dumpling (p40) $
99 Allen Street
(Map 4 F4)
Downtown/Lower East Side

HSF (p166) $$
46 Bowery
(Map 2 E1)
Downtown/Chinatown

Golden Unicorn (p29) $
18 East Broadway
(Map 2 F1)D
Downtown/Chinatown

Grand Sichuan
International (p43) $
229 9th Avenue
(Map 5 C5)
Midtown/Chelsea

Great NY Noodle Town (p166) $
281/2 Bowery at Bayard Street
(Map 2 E1)
Downtown/Chinatown

Peking Duck House (p29) $$
28 Mott Street
(Map 2 E1)
Downtown/Chinatown

Cuban

Cafe Habana (p31) $
17 Prince
(Map 4 E4)
Downtown/Nolita

Delis/Sandwich Shops

*See also Bakeries, Cafés, and
Tea Rooms*

Amish Fine Food (p166) $
17 Battery Place (Map 1 D5)
Downtown/Lower Manhattan

BB Sandwich Bar (p40) $
120 West 3rd Street (Map 3 C3)
Downtown/West Village

Cosi (p166) $
55 Broad Street (Map 1 D4)
Downtown/Lower Manhattan

Dean & DeLuca (p69) $
560 Broadway (Map 3 D4)
Downtown/SoHo

Pret a Manger (p166) $
60 Broad Street (Map 1 D4)
Downtown/Lower Manhattan

Sandwich Planet (p47) $
534 9th Avenue (Map 5 C2)
Midtown/Hell's Kitchen

Zabar's (p89) $
2245 Broadway (Map 7 B1)
Upper West Side

Eastern European

Café Arbat (p172) $
306 Brighton Beach Avenue
Brooklyn/Coney Island

Café Glechik (p172) $
3159 Coney Island Avenue
Brooklyn/Coney Island

European

Artisanal (p46) $$
2 Park Avenue (Map 6 F4)
Midtown/Gramercy

Blue Ribbon
Bakery (p37) $$$
33 Downing Street (Map 3 C4)
Downtown/West Village

Florent (p42) $
69 Gansevoort St. (Map 3 A2)
Downtown/Meatpacking District

Four Seasons (p42) $$$
99 East 52nd Street
(Map 7 D5) www.fourseasons
restaurant.com
Midtown/Theater District

Montrachet (p28) $$$
239 West Broadway (Map 1 C1)
Downtown/Tribeca

Picholine (p54) $$$
35 West 64th Street (Map 7 C3)
Upper West Side

French

Aix (p55) $$$
2398 Broadway (Map 9 B5)
Upper West Side

Balthazar (p29) $$
80 Spring Street (Map 3 D5)
Downtown/SoHo

Chanterelle (p42) $$$
2 Harrison Street (Map 1 C1)
212 966 6960 www.
chanterellenyc.com
Downtown/Tribeca

L'Ecole (p30) $$
462 Broadway (Map 3 D5)
Downtown/SoHo

The Elephant (p31) $$
58 East 1st Street (Map 4 F4)
Downtown/East Village

LouLou (p57) $$
222 DeKalb Avenue
(Map 13 C3)
Brooklyn/Fort Greene

Mercer Kitchen (p29) $$
99 Prince Street (Map 3 D4)
Downtown/SoHo

Pastis (p167) $$
9 9th Avenue (Map 3 A2)
212 929 4844
www.pastisny.com
Downtown/Meatpacking
District

Le Tableau (p33) $$
511 East 5th Street
(Map 4 F3)
Downtown/East Village

Tartine (p42) $
253 West 11th Street
(Map 3 B2)
Downtown/West Village

Greek

Pylos (p34) $$
128 East 7th Street (Map 4 F3)
Downtown/East Village

Symposium (p55) $$
544 West 113th Street
(Map 11 B5)
Above Central Park/Columbia
University

Ice Cream Parlors

Brooklyn Ice Cream $
Factory (p170)
Fulton Ferry Landing
(Map 13 A4)
Brooklyn/Brooklyn Heights

Chinatown Ice Cream $
Factory (p166)
65 Bayard Street (Map 2 E1)
Downtown/Chinatown

Cones (p40) $
272 Bleecker Street (3 C3)
Downtown/West Village

Indian

Tabla (p44) $$$
11 Madison Avenue (Map 6 E5)
Midtown/Flatiron

Tamarind (p45) $$
41–3 East 22nd Street
(Map 6 F5)
Midtown/Flatiron

International

Biltmore Room (p44) $$$
290 8th Avenue (Map 5 C5)
Midtown/Chelsea

Red Cat (p43) $$
227 10th Avenue (Map 5 B5)
Midtown/Chelsea

The River Café (p56) $$$
1 Water Street (Map 13 A3)
Brooklyn/Brooklyn Heights

Town (p50) $$$
Chambers Hotel, 15 West 56th
Street (Map 8 E5)
Midtown/Theater District

Italian

Acappella (p28) $$$
1 Hudson Street (Map 1 C2)
Downtown/Tribeca

Acqua Pazza (p49) $$$
36 West 52nd Street
(Map 8 E5)
Midtown/Theater District

Index by Type

Restaurants

Italian *continued...*

Al Di La (p57) $$
248 5th Avenue (Map 13 C4)
Brooklyn/Park Slope

Babbo (p38) $$$
110 Waverly Place (Map 3 C3)
Downtown/West Village

Bamonte's (p59) $$
32 Withers Street (Map 13 C1)
Brooklyn/Williamsburg

Convivium Osteria (p57) $$
68 5th Avenue (Map 13 C4)
Brooklyn/Park Slope

'inoteca (p32) $$
98 Rivington Street (Map 4 F4)
Downtown/Lower East Side

i Trulli (p46) $$$
122 East 27th Street
(Map 6 F4)
Midtown/Gramercy

Mezzaluna (p51) $$
1295 3rd Avenue (Map 8 F2)
Upper East Side

Noodle Pudding (p55) $$
38 Henry Street (Map 13 A3)
Brooklyn/Brooklyn Heights

Otto Enoteca and Pizzeria (p38) $
1 5th Avenue (Map 3 D3)
Downtown/West Village

Pepe Rosso's (p40) $
149 Sullivan Street
(Map 3 C4)
Downtown/West Village

Via Quadronno (p35) $
25 East 73rd Street (Map 8 F2)
www.viaquadronno.com
Upper East Side

Japanese

Blue Ribbon Sushi (p37) $$$
119 Sullivan Street
(Map 3 C4)
Downtown/SoHo

Cube 63 (p32) $$
63 Clinton Street
(Map 4 G4)
Downtown/Lower East Side

Geisha (p50) $$$
33 East 61st Street (Map 8 E4)
Upper East Side

Genki Sushi (p48) $
9 East 46th Street (Map 6 E1)
Midtown/Theater District

Nobu (p42) $$$
105 Hudson Street (Map 1 C2)
212 219 0500
www.myriadrestaurant
group.com
Downtown/Tribeca

Sobaya (p36) $
229 East 9th Street (Map 4 E2)
Downtown/East Village

Sumile (p42) $$$
154 West 13th Street (Map 3 C2)
Downtown/West Village

Sushi of Gari (p53) $$$
402 East 78th Street (Map 8 G1)
Upper East Side

Tomoe Sushi (p37) $$
172 Thompson Street (Map 3 C4)
Downtown/SoHo

Korean

Cho Dang Gol (p47) $
55 West 35th Street (Map 6 E3)
Midtown/Murray Hill

Mandoo Bar (p46) $
2 West 32nd Street (Map 6 E4)
Midtown/Flatiron

Mexican

Dos Caminos (p45) $$
373 Park Ave. South (Map 6 F5)
Midtown/Gramercy

Itzocan Café (p168) $
438 East 9th Street (Map 4 F2)
Downtown/East Village

Mi Nidito (p47) $$
852 8th Avenue (Map 5 C1)
Midtown/Theater District

La Palapa Rockola (p38) $$
359 6th Avenue (Map 3 C3)
Downtown/West Village

Middle Eastern

Mamoun's (p40) $
119 MacDougal St. (Map 3 C3)
Downtown/West Village

Yaffa Cafe (p34) $
97 St. Mark's Place (Map 4 F3)
Downtown/East Village

North African

Cafe Gitane (p31) $
242 Mott Street (Map 4 E4)
Downtown/Nolita

Le Souk (p33) $$
47 Avenue B (Map 4 G3)
Downtown/East Village

Pizzerias

Anna Maria's (p171) $
179 Bedford Avenue
718 559 4550 (Map 13 C2)
Brooklyn/Williamsburg

DiFara Pizzeria (p58) $
1424 Avenue J
Brooklyn/Midwood

John's of Bleecker Street (p39) $$
278 Bleecker Street
(Map 3 C3)
Downtown/West Village

Polish

S & B Polish (p171) $
194 Bedford Avenue
718 963 1536 (Map 13 C2)
Brooklyn/Williamsburg

Theresa's (p170) $
80 Montague Street
718 797 3996 (Map 13 A4)
Brooklyn/Brooklyn Heights

Seafood

Atlantic Grill (p52) $$
1341 3rd Avenue (Map 8 F1)
Upper East Side

Mary's Fish Camp (p41) $$
64 Charles Street
(Map 3 B3)
Downtown/West Village

Mermaid Inn (p35) $$
96 2nd Avenue
(Map 4 E3)
Downtown/East Village

South African

i-Shebeen Madiba (p58) $$
195 DeKalb Avenue (Map 13 C3)
Brooklyn/Fort Greene

South American

Churrascaria Plataforma (p48) $$$
316 West 49th Street
(Map 5 C1)
Midtown/Theater District

Spanish

Bolo (p44) $$$
23 East 22nd Street (Map 6 E5)
Midtown/Flatiron

Swedish

Aquavit (p49) $$$
65 East 55th Street
(Map 8 F5)
Midtown/Theater District

Tea Rooms

See also Bakeries, Cafés, and Delis

Lady Mendl's Tea Room (p35)
56 Irving Place
(Map 4 E1)
www.innatirving.com
Midtown/Gramercy

Palm Court Tea Room (p35)
Plaza Hotel, 768 5th Avenue
(Map 8 E4)
Midtown/Theater District

Rotunda at the Pierre (p180)
The Pierre Hotel, 2 East 61st
Street (Map 8 E4)
Upper East Side

Tea & Sympathy (p35)
108 Greenwich Avenue
(Map 3 C2)
www.teaandsympathy
newyork.com
Downtown/West Village

Teany (pp35 & 74)
90 Rivington Street
(Map 4 F4)
Downtown/Lower East Side

Wild Lily Tea Room (p177)
511a West 22nd Street
(Map 3 B5)
Midtown/Chelsea

Thai

The Elephant (p31) $$
58 East 1st Street (Map 4 F4)
Downtown/East Village

226

www.realcity.dk.com

Joya (p56) $
215 Court Street (Map 13 B4)
Brooklyn/Carroll Gardens

Planet Thailand (p59) $
133 North 7th Street
(Map 13 C2)
Brooklyn/Williamsburg

Turkish

Bereket (p31) $
187 East Houston Street
(Map 4 F4)
Downtown/Lower East Side

Pasha (p54) $$
70 W. 71st Street (Map 7 B2)
Upper West Side

Vegetarian

Angelica Kitchen (p36) $
300 East 12th Street
(Map 4 E2)
Downtown/East Village

Bliss Café (p171) $
191 Bedford Avenue
718 599 2547 (Map 13 C2)
Brooklyn/Williamsburg

Candle 79 (p52) $$
154 East 79th Street
(Map 8 F1)
Upper East Side

NY Dosas (p41) $
West 4th Street & Sullivan
Street (Map 3 C3)
Downtown/West Village

Vietnamese

Bao (p33) $
111 Avenue C (Map 4 G3)
Downtown/East Village

Shopping

Books

Heights Books (p170)
109 Montague Street
(Map 13 A4)
Brooklyn/Brooklyn Heights

Spoonbill & Sugartown
Booksellers (p92)
218 Bedford Avenue
(Map 13 B2)
Brooklyn/Williamsburg

The Strand (p81)
828 Broadway
(Map 3 D2)
Downtown/East Village

Department Stores

Barney's New York (p86)
660 Madison Avenue
(Map 8 E4)
Upper East Side

Bergdorf Goodman (p85)
754 5th Avenue
(Map 8 E4)
Midtown/Theater District

Bloomingdale's (p80)
1000 3rd Avenue
(Map 8 F4)
212 705 2000
www.bloomingdales.com
Upper East Side

Henri Bendel (p80)
712 5th Avenue at 56th Street
(Map 8 E5)
212 247 1100
Midtown/Theater District

Jeffrey (pp78 & 167)
449 West 14th Street (Map 3 A2)
*Downtown/Meatpacking
District*

Macy's (p80)
151 West 34th Street (Map 5 D3)
www.macys.com
Midtown/Chelsea

Pearl River Mart (p65)
477 Broadway (Map 3 D5)
Downtown/SoHo

Saks 5th Avenue (p80)
611 5th Avenue
(Map 6 E1)
212 753 4000
www.saksfifthavenue.com
Midtown/Flatiron

Takashimaya (p83)
693 5th Avenue
(Map 8 E5)
Midtown/Theater District

Fashion

Alexander McQueen (p167)
417 West 14th Street
(Map 3 A2)
www.alexandermcqueen.com
*Downtown/Meatpacking
District*

Anik (p87)
1122 Madison Ave. (Map 8 E2)
Upper East Side

A.P.C. (p66)
131 Mercer Street (Map 3 D4)
Downtown/SoHo

Banana Republic (p74)
1136 Madison Avenue between
84th and 85th street (Map 10 E5)
212 570 2465
www.bananarepublic.com
Upper East Side/Yorkville

Barney's CO-OP (p66)
116 Wooster Street (Map 3 D4)
Downtown/SoHo

Brooklyn Industries (p171)
162 Bedford Ave. (Map 13 C2)
www.brooklynindustries.com
Brooklyn/Williamsburg

Butter (p91)
407 Atlantic Avenue
(Map 13 B4)
Brooklyn/Boerum Hill

Calliope (p94)
135 Grand Street (Map 13 B2)
Brooklyn

Calypso (p71)
280 Mott Street (Map 4 E4)
Downtown/Nolita

Century 21 (p64)
22 Cortlandt Street (Map 1 D3)
Downtown/Lower Manhattan

Costume National (p67)
108 Wooster Street
(Map 3 D4)
Downtown/SoHo

Diane B (p87)
1414 3rd Avenue (Map 8 F2)
Upper East Side

Gap (p74)
60 West 34th Street
(Map 5 D3)
212 760 1268 www.gap.com
Midtown/Chelsea

Hotel Venus by
Patricia Field (p64)
382 W. Broadway (Map 3 D5)
Downtown/SoHo

INA (p71)
21 Prince Street (Map 4 E4)
Downtown/Little Italy

Intermix (p88)
210 Columbus Avenue
(Map 7 C3)
Upper West Side

J. Crew (p74)
347 Madison Ave.
(Map 6 E3) 212 949 0570
www.jcrew.com
Midtown/Theater District

Kirna Zabete (p67)
96 Greene Street
(Map 3 D4)
Downtown/SoHo

Malia Mills (p65)
199 Mulberry Street
(Map 4 E5)
Downtown/Little Italy

Marc by Marc Jacobs (p76)
403–405 Bleecker Street
(Map 3 B4)
Downtown/West Village

Marc Jacobs (p68)
163 Mercer Street
(Map 3 D4)
Downtown/West Village

Mayle (p72)
242 Elizabeth Street
(Map 4 E4)
Downtown/Little Italy

Metaphors (p171)
195 Bedford Avenue
(Map 13 C2)
Brooklyn/Williamsburg

Mini Minimarket (p92)
218 Bedford Avenue
(Map 13 B2)
Brooklyn/Williamsburg

Miu Miu (p67)
100 Prince Street
(Map 3 D4)
Downtown/SoHo

Nom de Guerre (p93)
88 North 6th Street
(Map 13 B2)
Brooklyn

Prada (p68)
575 Broadway
(Map 3 D4)
Downtown/SoHo

Sahil Sari Palace (p173)
37–55 74th Street
Queens/Jackson Heights

Index by Type

Shopping

Fashion continued...

Scoop (p69)
532 Broadway (Map 3 D4)
Downtown/SoHo

Searle (p88)
1124 Madison Ave. (Map 10 E5)
Upper East Side

Shop (p74)
105 Stanton Street (Map 4 F4)
Downtown/Lower East Side

Stella McCartney (p77)
429 West 14th St. (Map 3 A2)
Downtown/Meatpacking
District

TG-170 (p73)
170 Ludlow Street (Map 4 F4)
Downtown/Lower East Side

Urban Outfitters (p74)
2081 Broadway at 72nd Street
(Map 7 B2) 212 579 3912
www.urbanoutfitters.com
Upper West Side

Xukuma (p90)
183 Lenox Avenue (11 D4)
Above Central Park/Harlem

Food

Bedford Cheese Shop (p171)
218 Bedford Avenue
718 599 7588 (Map 13 C2)
Brooklyn/Williamsburg

Bonsignour (p76)
35 Jane Street (Map 3 B2)
Downtown/Meatpacking Dist.

**Borgatti's Ravioli &
Noodle Company** (p173)
632 East 187th Street
The Bronx

Brooklyn Lager Brewery (p171)
79 North 11th St. (Map 13 C2)
www.brooklynbrewery.com
Brooklyn/Williamsburg

Dean & DeLuca (p69)
560 Broadway (Map 3 D4)
Downtown/SoHo

Dylan's Candy Bar (p86)
1011 3rd Avenue (Map 8 F4)
Upper East Side

Egidio Pastry Shop (p173)
622 East 18th Street
The Bronx

Magnolia Bakery (p75)
401 Bleeker Street (Map 3 B3)
Downtown/West Village

**M & I International Food
Market** (p172)
249 Brighton Beach Avenue
Brooklyn/Coney Island

Patel Brothers Market (p173)
27–37 74th Street
Queens/Jackson Heights

Teany (p74)
90 Rivington Street (Map 4 F4)
Downtown/Lower East Side

Zabar's (p89)
2245 Broadway (Map 7 B1)
Upper West Side

Health & Beauty

Clyde's (p87)
926 Madison Ave. (Map 8 E2)
Upper East Side

Fresh (p75)
388 Bleecker Street (Map 3 B3)
Downtown/West Village

Kiehl's (p81)
109 3rd Avenue (Map 4 E2)
Downtown/East Village

LAFCO (p73)
285 Lafayette Street (Map 4 E4)
Downtown/Nolita

Oasis Day Spa (p79)
108 East 16th St. (Map 3 C1)
Downtown/Flatiron

Rescue Beauty Lounge (p70)
8 Centre Market Pl. (Map 4 E5)
Downtown/Little Italy

SCO (p71)
584 Broadway (Map 3 D4)
Downtown/SoHo

Interiors

ABC Carpet and Home (p79)
888 Broadway (Map 3 D1)
Midtown/Gramercy

ABH Designs (p88)
401 East 76th Street (Map 8 H1)
Upper East Side

The Apartment (p95)
101 Crosby Street (Map 3 D4)
Downtown/Little Italy

Astroturf (p95)
290 Smith Street (Map 13 B4)
Brooklyn/Boerum Hill

Bark (p91)
495 Atlantic Avenue (Map 13 B4)
Brooklyn/Boerum Hill

La Cafetiere (p78)
160 Ninth Avenue (Map 3 A1)
Midtown/Chelsea

Clio (p67)
92 Thompson Street (Map 3 C4)
Downtown/SoHo

Darr (p93)
369 Atlantic Ave. (Map 13 B4)
Brooklyn

Demolition Depot (p90)
216 East 125th Street
(Map 12 G3)
Above Central Park/Harlem

Felissimo (p84)
10 West 56th Street (Map 8 E5)
Midtown/Theater District

Hable Construction (p72)
230 Elizabeth Street (Map 4 E4)
Downtown/Little Italy

Karkula Gallery (p167)
68 Gansevoort St. (Map 3 A2)
www.karkula.com
Downtown/Meatpacking
District

Loom (p91)
115 7th Avenue (Map 13 C4)
Brooklyn/Park Slope

Moon River Chattel (p95)
62 Grand Street (Map 13 B2)
Brooklyn/Williamsburg

Moss (p68)
146 Greene Street (Map 3 D4)
Downtown/SoHo

MXYPLYZYK (p77)
125 Greenwich Avenue
(Map 3 B2)
Downtown/Meatpacking
District

Nest (p92)
396A 7th Avenue (Map 13 C5)
Brooklyn/Park Slope

Two Jakes (p95)
320 Wythe Ave. (Map 13 B2)
Brooklyn/Williamsburg

Vitra (p167)
29 9th Avenue (Map 3 A2)
www.vitra.com
Downtown/Meatpacking
District

Xukuma (p90)
183 Lenox Avenue (11 D4)
Above Central Park/Harlem

Lingerie

Bra Smyth (p86)
905 Madison Avenue
(Map 8 E2)
Upper East Side

Le Corset by Selima (p66)
80 Thompson Street (Map 3 C5)
Downtown/SoHo

La Perla (p86)
803 Madison Avenue (Map 8 E3)
Upper East Side

Markets

Chelsea Flea Market (p168)
24th Street and 6th Avenue
(Map 5 D5)
Midtown/Chelsea

Green Market (p166)
Bowling Green (Map 1 D4)
Downtown/Lower Manhattan

**Union Square
Green Market** (p168)
Union Square (Map 3 D1)
Midtown/Gramercy

Music

Earwax (p94)
218 Bedford Avenue
(Map 13 B2)
Brooklyn/Williamsburg

Fat Beats (p75)
406 6th Avenue (Map 3 C2)
Downtown/West Village

Jazz Record Center (p82)
236 West 26th Street,
8th Floor (Map 5 C5)
Midtown/Chelsea

St. Mark's Sounds (p82)
16 St. Mark's Place (Map 4 E3)
Downtown/East Village

Subterranean Records (p75)
5 Cornelia Street (Map 3 C3)
Downtown/West Village

Shoes & Accessories

ALife Rivington Club (p73)
158 Rivington Street (Map 4 G4)
Downtown/Lower East Side

Bond 07 by Selima (p72)
7 Bond Street (Map 3 D3)
Downtown/Nolita

Christian Louboutin (p87)
941 Madison Avenue (Map 8 E2)
Upper East Side

Flight 001 (p76)
96 Greenwich Ave. (Map 3 B2)
Downtown/West Village

Jimmy Choo (p82)
645 5th Avenue (Map 8 E5)
Midtown/Theater District

Kate Spade Travel (p64)
454 Broome Street (Map 3 D5)
Downtown/SoHo

Manolo Blahnik (p82)
31 West 54th Street (Map 8 E5)
Midtown/Theater District

Niketown (p84)
6 East 57th Street (Map 8 E5)
Midtown/Theater District

Rafe (p72)
1 Bleecker Street (Map 4 E4)
Downtown/Nolita

Sporting Goods

Blades Board & Skate (p88)
120 West 72nd St.
(Map 7 B2)
Upper West Side

Paragon Sporting Goods (p80)
867 Broadway (Map 3 D1)
Midtown/Gramercy

Super Runners (p89)
360 Amsterdam Ave.
(Map 7 B1)
Upper West Side

Stationery

Kate's Paperie (p70)
561 Broadway (Map 3 D4)
Downtown/SoHo

Thrift Stores

Beacon's Closet (p93)
88 North 11th St. (Map 13 B1)
Brooklyn/Williamsburg

Housing Works Thrift Shop (p89)
306 Columbus Ave. (Map 7 C2)
Upper West Side

Art & Architecture

Art Galleries

Asia Society (p109)
725 Park Avenue (Map 8 F2)
Upper East Side

Deitch Projects (p102)
18 Wooster Street (Map 3 D5)
212 941 9475
Downtown/SoHo

Forbes Magazine Gallery (p104)
60 5th Avenue at
West 12th Street
(Map 3 D2)
Downtown/West Village

Gagosian (p102)
555 West 24th Street
(Map 5 B5)
www.gagosian.com
Midtown/Chelsea

International Center of Photography (p106)
1133 Ave. of the Americas
(Map 5 D2)
Midtown/Theater District

Leo Koenig (p102)
249 Centre Street (Map 2 E2)
212 334 9255
Downtown/Chinatown

Mary Boone (p102)
541 West 24th St. (Map 5 B5)
www.maryboone.com
Midtown/Chelsea

Momenta Art (p114)
72 Berry Street (Map 13 B1)
www.momentaart.org
Brooklyn/Williamsburg

Noguchi Sculpture Museum (p183)
32–37 Vernon Boulevard
Queens/Long Island City

Pace Wildenstein (p102)
534 West 25th Street
(Map 5 B5)
www.pacewildenstein.com
Midtown/Chelsea

Pierogi 2000 (p114)
177 North 9th Street
(Map 13 B1)
www.pierogi2000.com
Brooklyn/Williamsburg

P.S.1 (p115)
22–5 Jackson Avenue
www.ps1.org
Queens

Williamsburg Art & Historical Center (p114)
135 Broadway at Bedford
Avenue (Map 13 B2)
718 486 7372
www.wahcenter.org
Brooklyn/Williamsburg

Historic Buildings

Block Beautiful (p104)
East 19th Street, between
Irving Place & 3rd Avenue
(Map 4 E1)
Midtown/Gramercy

Brooklyn Bridge (p13)
(Map 2 F3)
Downtown/Lower East Side

Federal Hall (p166)
26 Wall Street (Map 1 D4)
Downtown/Lower Manhattan

Flatiron Building (p106)
23rd St., 5th Ave. & Broadway
(Map 6 E5)
Midtown/Flatiron

Grand Central Terminal (p105)
42nd Street & Park Ave.
(Map 6 F2)
Midtown/Murray Hill

Jefferson Market Courthouse (p104)
425 6th Avenue
(Map 3 C2)
Downtown/West Village

Prospect Park West (p113)
Between Union and 15th Sts.
(Map 13 C5)
Brooklyn/Park Slope

Statue of Liberty (p13)
(Map 1 A5)

U.S. Custom House (p100)
1 Bowling Green
(Map 1 D5)
Downtown/Lower Manhattan

Williamsburg Savings Bank Building (p115)
1 Hanson Place, corner of
Flatbush & Atlantic Avenues
(Map 13 C4)
Brooklyn/Boerum Hill

Woolworth Building (p102)
233 Broadway at Barclay Street
(Map 1 D2)
Downtown/Lower Manhattan

Installations

Broken Kilometer (p102)
393 West Broadway
(Map 3 D5)
Downtown/SoHo

Earth Room (p102)
141 Wooster Street
(Map 3 D4)
Downtown/SoHo

Modern Architecture

*See also Museums:
Guggenheim and The Whitney*

Chanin Building (p105)
122 East 42nd Street at
Lexington Avenue (Map 6 F2)
Midtown/Murray Hill

Chrysler Building (p105)
405 Lexington Avenue
(Map 6 F2)
Midtown/Murray Hill

Daily News Building (p105)
220 East 42nd Street
(Map 6 G2)
Midtown/Murray Hill

Empire State Building (pp12 & 105)
350 5th Ave. (Map 6 E3)
Midtown/Murray Hill

General Electric Building (p105)
570 Lexington Avenue
at 51st Street
(Map 6 F1)
Midtown/Murray Hill

Ground Zero (pp15 & 101)
(Map 1 C3)
Downtown/Lower Manhattan

Index by Type

Art & Architecture

Museums

American Museum of Natural History (p14)
Central Park West & 79th St.
(Map 7 C1)
Central Park

Brooklyn Historical Society (p115)
128 Pierrepont Street
(Map 2 H5)
Brooklyn/Boerum Hill

Brooklyn Museum of Art (p114)
200 Eastern Parkway (13 D4)
Brooklyn/Crown Heights

The Cloisters (p112)
Fort Tryon Park (off map)
Above Central Park/Fort Tryon & Inwood

Cooper-Hewitt National Design Museum (p111)
2 East 91st Street
(Map 10 E4)
Upper East Side/Yorkville

Ellis Island (p13)
(Map 1 A5)
Upper West Side

Frick Collection (p108)
1 East 70th Street (Map 8 E2)
Upper East Side

Guggenheim Museum (p110)
1071 5th Avenue at 89th Street
(Map 10 E4)
Upper East Side/Yorkville

The Jewish Museum (p111)
1109 5th Avenue at 92nd Street (Map 10 E4)
Upper East Side/Yorkville

Lower East Side Tenement Museum (p103)
90 Orchard Street
(Map 4 F5)
Downtown/Lower East Side

Merchant's House Museum (p103)
29 East 4th Street
(Map 4 E3)
Downtown/Nolita

Metropolitan Museum of Art (pp15 &109)
1000 5th Avenue
(Map 8 E1) Upper East Side

El Museo del Barrio (p113)
1230 5th Avenue at 104th Street (Map 10 E2)
Upper E. Side/Spanish Harlem

Museum at the Fashion Institute of Technology (p104)
7th Avenue at 27th Street
(Map 5 D4)
Midtown/Chelsea

Museum of Chinese in the Americas (p166)
70 Mulberry Street, 2nd Floor
(Map 2 E1)
212 619 4785
Downtown/Chinatown

Museum of the City of New York (p111)
1250 5th Avenue at East 103rd Street (Map 10 E2)
Upper East Side

Museum of Modern Art (p107)
11 West 53rd Street (Map 8 E5)
Midtown/Theater District

Museum of Television and Radio (p109)
25 West 52nd St. (Map 8 E5)
Midtown/Theater District

Rose Museum at Carnegie Hall (p106)
154 West 57th Street, 2nd Floor
(Map 7 D5)
Midtown/Theater District

Skyscraper Museum (p101)
39 Battery Place (Map 1 D5)
Downtown/Lower Manhattan

Studio Museum in Harlem (p113)
144 West 125th St.
(Map 11 D3)
Above Central Park/Harlem

Whitney Museum of American Art (p107)
945 Madison Ave. (Map 8 E2)
Upper East Side

Whitney Museum of American Art at Altria (p106)
120 Park Avenue at 42nd Street (Map 6 F2)
Midtown/Murray Hill

Religious Buildings

Cathedral Church of St. John the Divine (p180)
1047 Amsterdam Avenue at 112th Street (Map 9 B1)
Upper West Side

Mahayana Buddhist Temple (p166)
133 Canal Street (Map 2 E1)
Downtown/Chinatown

St. Paul's Chapel (p100)
209 Broadway between Fulton & Vesey streets (Map 1 D3)
Downtown/Lower Manhattan

Walking Tours

Big Apple Jazz Tours (p169)
www.bigapplejazz.com
718 606 8442
Above Central Park/Harlem

Harlem Spirituals (p169)
www.harlemspirituals.com
212 391 0900
Above Central Park/Harlem

Performance

Ballrooms

Rainbow Room (p129)
30 Rockefeller Plaza, 65th Floor (Map 6 E1)
Midtown/Theater District

Swing 46 (p129)
349 West 46th St. (Map 5 C1)
Midtown/Theater District

Cabaret

Don't Tell Mama (p129)
343 West 46th St. (Map 5 C1)
Midtown/Theater District

Duplex (p122)
61 Christopher St. (Map 3 B3)
Downtown/West Village

Combined Arts

92nd Street Y (p131)
1395 Lexington Ave. (Map 10 F4)
Upper East Side/Yorkville

Apollo Theater (p134)
253 West 125th St. (Map 11 D3)
Above Central Park/Harlem

City Center (p129)
131 West 55th Street (Map 7 D5)
Midtown/Theater District

The Florence Gould Hall (p130)
55 East 59th Street
(Map 8 F4)
Upper East Side

The Kitchen (p126)
512 West 19th Street
(Map 3 A1)
Midtown/Chelsea

Makor (p133)
35 West 67th Street (Map 7 C3)
Upper West Side

P.S.122 (p126)
150 1st Avenue (Map 4 F2)
Downtown/East Village

Symphony Space (p133)
2537 Broadway (Map 9 B3)
Upper West Side

Comedy

The Comedy Cellar (p121)
117 MacDougal St. (Map 3 C3)
Downtown/West Village

The Comic Strip (p131)
1568 2nd Avenue (Map 8 G1)
Upper East Side

Gotham Comedy Club (p127)
34 West 22nd Street
(Map 6 E5)
Midtown/Flatiron

Stand-Up NY (p133)
236 West 78th St. (Map 7 B2)
Upper West Side

Upright Citizen's Brigade (p127)
307 West 26th Street (Map 5 C5)
Midtown/Chelsea

Concert Halls

See also Music Venues

Barge Music (p136)
Fulton Ferry Landing
(Map 2 G3)
Brooklyn/Brooklyn Heights

Brooklyn Academy of Music (p135)
30 Lafayette Avenue
(Map 13 C4)
Brooklyn/Fort Greene

Carnegie Hall (p131)
881 7th Avenue at
57th Street
(Map 7 D5)
Midtown/Theater District

Lincoln Center for the
Performing Arts (p132)
Straddling Broadway and
Amsterdam between 62nd
and 66th Streets (Map 7 B3)
Upper West Side

Merkin Concert Hall (p131)
129 West 67th Street
(Map 7 B3)
Upper West Side

New Jersey Performing Arts
Center (p137)
One Center Street
New Jersey/Newark

Dance

The Joyce Theater (p126)
175 8th Avenue
(Map 3 B1)
Midtown/Chelsea

Film Theaters

Film Forum (p120)
209 West Houston Street
(Map 3 C4)
Downtown/SoHo

Landmark's Sunshine
Theater (p124)
143 East Houston Street
(Map 4 F4)
Downtown/East Village

Jazz & Blues

55 Bar (p122)
55 Christopher Street
(Map 3 B3)
Downtown/West Village

B.B. King Blues Club (p128)
237 West 42nd Street
(Map 5 C2)
Midtown/Theater District

Blue Note (p121)
131 West 3rd Street
(Map 3 C3)
Downtown/West Village

Iridium (p128)
1650 Broadway
(Map 5 D1)
Midtown/Theater District

Jazz Standard (p127)
116 East 27th Street
(Map 6 F4)
Downtown/Gramercy

Lenox Lounge (p135)
288 Lenox Avenue between
124th & 125th Streets
(Map 11 D3)
Above Central Park/Harlem

Smoke (p133)
2751 Broadway (Map 9 B2)
Upper West Side

Village Vanguard (p122)
178 7th Avenue South
(Map 3 B2)
Downtown/West Village

Music Venues

Apollo Theater (p134)
253 West 125th Street
(Map 11 D3)
Above Central Park/Harlem

Arlene's Grocery (p123)
95 Stanton Street
(Map 4 F4)
Downtown/Lower East Side

Bowery Ballroom (p123)
6 Delancey Street (Map 4 E5)
Downtown/Lower East Side

Galapagos (p163)
70 North 6th Street (Map 13 B2)
Brooklyn/Williamsburg

Hammerstein Ballroom (p127)
311 West 34th Street
(Map 5 C3)
Midtown/Chelsea

Irving Plaza (p124)
17 Irving Place
(Map 4 E1)
Downtown/Union Square

Knitting Factory (p120)
74 Leonard Street
(Map 1 D1)
Downtown/Tribeca

Lit (p125)
93 2nd Ave.
(Map 4 E3)
Downtown/East Village

Mercury Lounge (p122)
217 East Houston Street
(Map 4 F4)
Downtown/Lower East Side

Rodeo Bar (p128)
375 3rd Avenue (Map 6 F5)
Midtown/Gramercy

S.O.B.'s (p120)
204 Varick Street (Map 3 C4)
Downtown/SoHo

Tonic (p123)
107 Norfolk Street (Map 4 G4)
Downtown/Lower East Side

Warsaw (p136)
261 Driggs Avenue (Map 13 C1)
Brooklyn/Greenpoint

Performing Arts

Brooklyn Academy
of Music (p135)
30 Lafayette Avenue
(Map 13 C4)
Brooklyn/Fort Green

Lincoln Center for the
Performing Arts (p132)
Straddling Broadway and
Amsterdam between 62nd
and 66th Streets (Map 7 B3)
Upper West side

New Jersey Performing Arts
Center (p137)
1 Center Street, Newark
New Jersey

Poetry

Bowery Poetry Club (p124)
308 Bowery
(Map 4 E4)
Downtown/East Village

Cornelia Street Cafe (p121)
29 Cornelia Street (Map 3 C3)
Downtown/West Village

Nuyorican Poets Cafe (p125)
236 East 3rd Street (Map 4 G3)
Downtown/East Village

Sports Arenas

Giants Stadium (p137)
50 State Route 120,East
Rutherford (special buses
from the Port Authority
Terminal at 8th Ave. & 41st
St.) www.giants.com
New Jersey

Madison Square Garden (p37)
(Map 6 E5)
Midtown/Flatiron

Shea Stadium (p137)
123 Roosevelt Avenue,
Flushing (7 IRT Flushing Line
Subway from Times Sq., 5th
Ave., and Grand Central)
www.mets.com
Queens/Flushing Meadows

Yankee Stadium (p137)
161st Street & River Avenue
(4, B, D subway trains from
Manhattan) www.yankees.com
Bronx

Theater

The Public Theater (p125)
425 Lafayette Street (Map 4 E3)
Downtown/Nolita

Roundabout Theatre Company
at the American Airlines
Theatre (p128)
227 West 42nd Street
(Map 5 D2)
Midtown/Theater District

TV Studios

Ed Sullivan Theater (p130)
1697 Broadway, at 52nd Street
(Map 7 D5)
Midtown/Theater District

NBC Studios (p130)
Between 5th Avenue & 7th
Avenue from 47th to 51st
Streets (Map 6 E1)
Midtown/Theater District

Bars & Clubs

Ale Houses

Blind Tiger Ale House (p153)
518 Hudson Street (Map 3 B3)
Downtown/West Village

The Ginger Man (p157)
11 East 36th Street Map 6 E3)
Midtown/Murray Hill

McSorley's Old Ale House
(p148)
15 East 7th Street
(Map 4 E3)
Downtown/East Village

Spuyten Duyvil (p162)
359 Metropolitan Ave.
(Map 13 C2)
Brooklyn/Williamsburg

Bars & Clubs

Ale Houses continued...

Swift (p148)
34 East 4th Street (Map 4 E3)
Downtown/East Village

Vol de Nuit (p152)
148 West 4th Street (Map 3 C3)
Downtown/West Village

White Horse Tavern (p153)
567 Hudson Street (Map 3 B3)
Downtown/West Village

Bars

2A (p147)
25 Avenue A (Map 4 F3)
Downtown/East Village

Antarctica (p142)
287 Hudson Street (Map 3 C5)
Downtown/SoHo

The Auction House (p160)
300 East 89th St. (Map 10 G4)
Upper East Side

Baraonda (p159)
1439 2nd Avenue (Map 8 G2)
Upper East Side

Barramundi (p146)
67 Clinton Steet (Map 4 F4)
Downtown/Lower East Side

Bar Veloce (p150)
175 2nd Avenue (Map 4 E2)
Downtown/East Village

B-Bar & Grill (p149)
40 East 4th Street (Map 4 E3)
Downtown/Nolita

Boat Basin Café (p161)
West 79th St. at Henry Hudson
Parkway (Map 7 A1)
Upper West Side

Bungalow 8 (p156)
515 West 27th Street (Map 5 B4)
Midtown/Chelsea

Buttermilk Bar (p162)
577 5th Avenue (Map 13 C5)
Brooklyn/Park Slope

**Cabin Club at Pine
Tree Lodge** (p154)
326 East 35th St. (Map 6 G3)
Midtown/Murray Hill

Campbell Apartment (p157)
15 Vanderbilt Ave., Southwest
Balcony, Grand Central
Terminal (Map 6 F2)
Midtown/Murray Hill

Chumley's (p152)
86 Bedford Street (Map 3 B3)
Downtown/West Village

Cubbyhole (p154)
281 West 12th Street
(Map 3 B2)
*Downtown/Meatpacking
District*

Eugene (p155)
27 West 24th St. (Map 6 E5)
Downtown/SoHo

Galapagos (p163)
70 North 6th Street (Map 13 B2)
Brooklyn/Williamsburg

Glass (p156)
287 10th Avenue (Map 5 B5)
Midtown/Chelsea

Gowanus Yacht Club (p161)
323 Smith Street (Map 13 B4)
Brooklyn/Boerum Hill

Great Lakes (p161)
284 5th Avenue (Map 13 C4)
Brooklyn/Park Slope

Hiro (p156)
366 West 17th Street (Map 3 A1)
Midtown/Chelsea

KGB (p148)
85 East 4th Street (Map 4 E3)
Downtown/East Village

Korova Milk Bar (p151)
200 Avenue A (Map 4 F2)
Downtown/East Village

Library Bar (p151)
Hudson Hotel, 356 West 58th
Street (Map 7 B4)
Upper West Side

Mica Bar (p154)
252 East 51st Street (Map 6 F1)
Midtown/Turtle Bay

ñ (p144)
33 Crosby Street (Map 3 D5)
Downtown/Little Italy

Nevada Smith's (p148)
74 3rd Avenue (Map 4 E2)
Downtown/East Village

Parkside Lounge (p147)
317 E. Houston St.
(Map 4 G4)
Downtown/East Village

Pianos (p147)
158 Ludlow Street (Map 4 F4)
Downtown/Lower East Side

Plunge Bar (p161)
18 9th Avenue (Map 3 A1)
Midtown/Chelsea

Pussycat Lounge (p142)
96 Greenwich Street
(Map 1 D4)
Downtown/Lower Manhattan

Ruby's (p161)
Coney Island Boardwalk
(F, D, Q subway trains to
Coney Island/Stillwell Avenue)
Brooklyn

Rudy's Bar & Grill (p154)
627 9th Avenue (Map 5 C1)
Midtown/Hell's Kitchen

Rue B (p151)
188 Avenue B (Map 4 G2)
Downtown/East Village

Russian Vodka Room (p159)
265 West 52nd Street
(Map 7 C5)
Midtown/Theater District

Serena (p155)
Chelsea Hotel, 222 West 23rd
Street (Map 5 C5)
Midtown/Chelsea

Single Room Occupancy (p158)
360 West 53rd Street
(Map 7 C5)
Midtown/Theater District

Sky Bar (p161)
17 West 32nd Street
(Map 6 E4)
Midtown/Flatiron

Slipper Room (p147)
167 Orchard Street (Map 4 F4)
Downtown/Lower East Side

Stonewall (p153)
53 Christopher Street (Map 3 B3)
Downtown/West Village

**The View, Marriott Marquis
Hotel** (p161)
1535 Broadway(Map 5 D1)
Midtown/Theater District

Trash (p162)
256 Grand Street (Map 13 C2)
Brooklyn/Williamsburg

Welcome to the Johnson's
(p146)
123 Rivington Street (Map 4 F4)
Downtown/Lower East Side

Winnie's (p142)
104 Bayard Street (Map 2 E1)
Downtown/Chinatown

Clubs

Avalon (p155)
47 West 20th Street (Map 3 C1)
Midtown/Chelsea

Black Betty (p162)
366 Metropolitan Avenue at
Havermeyer Street (Map 13 C2)
Brooklyn/Williamsburg

Cielo (p154)
18 Little West 12th Street
(Map 3 A2)
*Downtown/Meatpacking
District*

Copacabana (p157)
560 West 34th Street
(Map 5 B3)
Midtown/Chelsea

Eugene (p155)
27 West 24th Street
(Map 6 E5)
Midtown/Flatiron

Roxy (p155)
515 West 18th Street (Map 3 A1)
Midtown/Chelsea

Spirit (p156)
530 West 27th Street
(Map 5 B4)
Midtown/Chelsea

Cocktail Lounges

Angel's Share (p148)
8 Stuyvesant Street
(Map 4 E2)
Downtown/East Village

Ava Lounge (p158)
210 West 55th Street (Map 7 D5)
Midtown/Theater District

Beauty Bar (p150)
231 East 14th Street
(Map 4 E2)
Downtown/East Village

Bemelmans Bar (p159)
Carlyle Hotel, 35 East 76th
Street (Map 8 E1)
Upper East Side

Lansky Lounge (p145)
104 Norfolk Street (Map 4 G4)
Downtown/Lower East Side

Larry Lawrence (p162)
295 Grand Street (Map 13 C2)
Brooklyn/Williamsburg

Level V (p154)
675 Hudson Street (Map 3 A2)
Midtown/Meatpacking District

Métrazur (p158)
East Balcony, Grand Central
Terminal (Map 6 F2)
Midtown/Murray Hill

Pravda (p145)
281 Lafayette Street
(Map 4 E4)
Downtown/Nolita

Temple Bar (p144)
332 Lafayette Street (Map 4 E4)
Downtown/Nolita

THOM's Bar (p143)
60 Thompson Street (Map 3 C5)
Downtown/SoHo

**Top of the Tower @ Beekman
Tower Hotel** (p178)
3 Mitchell Place at 49th Street
& 1st Avenue (Map 6 G1)
Midtown/Turtle Bay

Zombie Hut (p160)
261 Smith Street (Map 13 B4)
Brooklyn/Boerum Hill

DJ Bars

Beauty Bar (p150)
231 East 14th Street
(Map 4 E2)
Downtown/East Village

Flûte (p158)
205 West 54th Street
(Map 7 D5)
Midtown/Theater District

Frank's Lounge (p160)
660 Fulton Street (Map 13 B4)
Brooklyn/Boerum Hill

Lansky Lounge (p145)
104 Norfolk Street (Map 4 G4)
Downtown/Lower East Side

Lotus (p150)
409 West 14th Street
(Map 3 A2)
*Downtown/Meatpacking
District*

Sullivan Room (p152)
218 Sullivan Street
(Map 3 C3)
Downtown/West Village

Uncle Ming's (p152)
225 Avenue B, 2nd Floor
(Map 4 G2)
Downtown/East Village

Hotels

Expensive

60 Thompson (p188)
60 Thompson Street
(Map 3 C5)
Downtown/SoHo

Carlyle (p189)
Madison Avenue at 76th Street
Upper East Side

Four Seasons (p194)
57 East 57th Street
(Map 8 E5)
Midtown/Theater District

The Lowell (p195)
28 East 63rd Street
(Map 8 F4)
Upper East Side

The Mark (p195)
25 East 77th Street (Map 8 E1)
Upper East Side

Mercer Hotel (p188)
147 Mercer Street (Map 3 D4)
Downtown/SoHo

The Peninsula (p192)
700 5th Avenue at 55th Street
(Map 8 E5)
Midtown/Theater District

The Pierre (p195)
5th Avenue at 61st Street
(Map 8 E4)
Upper East Side

Soho House New York (p190)
29–35 9th Avenue
(Map 3 A2)
*Downtown/Meatpacking
District*

St. Regis (p192)
2 East 55th Street
(Map 8 E5)
Midtown/Theater District

Tribeca Grand Hotel (p189)
2 Avenue of the Americas
(Map 3 C5)
Downtown/SoHo

Moderate

Affinia Shelburne (p192)
303 Lexington Ave. (Map 6 F3)
Midtown/Murray Hill

**Bed & Breakfast
on the Park** (p197)
113 Prospect Park West
(Map 13 C5)
Brooklyn/Park Slope

Hotel Chelsea (p189)
222 West 23rd Street
(Map 5 C5)
Midtown/Chelsea

Hotel Surrey (p195)
20 East 76th St. (Map 8 E1)
Upper East Side

Hotel Wales (p196)
1295 Madison Avenue
(Map 10 E4)
Upper East Side/Yorkville

Hudson Hotel (p193)
356 West 58th St. (Map 7 C4)
Upper West Side

Maritime Hotel (p191)
363 West 16th St. (Map 3 A1)
Midtown/Chelsea

Morgans (p193)
237 Madison Avenue
(Map 6 E3)
Midtown/Murray Hill

Royalton (p192)
44 West 44th Street
(Map 6 E2)
Midtown/Theater District

SoHo Grand Hotel (p188)
310 West Broadway
(Map 3 D5)
Downtown/SoHo

**W New York,
Union Square** (p191)
201 Park Avenue South
(Map 3 D1)
Midtown/Gramercy

Cheap

1871 House (p194)
130 East 62nd Street
(Map 8 F4)
Upper East Side

Abingdon Guest House (p189)
13 8th Avenue
(Map 3 B2)
*Downtown/Meatpacking
District*

Akwaaba Mansion (p197)
347 MacDonough Street (Utica
Ave. stop)
Downtown/SoHo

Bevy's SoHo Loft (p188)
70 Mercer Street
(Map 3 D5)
Downtown/SoHo

Chelsea Inn (p191)
46 West 17th Street
(Map 3 C1)
Midtown/Flatiron

Chelsea Lodge (p191)
318 West 20th Street
(Map 3 B1)
Midtown/Chelsea

Harlem Flophouse (p196)
242 West 123rd Street
(Map 11 D4)
Above Central Park/Harlem

Union Street B&B (p197)
405 Union Street
(Map 13 B4)
Brooklyn/Boerum Hill

Washington Square Hotel
(p189)
103 Waverly Place
(Map 3 C3)
Downtown/West Village

>> (For hotel price ranges, *see p189*)

233

General Index

General Index

General Index

Acknowledgments

Produced by Blue Island Publishing
www.blueisland.co.uk
Editorial Director Rosalyn Thiro
Art Director Stephen Bere
Commissioning Editor Michael Ellis
Editorial Assistant Allen Stone
Proofreader Jane Simmonds
Picture Researcher Chrissy McIntyre

Published by DK
Publishing Managers Jane Ewart and Scarlett O'Hara
Senior Editor Christine Stroyan
Senior Designers Paul Jackson and Marisa Renzullo
Website Editor Gouri Banerji
Cartographic Editor Casper Morris
Senior Cartographer Uma Bhattacharya
Fact Checker Michelle Haimoff
DTP Designers Jason Little and Natasha Lu
Production Controller Rita Sinha

PHOTOGRAPHY PERMISSIONS

The publishers would like to thank all the museums, hotels, restaurants, bars, clubs, shops, galleries and other sights for their assistance and kind permission to photograph at their establishments.

Placement Key: tc = top centre; tl = top left; tr = top right; c = centre; ca = centre above; cl = centre left; cla = centre left above; clb = centre left below; cr = centre right; cra = centre right above; crb = centre right below; b = bottom; bl = bottom left; br = bottom right; r = right.

The publishers would like to thank the following companies and picture libraries for permission to reproduce their photographs:

66: 27tr, 28tl; 1871 HOUSE: 194br; AFFINIA SHELBOURNE: 192tr, ANIK: 87tr; A.P.C.: 66tl; AQUAVIT: 27tl; 49bl/br; AUCTION HOUSE: 160tl; AKWAABA: 191tl; ASIA SOCIETY: Frank Oudeman 109bl; BEVY'S SOHO LOFT: 186bl, 188tl; BLACK BETTY: Marike Voss 162br; BLISS SOHO: 176ca/clb/crb; BROKEN KILOMETER, Walter De Maria 102cl;

BROOKLYN ACADEMY OF MUSIC: 135br; BROOKLYN BOTANICAL GARDENS: 5b, 17tl; BROOKLYN HISTORICAL SOCIETY: 115tl; BROOKLYN MUSEUM OF ART: Adam Husted 98cr, 114tl/tc; BUNGALOW 8: 156clb; CALLIOPE: 94cl; CAMPBELL APARTMENT: 157br; CHELSEA LODGE: 191cla; CITY CENTER: 129br; CORBIS: Bettmann 15cra, 19r; Seth Cohen 15cl; Jose Fuste Raga 11tl, 13cra; Jon Hicks 13br; Viviane Moore 17tr; Mark Peterson 19tl; Louie Psihoyos 1; Reuters 12tl; Reuters/Mike Segar 98bl; Adam Woolfit 19tc; DARR: 93tr; Bo Zaunders 106br; DK IMAGES: 13tr/tc/clb, 105bl, 118cr; Guggenheim 96–7, 110t; Dave King 12cr, 14tr, 15crb, 98tl, 99tc, 103tr; David King/Tim Knox 169br; Sal Marsh 14c; Norman McGrath 178bl; Courtesy of The American Museum of Natural History/Dave King 14br; Rough Guides/Nelson Hancock: 12bl, 13tl, 15tl/tr/bl, 99tl/ bl, 118tl; Chris Stevens 15tc; Studio Museum Harlem 113cl; Trinity Church 166tl; EARTH ROOM: Walter De Maria 102br; FOUR SEASONS: 184–5, 187bl, 194tl; FREEMANS: 34br; THE FRICK COLLECTION: John Bigelow Tayler 108cr/bl/br; GETTY IMAGES: Mitchell Funk/Stone, 6–7; HOTEL SURREY: 195cla; IRIDIUM JAZZ CLUB: 116-17, 128cla; JAZZ STANDARD: 6bl, 127cra; LEVEL V: 154cl; LOTUS: 150br; THE MARK: 186cl; MERCER HOTEL: 188crb; MORGANS: 187tl/crb, 193tr/cr; MUSEUM OF MODERN ART: 107tr; MUSEUM OF THE CITY OF NEW YORK: 111tl; NEW JERSEY PERFORMING ARTS CENTER: 137tl/tr; NOM DE GUERRE: 93cl; OASIS DAY SPA: 79tr; PIANOS: 147crb; RAINBOW ROOM: 129crb; ROYALTON: 192cla; SKYSCRAPER MUSEUM: 101bl; SOHO GRAND HOTEL: 188cl; SOHO HOUSE: 186tl, 187tc, 190tr/c; THE SPA AT THE MANDARIN ORIENTAL: 178tl; SPOTTED PIG: 37tr; STAN'S PLACE: 58cr; THE STRAND BOOKSTORE: 81bl; STUDIO MUSEUM IN HARLEM: 99cla, 113cl; WHITNEY MUSEUM OF AMERICAN ART AT ALTRIA: 106cl; WHITNEY MUSEUM OF MODERN ART: 17tc, 107bl.

Full Page Picture Captions Relish: 2; The River Café: 8–9; Tamarind: 24–5; Liliblue: 60–61; Guggenheim Museum: 96–7; Iridium Jazz Club: 116–17; Spirit: 138–9; Union Square Market: 164–5; Noguchi Sculpture Museum: 174–5; Four Seasons Hotel: 186–7; China Town: 198.

Jacket Images
Front and Spine: CORBIS: Louie Psihoyos.
Back: DK IMAGES: cla, cra; FOUR SEASONS, New York: ca.

Special Editions of DK Travel Guides

DK Travel Guides can be purchased in bulk quantities at discounted prices for use in promotions or as premiums. a We are also able to offer special editions and personalized jackets, corporate imprints, and excerpts from all of our books, tailored specifically to meet your own needs.

To find out more, please contact:
(in the United States) SpecialSales@dk.com
(in the UK) Sarah.Burgess@dk.com
(in Canada) DK Special Sales at general@tourmaline.ca
(in Australia) business.development@pearson.com.au

The Manhattan Subway

The Metropolitan Transit Authority subway service operates 24 hours a day. On this map, **bold** identification letters or numbers below station names indicate that trains always operate between 6am and midnight. A light letter or number shows that the train does not run at all times or skips a station. Following the destruction of the World Trade Center, Cortlandt Street Station is temporarily closed.

For more information call (718) 330 1234 or visit www.mta.nyc.ny.us/nyct/subway/index.

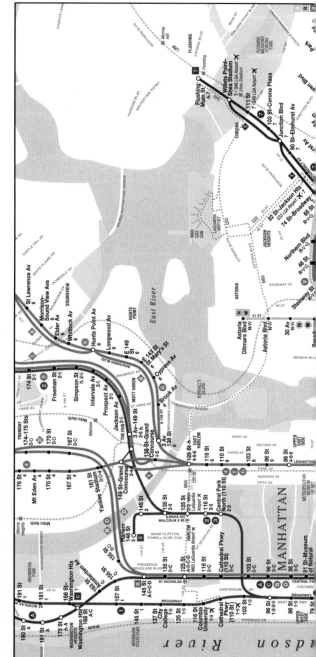